ERRATUM

The Eagle and the Small Birds

Page 20. Nine lines from the bottom

for 'with Hitler' read 'against Hitler'

The Eagle and the Small Birds

The Eagle and the Small Birds

Crisis in the Soviet Empire: from Yalta to Solidarity

Michael Charlton

'*The Eagle should permit the small birds
to sing, and care not wherefore they sang.*'

Winston Churchill to Josef Stalin, Yalta 1945

THE UNIVERSITY OF CHICAGO PRESS

The University of Chicago Press,
Chicago 60637
British Broadcasting Corporation,
London W1M 4AA

ISBN 0-226-10154-1

Set in 10/12pt Linotron Sabon
by Phoenix Photosetting, Chatham
Printed in England
by Mackays of Chatham Ltd

93 92 91 90 89 88 87 86 85 84   5 4 3 2 1

Contents

Introduction

THE EAGLE AND THE SMALL BIRDS is oral history, and a survey over several decades of a particularly turbulent part of Europe.

It recalls with evidence at first hand the once secret diplomacy of great power politics – those 'realities of facts and force' as Churchill described them, which led to the creation and consolidation of the Soviet Union's empire in Eastern Europe. With such first-hand evidence it has attempted to explore the nature and degree of the subsequent antipathies to the Soviet Union as the imperial governor of this – 'the other half of Europe'.

It is therefore an account, given to me in their own words, by men who helped to make, have a particular knowledge of, or directly bore the consequences of great decisions. These decisions were themselves indivisible from the events which imposed a new order behind that central fracture in the cultural and spiritual affinities of the European continent which Churchill called the Iron Curtain.

Although it complements an earlier enterprise in oral history for the BBC's Radio 3 (British diplomacy in Europe after the Second World War, 'The Price of Victory', subsequently published under that title) the present undertaking was largely prompted by the huge political earthquake which struck Poland in the summer of 1980. The significance of Solidarity still reverberates in the countries of the Communist bloc and in the West. It made a huge rent in the seamless robe of Stalin's fabric of totalitarian Communism, imposed by him in the old nation states east of the Elbe. And in Poland, so often in its history the key to Eastern Europe, Solidarity spelt the utter ruin of Marxist–Leninist ideology.

The interviews which comprise, for the most part, this oral history set out to establish the political background to the sustained effervescence in the centre of Europe, and in Poland particularly. Their purpose has been to try and throw some light on the corollary of these persistent challenges to the status quo: whether the political and military architecture built upon the outcome of the Second World War – and which it has been taken for granted would mean another (and this time probably nuclear) war to dismantle – is nonetheless being eroded by forces which will bring about either change or destruction.

The recording of the interviews took place in Britain, the United States and Eastern Europe, in the course of 1982. They were broadcast originally in a series of documentary programmes for Radio 4 under the same title. Without the more exacting constraints of time and space in radio it has been possible to expand substantially the use of the recorded material for this book.

The participants were given notice of the areas of questions to enable them to refresh their memories (where possible from personal diaries of the time) and to expand upon their original advice and opinions now available in, for example, the Foreign Office archives. The interviews then took the form of conversations. The questions and answers in the following pages were those on the spot and at the time. No subsequent alterations have been made other than the minor ones necessary for clarification in print and where, in free speech, the inflexion of the voice may have conveyed a particular emphasis or meaning.

With the passing of the generation involved at the time of Yalta, which is now almost forty years ago, the link with the past must soon be broken in terms of a direct and informed personal knowledge at the highest level of all those issues in which the present discontents in the centre of Europe have their origin. Among the principal contributors to *The Eagle and the Small Birds* the BBC has been fortunate indeed to have been able to call upon men who were crucially important aides and advisers to Churchill and Roosevelt when they met Stalin at Yalta for the famous conference which gave such an ambiguous benediction to the political reach of armies in the field and the reality of a Europe split between wartime allies and their opposing ideologies.

Sir Ian Jacob (Military Secretary to the War Cabinet led by Churchill and with him throughout the war), Sir Frank Roberts and Lord Gladwyn of the Foreign Office were all present and 'looking over the shoulders' as it were of the wartime leaders at Teheran, Yalta or the other vital conferences. They reflect here upon the hopes and beliefs of the period when it was clear that one totalitarian tyranny, Hitler's, would be vanquished and when the future was seen to lie in a manageable relationship with another, Stalin's, without whom the war could not have been won. They add to and clarify what we know from the official record today of how Churchill and Eden came to concentrate upon the Polish question. Why for Churchill it was 'a matter of honour' and why, after Yalta, he was troubled by what the judgement of history would be upon him for his handling of it.

There is also the evidence of Alger Hiss, speaking here in old age of his time when, as a most highly regarded young State Department official, he helped to draft the famous Declaration on Liberated Europe, uttered at Yalta. Hiss, who subsequently stood trial in the 1950s in the United States, accused of spying for the Soviet Union, complements his own eyewitness evidence of official American attitudes at the time of Yalta with fresh anecdotal references, and things 'not in the history books'. And there are, too, the personal narratives of astonishing figures like Professor Stanislaw Swaniewicz, who survived, with his chilling evidence of a certain spring day and the infamous episode which remains a central block in any statement of Soviet–Polish relations to the present time – Stalin's attempted decapitation of a nation – the massacre in the Katyn Forest.

The period immediately following Yalta introduces new evidence 'from the horse's mouth' of how Marxist–Leninist methods of political organisation, 'salami tactics', were put into effect throughout Eastern Europe. It includes the disarming personal testimony of a high-ranking Communist in Hungary of how the 'free and unfettered elections', for which Yalta provided, were rigged. It is evidence which accompanies the oral witness of what happened when Stalin's 'confessors' arrived in the capitals of these eastern states during the 'carnivorous' period of the establishment of Soviet authority. And General Bela Kiraly discloses his insider's account of the invasion Stalin planned of Tito's heretic Communist state – an invasion which Kiraly helped to plan and would have commanded. It was an enterprise which was stood down only when the Americans 'stood up' and went to war in far-away Korea.

The chapter called 'The Eclipse of Ideology' is an outline of the recantations of the Communist faith which have emerged in recent years from within the fold itself – the personal evidence of influential Communists, men who have 'stormed heaven' only to find it empty.

They put on record here their powerful reconsiderations. They might be judged in the light of what a former Communist, Ignazio Silone, said in an often quoted exchange to the Italian Communist leader Palmiro Togliatti: Silone's ironic variant of the famous call of the International, 'The final struggle will be between the Communists and the ex-Communists!' In other words one has to have *believed* in order to comprehend the final struggle and to have the power and will to demolish the once-held faith.

The final chapter deals with the contemporary flux of events and the kind of advice which has been reaching the ears of successive American Presidents about developments in Eastern Europe. The White House advisers on these matters to Presidents Johnson, Nixon, Carter and Reagan contribute their insights and appraisals alongside those of the most high-ranking Soviet diplomat to have come to the West, Arkady Shevchenko, who for many years was a personal aide to the Soviet Foreign Minister, Mr Gromyko.

It has been a constant Soviet theme that the Soviet Union is helping us all by sitting in command of Eastern Europe and its fractious and unruly populations. On the whole, the cause of these states has aroused no sustained Western indignation. The feeling is strong that they have made their contribution to two World Wars. But the unresolved issue in Eastern and Central Europe is the legacy of our time since Yalta. The Soviet presence there invests all these problems with an earth-shaking potential. It follows that we can no longer delude ourselves that there is no connection between their plight and the prospects of our own countries. Just as it can now also no longer be said that these states are cemented into an imperial system which ensures their impotence. The self-assurance of a shipyard electrician called Lech Walesa in unravelling what Lenin and Stalin put together bears witness to that. Slowly they are gaining a degree of freedom. How and why has been the objective of this oral history to explore.

I would like to make clear my gratitude on more than one count. Firstly for 'other men's flowers' – to the contributors themselves who gave to me and the BBC their time and memory. To the BBC itself of course and in particular George Fischer, the Head of its Talks and Documentaries Department, for their continued cultivation of enterprises such as this. And I would also like to make clear my thanks to my colleague David Morton (who produced the original series of programmes for the BBC's Radio 4) for a most agreeable collaboration. Not least for his personal exertions by the shores of Lake Balaton which produced the historically interesting 'confession' of Zoltan Vas – a rare bird among the small birds.

Michael Charlton
Broadcasting House
London

1

THE SPECTRE OF YALTA

In FEBRUARY 1945, a huge delegation of more than 600 British and American officials set out for Yalta in the Crimea. Roosevelt and Churchill were to sit down with Stalin and write the peace to follow the Second World War. 'Ursus Major', as Churchill called Stalin in letters to his wife Clementine, had refused to leave home. The leaders of the West therefore had to go to him.

Of Yalta itself Churchill lamented to Roosevelt before the conference, 'We could not have found a worse place for a meeting if we had spent ten years in looking for it!'

Now, forty years on, and in the enlarged perspectives of the present day, with its new horizons out among the stars, it is easy to overlook what formidable, outlandish journeys the crucial conferences of the war entailed.

Among those who were centrally involved in the Yalta Conference was Gladwyn Jebb of the Foreign Office, now Lord Gladwyn.

GLADWYN: The most vivid thing about it was getting there. We were divided into two groups and we were all going to Malta on the way to Yalta. My group went in one old-fashioned 'York' aeroplane, the second group of us in another. This other one did not get to Malta but crashed at Lampedusa, in the Pelagian Islands in the Mediterranean. Everybody on it was killed, including the admirable Peter Loxley of the Foreign Office and all my friends. A terrible thing. However, we got to Naples, then went on and on, gradually over the Aegean – there were supposed to be German fighters off Samothrace but we avoided them – and so over the Black Sea, and after a very long and tiring journey got to Simferopol. First of all we were told that all our friends had been killed – and that was not very encouraging – then we were borne off to a sort of local cocktail party by some Cossacks. We were given an enormous amount of vodka and general jollification of a very Russian kind. Then, when we were quite exhausted we got into cars and went south, over a mountain range to Yalta. That was another eight or nine hours, a very tiring, very winding, curving trip. Every ten yards there was a Russian soldier. Then we got down finally, absolutely exhausted, to the coast.

A CENTURY BEFORE, in these parts Imperial Britain had waged war against Imperial Russia. Britain had lost the Light Brigade at Balaclava but won the contest for influence in Europe. Blocked to the West, Russia had begun then an advance on a different axis – into Central Asia, to match that of the British in India, absorbing the great Khanates of Islam as she went, the lands of the Turkmen and Kazakhs. It was an advance which by the last decades of the last century had carried her down to the northern frontiers of Afghanistan, once more to contest influence with Britain in the outcome of the two Afghan wars.

By the time of Yalta in 1945, the whole balance of power in the world had been overthrown by the consequences of Hitler's war. In Europe the prospect was that nations newly liberated by the Soviet Union were about to exchange one totalitarian captivity for another – among them Poland, Britain's first ally after the Fall of France in the war against Hitler. Stalin's armies were poised to control an unknown extent of Europe. The Russians were not yet masters in what is now their famous glacis, but at Yalta they were masterful from the first day, in matters great and small.

GLADWYN: There was said to be a bath. 'Where is the bath?' It was 'on the other side of the courtyard'. When we all arrived, there it was: a Russian bath. We said, 'What do we do?' Well, 'You take your clothes off and go into the steam!' So we took our clothes off and then we were assaulted by an enormous Russian woman who scrubbed us with a scrubbing-brush! We arrived even more exhausted after this for dinner and had an enormous meal. Then they said, 'What about breakfast?' I said I'd like a boiled egg. So we arrived at breakfast – this was already fairly early in the morning – and they brought in first of all an enormous sturgeon which was served around, and then a sucking pig and lots of vodka and Russian champagne, and finally at the end of all this was proudly brought in one boiled egg! We survived all that and then went up to the Livadia Palace, and the conference started. That was my initial experience of Yalta.

CHARLTON: Finding yourself in this part of the Crimea how conscious would you say you all were, the British, and one imagines the Russians, of the flux of history? After all, it was the outcome of the Crimean War which had denied Russia under the Tsars movement or expansion westward into Europe and down to the Mediterranean.

GLADWYN: Well I am not sure if we thought very much about that. I suppose that the Russians did.

'The Russ would cry with gleaming eye, "Sebastopol!" and groan. . . .'

The Russian with his 'gleaming eye'? I think he thought deeply about it in his subconscious, but I am not sure that the Bolsheviks were very conscious of it at that moment.

CHARLTON: Well, how conscious were the British from the outset that there was a great reversal in the tides of history and that the boot was now very much on the other foot, as far as the Russians were concerned?

GLADWYN: I think we knew, you see, by the time we got to Yalta that the Russians were just getting into Poland, and it was pretty clear that they were going to go deep into Germany. Nobody knew quite how deep even then, but we had to reckon with the fact that they would be occupying most of Eastern Europe and that it was absolutely inevitable. It was quite evident that the war was very quickly going to come to an end.

IT WAS AFTER DINNER on 4 February 1945, at the end of the first day, that, following a toast by Winston Churchill to 'the Proletariat Masses of the World', the minutes disclose there was a considerable discussion about the rights of people to govern themselves in relation to their leaders. When Stalin said that he would never agree to having any action of a great power submitted to the judgement of the small powers, Churchill answered him in these words: 'The Eagle should permit the small birds to sing, and care not wherefore they sang.'

In his generous allegory Churchill was acknowledging that the Soviet Union had unassailable security interests, but he was also disputing Stalin's concept of that security, so soon to be made manifest, as being indivisible from dictatorship by the Communist Party over occupied territory, and the imposition there of an alien ideology.

That issue divided Europe. It divides it still. Almost forty years later the hopes that the situation in Eastern Europe, which Yalta so ambiguously endorsed, would come to be accepted as the only available prescription for peace are being refuted in the recurring upheavals and resistance to Soviet domination. There is now a pattern discernible in these events. Each time they occur they pose a sharper and a more comprehensive challenge to the Russians. This pattern is matched by a progressive collapse in the appeal of the Communist claim to an ideology innately possessed of an historical inevitability.

A third warning has now come from Poland to be set beside the earlier warnings from Hungary in 1956, and Czechoslovakia in 1968, that the degree and nature of Soviet control in Eastern Europe is unacceptable to the peoples concerned. The balance of power in this world is still determined largely by what happens at the heart of Europe. The failure to comprehend that adequately led to two world wars.

Today there is a crisis developing in the Soviet Empire. Inevitably, the spectre of Yalta has been revived. In essence, the charge against the outcome of the famous conference in the Crimea is that a pragmatic, but ultimately disastrous, disregard for Stalin's underlying ideological and strategic ambitions allowed him, at Yalta, to secure the Soviet Union's advantage with impunity. Lord Gladwyn.

GLADWYN: The suggestion that Europe was carved up at Yalta is an illusion. It wasn't carved up at Yalta: it was carved up by the advance of the Soviet armies into Eastern Europe – that's what carved Europe up. At Yalta efforts were made to make the situation less intolerable, as far as we could, for the Poles and other nationalities. We didn't succeed, but I don't think you can criticise Yalta for having carved Europe up. I think it is really in itself an illusion.

A FIERCELY ARGUED controversy took place recently in the magazine *Encounter*, where Lord Gladwyn's pragmatic view was challenged by the Editor of *Survey*, Leo Labedz, who for many years has published an authoritative commentary on Eastern Europe.

LABEDZ: The events in Poland revived Yalta, because after all Poland was the beginning of the Cold War. And now, after Solidarity, when the Polish population made it quite clear what its attitudes are, there is very little room for any kind of doubt about the outcome of Yalta.

The fact is that Yalta gave the opportunity for the Soviet Union to swallow Eastern Europe. Now, thirty-seven years later, it is perfectly clear that they have been able to swallow but are not able to digest it. And that is why, at present, the discussion in the West must touch the question of Yalta, because the illusion of Yalta about Eastern Europe has now become part of the overall discussion about East–West relations. Some of these illusions were resuscitated during the period of *détente*.

The results of Yalta now are clear, not only vis-à-vis Eastern Europe but vis-à-vis the possibilities in Western Europe. The same policy, and the same attitude behind the policy, may result in the eventual loss of Western Europe in the same way that Eastern Europe was lost. I am not of course comparing the situation in the sense that there is going to be occupation by military means, in the same way as the Red Army occupied the East. There are some basic differences in this situation. But within the framework of the policy there are some points of comparison, as far as the attitudes of some Western politicians are concerned.

CHARLTON: You say that Yalta gave the opportunity to the Soviet Union under Stalin to swallow Eastern Europe, but what do you say to the argument that it was not diplomacy but the march of events, the march of armies, which determined the division of Europe?

LABEDZ: Well I would say one or two things! One is that at the time the discussion started, from the word go, there were differing attitudes between those who had both the experience and the historical perspective of Soviet foreign policy and those who did not. The prospective victims knew much better what was going to happen to them than those who assured them that everything would be fine because Stalin had signed the Declaration on Liberated Europe.

Of course you can say that it was not the diplomacy which was decisive, but the march of armies, and of course it is obvious that this is the case. But it does not detract from the fact that this diplomacy helped; and that those who were pursuing the Yalta policy were full of illusions, illusions for which there is no longer any room.

THERE HAS BEEN an enduring challenge to the 'realistic' thesis from the Poles. Solidarity in 1980 was seeking what Poland was promised in 1945 at Yalta – 'free elections'. Roosevelt had said to Stalin that 'they should be, like Caesar's wife, "above suspicion".' But in the end the promise was hedged about with ambiguity.

The 'realistic' view – that is, the one which came to prevail among the foreign policy advisers to the British and American governments (and which is put forward in essentials by Lord Gladwyn) – is held by opponents to overlook the vital influence upon Western policy of a whole attitude of mind. First, that there was a climate of public opinion in the West, largely due to government propaganda and officially inspired, which had kindled the image of Stalin as 'Uncle Joe' and of the Soviet Union ruled by him as a benign state. Second, that this obscured the opposite meanings in the use of words like 'Democracy' and 'Freedom' on either side of what became the Iron Curtain; and, further, that this had important consequences in decisions and agreements which had no real chance of being implemented.

Poland was the key issue. Seventeen hours, and thousands of words of discussion were devoted to it at Yalta. It was, as Churchill said, the first of the great causes which led, at the war's end, to the disintegration of the alliance against Hitler.

A courier from Warsaw, from the Underground Army (fighting there during the war against the Germans) to the Polish Government-in-Exile in London, was Jan Nowak.

NOWAK: Yalta came as a terrible shock. I would say the perception of Yalta among the Poles in England was slightly different from the one in Poland itself. In Poland it was a shock because the faith and trust in the Allies was so strong that, even up to the last moment, nobody expected that the United States and Great Britain could become accomplices, could share responsibility for the subjugation and partition of Poland with the Soviets. And people could really not understand why.

The Poles in England had no illusions whatsoever. They knew that an agreement where both sides put entirely different interpretations on the words is worthless.

A few days after Yalta, I visited one of the Polish squadrons in England. The shock of Yalta among these pilots was terrible. They had lost so many of their colleagues and suddenly they could see that all was in vain, that all is lost. On that very evening the order came: all-out effort to bomb Chemnitz [in East Germany] to help the advance of the Red Army. And they refused. They said, 'We are not going to go, we will refuse. Because, after all, why should we put our lives in danger when it is all lost, when Poland is lost? Our fight is in vain.' And, just before the critical hour, the letter from the President of the Polish Republic, Raczkiewicz, arrived persuading them, in a quiet way, that if they refused the order, then all their sacrifices will be really destroyed, eliminated, if at the last moment they showed a lack of discipline.

And they all went; and there were some losses.

I thought that was probably the greatest act of heroism of my country-men that I saw in the last war.

It can have been only one among many reasons why Churchill said memorably to Stalin at Yalta that for Britain, 'Poland was a matter of honour: it was for Poland that Britain had drawn the sword against Hitler.'

But it was well before Yalta, following the German invasion of Russia – and even before it was clear that the Russians would withstand the shock – that the Foreign Secretary, Anthony Eden, was urging, in 1942, the need to bring the Poles to make legally defined concessions of their Eastern territory to Stalin. British policy was directed to a para-mount necessity – keeping the Soviet Union in the war. It was only at a later stage that both Churchill and Eden urged the Poles to take 'the realistic view' and make such territorial concessions *in time* rather than see Poland confronted with unwelcome new 'facts' created by the Red Army. Notwithstanding the recent British experience of this appeasing attitude in dealing with Hitler, the Foreign Office considered such legally-defined concessions as the only practical basis for conducting policy with Stalin, a now indispensable ally. It was urged upon the Poles as offering the only prospect of salvaging, if not Poland's territorial integrity, then Polish independence.

But the savagery and desolation brought upon Poland by the decision of Hitler and Stalin together to invade and destroy the Polish nation – their pact had only recently been discarded – made insurmountable demands upon Polish pragmatism. The Foreign Minister of the Polish government then in exile in London, now in his ninety-first year, was Edward Raczynski.

Raczynski: My feeling is that maybe, in this country, people did not realise the way the Russians acted. First of all their cruelty was totally inhumane. People did not realise that it was not only Katyn (which was not known at the time) but that there were millions of people who had been taken by the Russians from the eastern provinces and sent to Siberia and so on. The total number was never fully ascertained, but it was nearly two million people in fact who were removed from those eastern provinces and sent to their death.

Russian behaviour, Russian rule, in the parts of Poland which were in their hands before Hitler attacked Russia in 1941 was cold-blooded cruelty. So the Polish nation itself had a very good proof and a very good taste of what would be in store for them should they become subjects, or part of the Soviet Union. This was not fully understood in this country.

CHARLTON: But in this matter of territorial concessions, to what extent were you aware that there was something of an historical continuity in British attitudes over Poland? One goes back to what we know from the records of how the British thought about Poland at the time of the First World War and Versailles. Lloyd George quotes in his memoirs the paper drawn up by Balfour for the Cabinet then, which said that 'the solution of the Polish question which would best suit our interests would be the constitution of a Poland *endowed with a large measure of autonomy while remaining an integral part of the Russian Empire*'. Did you have the feeling that the British still supposed, twenty-five years later, that a peaceful future lay in 'Home Rule' for Poland: autonomy, but essentially a Poland which had to accept a friendly relationship with the Russians?

RACZYNSKI: I hoped that it was not so. You must understand that Poland was a considerable country. *In potentia*, Poland from the Middle Ages onwards was a kind of *sui generis* great power, and at the same time endowed with a very strong sense of independence. Furthermore, the whole nature of our country was so totally different from the Russians, who were submitted to an absolute ruler and accustomed to obey. The two races were so widely different, with the Poles feeling always more attracted to Western civilisation. With the Russians it was completely different – it was at first Byzantium and later on in any case it was 'the East'. So the difference between the two nations; and the attitude of the two nations was so fundamentally different. Maybe we could be on friendly terms with a peaceful neighbour, but the idea of Poland being subject to Russian rule in any form was, I think, an impossibility. I think Churchill understood that quite well.

The other view that you put forward was really held by another gentleman whom we disliked cordially, Lloyd George. Lloyd George published an article, in the *Sunday Express* I think it was, on 23 September 1939, in which he said that fortunately the reactionary Poles were now defeated. The populations of Eastern Poland would now have a pleasant life under the paternal rule of the Soviet Union – more or less: I'm paraphrasing of course. But we were accused of being 'reactionary', a landowners' government, aristocratic and so on.

CHARLTON: How damaging do you believe such perceptions of the Polish Government-in-Exile were? You remind us that Lloyd George had spoken of – and that you took up the issue publicly with him – 'this wretched class government'. But as late as 1944 we find Harriman, Roosevelt's principal Russian adviser, saying – and this is after Katyn, after the Hitler–Stalin Pact – 'I do not know what the Poles in Poland think but we know very well what the Polish Government in London thinks. It is predominantly a group of aristocrats looking to the Americans and British to restore the position and landed properties and the feudalistic system of the periods before and after the last war'; meaning the First World War.

RACZYNSKI: Which was totally and absolutely untrue. The Polish nation was never as united as it was during the war. We had nothing left of our freedom, of our property, of our political life and so the nation was really one bloc. During those war years the contact between the Poles at home and abroad was constant and the solidarity and sense of devotion to one's country was unique. The country was one bloc at that time.

CHARLTON: Nonetheless, how influential do you believe it was as forming a basis for decisions by the leaders of the West, this perception of you as a government that was out of touch, a 'reactionary' government, and that some kind of radical reform was overdue in Poland?

RACZYNSKI: Never. That I do not believe. As I say with the exception of two persons in this country who I remember as unfriendly. Lloyd George was one and another was Lord Beaverbrook.

CHARLTON: It is the British position I think – the conventional historical wisdom – that it was Polish intransigence (the intransigence of the Polish Government-in-Exile in London) on this frontier question that prevented Churchill and Eden and Roosevelt getting any very clear idea at an early stage of what Stalin's ultimate intentions over Poland really were.

RACZYNSKI: Maybe. But I do not think they understood the Russian mentality. I do not think they understood that the Soviet Russian mentality was one of more or less permanent conquest. It was first, as you know during the Tsarist period that the Tsarist government was always proclaiming the defence of the Orthodox faith in the union of all the Russian tribes. In other words they considered the Ukrainians and the others should all come under Russian domination. In the time of the Soviets this was extended, not only to all the Slav countries but to all the countries which were to accept the Communist creed. The expansionist nature of the Soviet Union was not understood at the time. Not fully understood.

CHARLTON: By Churchill?

RACZYNSKI: Churchill disliked them. He understood them better than others.

CHARLTON: And Eden?

RACZYNSKI: Eden was more the diplomat. I do not think, you know, that Eden had a very strong view himself.

CHARLTON: Roosevelt?

RACZYNSKI: Roosevelt was very weak. Not determined. But at the same time he was more of a politician than Churchill. When he received us in Washington he was full of sweet words as regards our situation. Towards the end he conceded the town of Lwów to the Russians but at the same time he would not say it to us. He was shifty as regards Polish questions.

IT WAS ONLY IN 1948 that the two 'secret protocols' in the Hitler–Stalin Pact became known, when the captured German archives were published by the Americans at the beginning of the Cold War.

The secret protocols make the more familiar explanation of this remarkable alliance as one forced upon the Russians by the Western democracies' appeasement of Hitler at Munich – a popular view during and since the war – something less than complete. They show that it was only Hitler who met Stalin's exacting demands – the Baltic States, half Poland, Bessarabia and an agreed sphere of influence south and east. (The latter revised and defined between them later, in November 1939, as south towards the Indian Ocean, and 'towards the Persian Gulf as a centre of Soviet aspirations'.)

In the two words which Hitler telephoned to Moscow in August 1939, 'Yes. Agreed', he gave to Stalin half of Eastern Europe. It was in collusion with Hitler that Stalin formulated his design for Eastern Europe and forged the means of achieving it. The much-vaunted 'Non-Aggression Pact' between Hitler and Stalin was, in reality, the opposite. It embodied the partition and destruction of the Polish State, agreed upon between them before hostilities even began. Robert Conquest is one of the authoritative historians of this period in Stalin's Russia – a time when a far-reaching agreement was made which contained elements of intimate collaboration expressed in phrases more typical of treaties of alliance or friendship. Stalin and Hitler had learned much from each other. Both used the same methods against enemies, real and imagined. Soviet and Nazi propaganda were strikingly similar.

CONQUEST: Perhaps it is best expressed by Molotov in a speech to the Supreme Soviet in October 1939, after the invasion of Poland, when he said: 'One blow from the German army and another from the Soviet army put an end to this ugly product of Versailles' – Poland. This was traditional. There was always a pro-German policy from the Rapallo Treaty onwards, and from the earliest days, when both Germany and Russia were the outcast states after the First World War – and that was strongly felt in one section, at least, of the Soviet foreign policy establishment. We know more about it now than we did, because there have been books by Russians like Gnedin, who was a prominent figure in the Soviet foreign ministry up to his arrest in 1939, and a lot more is known about the negotiations.

CHARLTON: But Western public opinion is, I think, accustomed to the idea that Hitler certainly thought that nations were expendable. What is the evidence that the Marxists (in this case Stalin) also thought so?

CONQUEST: Well, it goes back to Lenin, the notion that there are nations which are 'reactionary' and would disappear. Stalin showed it in his deportation of all those Caucasian nations in 1943–4, when entire nations were sent to the Far East and Siberia, and it was clearly intended that they should die out. But this is certainly, I think, quite different from the Nazi attitude: their 'blood theory' means that you cannot assimilate them. Stalin was more old-fashioned, in fact rather like Pobedonostsev under the Tsars, who looked forward to getting rid of the Jews in Russia by killing a third of them, letting a third emigrate, and assimilating a third. I'm sure Stalin would quite have approved of that.

CHARLTON: What would you say were the common points of agreement between Hitler and Stalin in addressing the issue of the Polish nation and its partition?

CONQUEST: There is, of course, a difference, in the sense that the Nazis officially regarded the Poles as 'sub-men' and this was certainly not so in the case of Stalin and the Communist Party. On the other hand, he'd dissolved the Polish Communist Party already and shot all its members of both factions, in the Soviet Union, as 'agents of the Polish fascist police'. So, there is a certain anti-Polish tone to his general attitudes. And then, Stalin was a great believer in destroying groups and classes which would prevent him from taking over a nation. He had a lot of Polish prisoners of war and others; he winnowed out the intellectual and other leadership and of course shot them at Katyn and Starobielsk in the north.

ALMOST FORTY YEARS after Yalta, the political landscape in Eastern Europe, and in Poland in particular, is like some exposed beach following storm and high tide. Issues and events which were either submerged or lost sight of in the huge scale and savagery of the Second World War and the fighting in the East – and the knowledge of which was repressed in the West in terms of conducting the alliance with Hitler in a war for joint survival – lie today like tidal rocks in the way of hope for improved relations between Poland and the Soviet Union as nations.

The realities of the Hiter–Stalin Pact and its brutal aftermath, as with the fate of the Warsaw Uprising, are still successfully confined by Soviet policy to an Orwellian limbo where they are neither acknowledged nor discussable. Above all there is the stupendous crime of Katyn.

Professor Stanislaw Swaniewicz (who now lives in London) was the last man to see alive some 5000 of his fellow Polish officers whose bodies were found subsequently by the German army in graves covered by small conifers in the Katyn Forest, near Smolensk, in Russia in 1943.

After the joint Nazi–Soviet invasion and partition of Poland in 1939, 250,000 officers and men of the Polish army – which had been resisting Hitler's invasion of Poland – were rounded up and sent into camps in the Soviet Union. There were 15,000 officers in all. They were separated from the rest into three camps. They were guarded as prisoners of war, not by the Red Army, but by detachments of the NKVD, as it was then known – the Secret Police.

After April 1940, and a story ending with a journey like the one Swaniewicz describes, the 5000 from his own camp, as well as the other 10,000, were never seen alive again.

Swaniewicz himself survived that final journey apparently because, at the very last moment, the Russians discovered that he was the author of an economic study of the German Reich which was of interest to Soviet intelligence. He was taken off the train for further interrogation. And so lived.

SWANIEWICZ: In 1939 I had been called up to my old regiment in which I had been a volunteer in 1919. This was a few days before the beginning of the war, and so at the very beginning of the war I was already in the western part of Poland. We fought against the Germans, and my divisional commander was taken prisoner. But some remnants managed to get across the Vistula, to the East, and we fought against the Germans again near the river Bug. There, ultimately, we learned that the Soviet Union had joined the attack against Poland and then we tried to reach the Hungarian border. This was just the remnants of my unit. During this effort I was taken prisoner by Russian cavalry, not very far from the Hungarian frontier.

CHARLTON: Then what happened?

SWANIEWICZ: Ultimately all the officers in Soviet hands were concentrated in three camps. It was cold: the beginning of November 1939. One camp was Kozielsk. I was there. It is a very famous place in Russia – if you know *The Brothers Karamazov*. There was a famous monastery, and one of Dostoevsky's main characters lived there as a hermit, near that monastery. Anyway, I was kept there together with my comrades. There were more than 4000 officers and also civilians – mainly judges and doctors. Getting on for 5000 people. There we stayed until April 1940. We were not treated badly. There was enough food to survive. Probably we felt hungry but it was not so bad. And there was a very thorough investigation. They asked everybody about his past, his family, everything. Everybody was in those files.

By the end of March we were told by the Soviet personnel of the camp that some major decision concerning our fate had been taken. Generally, you've probably noticed, Poles are very optimistic and I don't remember anybody who had any gloomy expectations. The worst thing we expected was that we would be handed over to the Germans. No one expected execution.

CHARLTON: But when you asked, 'What is going to happen to us?', what did the Russians say to you?

SWANIEWICZ: That they did not know – and it was certainly a sincere answer, because the Soviet system is one of very considerable secrecy. Perhaps there were some – a few people among the personnel of the camp – who knew, but very few.

I remember very well the date: 3 April. The first group was taken in an unknown direction, about 300 people. And then every few days they took another 300 – generally in the morning. On the previous day already the transport was prepared for them, and the Russian workers in the camp told us.

CHARLTON: What did they say?

SWANIEWICZ: Oh, they said there will be new transport and the cars are ready for you. They had a special kind of railway car, you see, called 'Stolypin cars'. They were for prisoners and were introduced in the old time of Prime Minister Stolypin. There were prison compartments inside the cars, with iron bars. There were always six cars prepared for a group of prisoners to be taken.

CHARLTON: Didn't that make you all rather apprehensive?

SWANIEWICZ: I would not say so. People were rather happy that something was happening. Something is changing! It was spring. Beautiful sun . . . and this certainly had some influence on our state of mind. The general feeling was of a certain excitement. The most optimistic people expected that we would be handed over somewhere outside the Soviet Union, maybe into the hands of the Allies. The less optimistic ones thought that we would be sent home to the place where we lived before the war. Others expected we might be handed over to the Germans, because there was the German–Russian alliance. We just said goodbye. Sometimes there was an expression of various feelings, but nobody really expected that it meant execution.

My own turn came rather late, on 29 April 1940. I was taken together with about 300 others to the lorries which took us to the railway station. The cars were waiting for us, not in the station but in the siding; and we were put in those cars. Usually we had travelled in ordinary cattle-cars, but this time we were put in these particular prison cars. There was very little room in the compartment. The compartment was for eight people. There were thirteen or fourteen, however, in the compartment. We travelled throughout the night.

In the morning, just as the sun was rising – we had no windows in our compartment but one could see something through the side-windows in the corridor where our guards were – I recognised that we were in Smolensk. Smolensk was a place I knew from the *First* World War, because I had spent most of 1914–18 in Russia. It was a very great surprise to all of us, because we did did not expect to be sent at once to the west, and Smolensk is about 200 miles to the west from Kozielsk. So there was an assumption that they were bringing us to be handed over to the Germans.

We stayed in Smolensk for a very short time, probably a quarter of an hour only. Then the train started again in the direction of the west. This we could determine from the position of the sun. To our very great surprise the train stopped very soon after that, and the unloading of the train started. At a certain moment the Soviet colonel – which is a very high rank in the NKVD – came into our car and called out my name, and I was told, 'We shall separate you from all your comrades. Take your belongings!' He brought me to another car, put me in an empty compartment, put a guard on my door and asked me, 'Would you like some tea?' I cannot explain it but, in Russian, it was a very friendly way of approach. The guard had no tea but he brought me plenty of hot water, and I also got something to eat. A herring and a bit of bread. Then I heard the cars being unloaded. I managed to get up on the luggage-rack of my car, and there was a small opening in the side and through this opening I could see what happened. There was a bus – not very large, for about thirty or forty persons, no more. There was an open space in front of it – very heavily guarded by guards with fixed bayonets. This made an impression on me because, you know, bayonets are very seldom used, except on ceremonial occasions. So, I saw my comrades being loaded into that bus. The bus left, and came back after about half an hour, and so on.

CHARLTON: It made several trips, this bus?

SWANIEWICZ: Several trips. There were 300 people and so – several trips.

CHARLTON: And we know now that the bus was going into the Katyn Forest?

SWANIEWICZ: It appears now that it was. At that time I did not know. There were trees and a bit of forest, so I did not see directly where the bus was going. But the question which interested me was why – this place was obviously very near – they did not simply ask us to go on foot, and yet there was a convoy. The day was really beautiful, a spring day. There was still a bit of snow on the fields. . . .

Another particular feature of this bus was that the windows were painted.

CHARLTON: Blacked out?

SWANIEWICZ: Blacked out. It was obviously so that the local population could not see who was inside the bus.

CHARLTON: You are the last man to have seen alive those who were executed in the Katyn Forest?

SWANIEWICZ: Yes.

CHARLTON: When you saw your brother officers, the last of them, being loaded into this bus what impression did they make on you? Were they uneasy? Were they beginning to put up some kind of resistance?

SWANIEWICZ: My impression was that this was something very bad for *me*! That *I* had been separated! I expected that the fate of my comrades was better than mine. I could not speak to them. I had a feeling that something bad would happen to me, that I might ultimately be shot because I realised that they knew about me in the Soviet Union. But, not concerning my comrades. For my comrades I had no impression that anybody would suspect something, or what really happened. The general attitude was rather optimistic. This is what I remember of those last moments with my comrades. I could not speak to them, but I did not see that anybody had any premonition.

CHARLTON: The Russians seem to have been successful in keeping what happened quite remarkably secret. Did you have no inkling, you who survived almost uniquely, of what had happened until the bodies were found by the Germans?

SWANIEWICZ: You see my case is very special. I was released from the Soviet camp in April 1942. The agreement between Poland and Russia had been signed in August 1941. But they did not release me. When I was released and sent to the Polish Embassy (then in Kuibyshev) I submitted my report. The Polish army authorities were then looking for some evidence about this 15,000 who had disappeared – and they had one name, my name, and that I was in some camp in the north of Russia. So they expected me to have some kind of information.

In this report I described everything which I have told to you about the direction, about Smolensk, about the unloading in Smolensk and so on. It was a very great surprise to everybody, because the Polish authorities, General Anders and his staff, were looking somewhere in the *east* of Russia. Now my report was that the direction was to the west, that it was there – a few miles to the *west* from Smolensk – that we were unloaded. This came as a very great surprise. The surprise was also because they had asked the Soviet authorities, 'Tell us please what was the direction of transport from the camps of Kozielsk, Starobielsk, and Ostashkov?' And do you know what the answer was? 'They were released. We have released them.'

Now, according to my evidence, they kept the files on everybody in Moscow, and the extremely important thing is that the lists of people who went on a given date from the camps were dictated by telephone from Moscow. So files on everybody were in the central NKVD offices in Moscow. We knew that. We knew it very simply because, when there was transport – on the day when transport was expected – they gave the orders from Moscow who to take, personally. We could hear it. People who worked in the office of the camp heard it. We could hear it because it was a beautiful spring day and the window was open. This was a very complicated operation, the giving of so many foreign names over the telephone from Moscow, and they had to repeat them. So we knew, usually a few hours in advance, who would be sent on this date. Everything was regulated from Moscow. I described all these things in my report to the Military Attaché. I did not suspect Katyn then.

KATYN, WHERE THE POLISH officers were shot in the back of the neck in 1940, was a massacre carried out in secrecy and as a routine administrative measure in what was then peacetime in the East – the time between the crushing of Poland, and Hitler's invasion of the Soviet Union in June 1941.

The efforts made by the Russians at the Nuremberg Trials to blame the Germans for the killings at Katyn were mysteriously dropped; and Katyn remains the only 'German war crime on Soviet territory' which the Russians no longer even mention. Airey Neave (who served on the excutive of the International War Crimes Tribunal, assisting the judges who tried the German war criminals) wrote later that the evidence before the court demonstrated quite clearly that it was the Russians who were responsible. In the end, as Churchill put it in his memoirs, 'it was decided that the issue should be avoided.' The revelation of what had happened at Katyn came at a moment of critical importance – as the fortunes of war (following the Soviet Union's decisive victory at Stalingrad) had been reversed. It seemed clearer that Hitler would now be beaten. The Allied leaders were looking more intently to the future design of Europe.

Katyn therefore presented itself as a startling prism through which the nature of the Soviet state and the chances of common purpose and cooperation with Stalin had to be viewed and assessed – and not just by the Polish Government-in-Exile in London, led by General Sikorski, but also by Churchill and Roosevelt.

Advice on Polish and Soviet questions to the British Cabinet was a principal responsibility of the Central Department of the Foreign Office, whose Acting Head at the time was Sir Frank Roberts.

ROBERTS: Katyn suddenly blew up, I think it was in 1943 wasn't it? And that was a major disaster obviously. Because the Poles at once jumped to the conclusion, I think myself the right conclusion, that it was the Russians who had done it. But the Russians were our wartime allies. We hadn't chosen them but, after all, there they were!
CHARLTON: Why then did Eden say exactly the opposite in the House of Commons when asked that question? He said, 'We have no wish to apportion the blame for this tragedy on anybody other than the common enemy.'
ROBERTS: Of course there wasn't any *evidence* at that point. One of the main reasons for the Polish assumption that it was the Russians was that they had been making enquiries of the Russians about these officers when they were rebuilding their army, and they could never get any kind of

satisfactory answers. But still, in London, we had to assume that the Poles would think the worst of the Russians in any circumstances.

If you remember, the Germans did get a theoretically. . . . It was a neutral commission, Swiss and others, to come and look at Katyn who gave a rather anodyne report. We could not get up in the House of Commons and say, 'We *know* that this was our Allies the Russians.' And there was an advantage at that time, I think, in trying to keep the alliance going, trying to keep the possibility of Sikorski and the Russians reaching an eventual agreement. After all this horrible thing had been done, *before* the resumption of relations between Poland and Russia. So it really knocked the bottom out of what was, to us, the sole hope of getting a Polish agreement with Russia, and therefore an independent Poland after the war.

CHARLTON: You were in the thick of Polish affairs at this time. Can you remember the impact Katyn made on you personally?

ROBERTS: I personally jumped to the same conclusion as the Poles. And of course my first feeling was: 'How absolutely horrible,' and my second feeling, naturally, was: 'Oh God, this does ruin the chances we were working on with Sikorski of getting some reasonable arrangement between Russia and Poland.' I think this really did undermine it. Later of course, the following year, the Warsaw Uprising more or less completed the operation of ruining any possibility of relations.

CHARLTON: I think it must be on almost the same day that the Foreign Office records indicate that Katyn was being discussed among you all there (18 June 1943) that Sir Alexander Cadogan, the head of the Foreign Office, writes in his diary about 'an extremely well done despatch' by Sir Owen O'Malley at the Foreign Office. . . .

ROBERTS: . . . Owen was absolutely convinced, rightly I think, that it was the doing of the Russians. We got despatches almost daily on the subject.

CHARLTON: Cadogan says, '. . . an extremely well done despatch by O'Malley making the case against the Russians for the Katyn murders and drawing the inference that it was terrible to be on friendly terms with a government which can do such things.'

ROBERTS: And I would agree wholeheartedly. But after all, it was at the beginning of 1941, wasn't it, that Churchill said, 'I will sup with the Devil if I have to', or words to that effect?

CHARLTON: Yes, Churchill (I have it here) saying at the time that if Hitler invaded Hell he would feel that he would have to make at least one favourable reference to the Devil in the House of Commons!

ROBERTS: Yes, indeed. We were allied to an unpleasant dictator in Stalin. But on this particular issue it was not the idea of 'don't let's be beastly to the Russians', it was very much more, I repeat, that we felt it might knock the bottom out of any hopes of continued agreement between Sikorski and Stalin on which the only hopes of ever getting a viable and independent Poland after the war were based.

CHARLTON: Why was it that Churchill sought, as we know he did, the special guidance of the Foreign Office on this issue? 'Merely,' as he said, 'to ascertain the facts, because we should none of us speak a word about it'? The point is, it was never made public.

ROBERTS: Well, because of the wartime alliance undoubtedly. We felt, and as it happened we rightly felt, that it was going to ruin – well, the Russians broke off relations with the Poles over Katyn. And from then on there were no relationships. We were trying hard to recreate them. And then of course we had the subsequent disaster (it was in the same year) of Sikorski's death. From then on the chances of doing a deal between the Poles and the Russians were minimal in my view, but we had to go on trying. Sikorski's death was a major disaster. I took the news, I remember, to Churchill, who wept. He was very fond of Sikorski, who was a very attractive character. As I say all our Polish policies were based on Sikorski who was the only leader, a leader of authority and one who saw the need for an agreement with Russia.

CHARLTON: Yes. I suppose the charge might be, in historical terms, that you put Katyn out of your minds, rather than reflecting more deeply upon the lessons of it?

ROBERTS: No, I don't think so. We certainly reflected on the lessons. But you see we were fighting a *war* at that time, and we were not able to *do* anything in Eastern Europe. The only people who *could* do anything in Eastern Europe were the Russians who were engaging, after all, two-thirds or more of the German army.

CHARLTON: It has no place at all, this whole affair, in Eden's memoirs and has been consistently played down – not just during the war; but it is played down even today. It is still more or less a taboo subject it seems. Why is it?

ROBERTS: I had no idea it was. I mean, to me it's not a taboo subject, but I didn't really . . . I mean I'm not trying to cover up, but I didn't realise it was. At that time, I entirely agree with you – I mean Churchill and Eden said, really, 'For God's sake, don't let us talk too much about this.'

IT HAD BEEN British policy to encourage reconciliation between the Poles and the Russians and to avoid having to make choices between the two. Katyn dictated the necessity for choice. It had sent a disturbing, even awesome signal that an agreement over frontiers was not (as the British had hoped and supposed) at the root of disagreement between Stalin's Russia and Poland. But: '*Clearly we must try and plaster it over*,' Sir Alexander Cadogan confided to his diary at the time. There can be no doubt that Churchill accepted at the outset the probability of Soviet guilt for Katyn. The Polish Foreign Minister, Edward Raczynski, who was in personal touch with him, recalls Churchill's first reactions to Katyn.

RACZYNSKI: My feeling was that he understood it fully, as we did. It was obvious that it was a Russian doing. There was not the slightest possibility of explaining it otherwise. So that when we met, soon after the news was released, Churchill said to us, 'Oh, the Soviets can be very cruel.' So he knew very well. Sikorski explained at length why we were fully convinced of who the culprit was. Churchill kind of listened carefully to what we had to say, and I think he never tried to discuss it, or to oppose another view. I think he understood it fully. I am personally well informed because I remember a telephone call from him (whether it was from Chequers or London, I don't know) and he was in a state of great excitement because he knew that Stalin had broken off relations with Poland, and of course he was very cross with the Polish government for having appealed to the Red Cross over Katyn.

CHARLTON: It is a crucial moment this, isn't it? The British are urging you to forget Katyn, publicly at least, in the interests of *not* giving Stalin the excuse to break off relations with the Government-in-Exile in London?

RACZYNSKI: Which to a Polish government was practically impossible – to forget about it, to leave it alone. The Katyn massacre was such a dishonourable thing. The whole thing was such a blow that even today, after so many years, it is very difficult for the Polish nation to forget and it is still very difficult for the Russians to confess to their deed. It was a catastrophic affair.

STALIN BROKE OFF RELATIONS with the Polish government in London over Katyn. Eden had told the Poles that Stalin would agree not to do so if they blamed the Germans for the massacre. Sikorski, the Polish Prime Minister, refused. In the closest secrecy ('We should none of us speak a word of it,' in Churchill's words) the official British report on Katyn, drawn up by Sir Owen O'Malley of the Foreign Office, was sent by Winston Churchill to Roosevelt. It has never been published. But it was seen at the time, in unusual circumstances, by Edward Raczynski.

RACZYNSKI: O'Malley once invited me to his private apartment. We sat on the bed, and he read out to me his report to the British Cabinet, in which he gave all his arguments, and finished by saying that we should not allow this crime to pass unpunished, forgotten like the poor officers now under the trees planted on their graves.

CHARLTON: Under the conifers.

RACZYNSKI: Yes. And the whole report of O'Malley was that there was not the slightest doubt that it was Russian work.

CHARLTON: What were your reactions therefore when Eden spoke in the House of Commons and said that the United Kingdom – I think I'm quoting him accurately – had no wish to attribute this crime other than to the *common enemy*? He did not say the Germans, but the implication was clear.'

RACZYNSKI: Yes. We were very critical. We considered that to be shifty. It was as clear and as obvious as it could be.

KATYN HAS BEEN called the most puzzling and atrocious of Stalin's crimes. It was the murder of men who had surrendered to the Soviet Union and the Red Army in the field, and on terms. The coercive instrument Stalin alone wielded was that 'state within the state', the NKVD, the secret police, led at the time by Lavrenti Beria; and it carried out the Katyn murders.

A classic analysis of the objectives of Stalin's uses of terror has been written by Robert Conquest.

CONQUEST: I would certainly view it as decapitating the Polish nation. When Stalin occupied Lithuania, Latvia and Estonia, they deported about twenty per cent of the population – a broader spread than the mere 15,000 Poles he shot, but the categories which are listed include all former politicians, and intellectuals . . . anything resembling a cultural or political or national leadership. And Stalin is quoted once as saying, curiously enough, of the Poles and of the Hungarians, that they are 'strong nations' because they had an aristocracy – it was a very general sort of expression but there is the implication that if you kill off the officer class, it's easier to run them. I think he misunderstood Poland as many men in Moscow had done before.

But remember: it sounds exceptional to us, but it wasn't. There are mass graves of *Soviet* citizens in Vinnitsa in the Ukraine, for example. They discovered where they'd shot 7000 or 8000 people in the summer of 1938 and, once again, in peacetime. In fact Stalin's son, the one who was captured by the Germans . . .
CHARLTON: Yakov.
CONQUEST: . . . Yakov is quoted when they heard about Katyn, when it became public in 1943, as saying to fellow prisoners, Western ones: 'What are you making a fuss about – shooting 5000 people? What's *that?*'
CHARLTON: One recalls Stalin's famous rejoinder about his own son, 'I *have* no son called Yakov,' when told he was a prisoner. Is there any evidence for the belief that there may have been an additional motive with Stalin over the Polish officers – that it was in some way retributive? When in 1920 the Red Army was defeated by the Poles who resisted its arrival in Poland, the political commissar involved was Stalin himself.
CONQUEST: Possibly, but on the other hand the ones he shot at Katyn were not the leaders of 'the anti-Soviet War' in 1920. Those who were particularly anti-Soviet were kept in Soviet prisons. The ones who were shot at Katyn were simply shot on a class basis. They were simply shooting a category. And some of the anti-Soviet ones survived, got out.
CHARLTON: There are surviving scraps of evidence, aren't there, of what members of the NKVD hierarchy – the Berias and Merkulovs and

the Raikhmans, who were actually responsible, so it is thought, for this operation – are alleged to have said at one time or another: 'It was a great mistake.' Was there an element of caprice about Stalin's decisions? CONQUEST: I think there was, very much; I think you can say afterwards: 'We made a mistake,' when the *policy* changes and they need a Polish army, when they were trying to *build up* the Polish army. It was Merkulov, the Vice-Minister of State Security, who said that, that it was 'a big mistake'. But these people like Beria, Merkulov and Raikhman . . . they're really criminal types. They'd come up in the frightful massacres both by, and within, the NKVD in the thirties. But more striking to me is, when the Poles were trying to find out, the lies they were told, the complicated but childish lies: 'Perhaps they fled across the Manchurian border.' Stuff like that.
CHARLTON: Stalin himself said that to the Polish Ambassador, Kot.
CONQUEST: Yes. The Poles were allowed to go and ask, but they were told all sorts of damn silly stories, whereas the officials knew perfectly well what had happened. They had been involved in it themselves! There is a sort of element of automatic falsification in the Soviet system, or was then certainly.

AS THE ULTIMATE PHASE of the war advanced Katyn had raised – long before Yalta – the probability that Stalin wanted in Poland not just a friendly government (as he constantly maintained, and which Roosevelt and Churchill readily conceded was the Soviet Union's rightful expectation) but one which could be depended upon to support him in suppressing the knowledge, and snuffing out discussion, of what had happened. Katyn was an affair which could not be redeemed by any honourable explanation, and ever since it has been the Achilles' heel of Polish Communist governments.

Today we know that despite the heat and burden of the daily conduct of war on a global dimension, the episode of Katyn weighed heavily with Winston Churchill. Martin Gilbert is Churchill's official biographer, with a privileged access to the former Prime Minister's papers and correspondence.

GILBERT: I don't think he ever put it out of his mind. I think as an image in his mind it remained very strong, a rather horrific image. And he does come back to it again and again, always curious to know what new facts are coming to light, what sort of inquiries are being made. So on the personal side I think it had an effect.

When one looks at his discussions with Stalin subsequently, and his discussions with the Poles, I think one would be right to see Churchill feeling and rather fearing this thing of which Stalin and his people are capable. Of course, he had a very long history of knowing and having spoken against and denounced Soviet behaviour, and before that

Bolshevik behaviour. There is this aspect of Churchill – the lack of any illusions about Soviet behaviour – which underpins everything.

But then there is the other side of the coin: the realisation that without an intimate working relationship with the Soviets at every level – geographic, territorial and military – the Allies were in trouble. That somehow a relationship *had* to be found with Stalin, there *had* to be a chink, there *had* to be a way whereby these controversial issues could be resolved by some sort of compromise.

I think in his psychology, because he was a forceful personality, because he had many years – decades – of experience of succeeding (whether it was the Irish Nationalists, the terrorists of the 1920s, whether it was with the Arabs and the Jews in the 1930s), because he had dealt with very tricky situations and people, and had secured compromises – he felt, now, was it possible that Stalin and his people *alone* were incapable of being persuaded? Of being perhaps even forced into a position where they would commit themselves to something not entirely, not one hundred per cent, in their interests? I mean hence, as it were, his famous attempt to define the 'percentages' – that is, to find the chinks in the armour. Is Stalin prepared to accept only 50 per cent in Yugoslavia? In other words this would mean that we would have there some area of manoeuvre – we then have 50 per cent pressure.

After the war Churchill set down various musings about this period which were intended to guide him when he was writing his memoirs. And he writes of the Polish imbroglio – that is, the period of, say, Katyn to Yalta – was there really *no* way that we could somehow get through? Was there *no* way that we could achieve something? It would never be everything we wished to achieve obviously, but *surely* this man was capable of budging? As you know at Yalta, he felt momentarily that he had succeeded, and after Yalta asked many of his close advisers whether they thought that when Stalin got back to Moscow his people had forced him to renege on what he had agreed. Surely the whole thing could not have been 100 per cent deception? In other words even he, in his mind, created a Stalin who had other pressures on him, not merely his own decisions.

CHARLTON: Doesn't that make this Katyn episode even less easy to relegate, although it is in a category by itself. It seems to me that he does recognise at once, within a day or so, the central challenge it represents to the possibility of conducting an alliance with the Soviet Union. He sees the Russians as responsible for Katyn at once, and if that is so it means that the Russians from the very earliest time had no intention of seeing any government installed in Poland, other than a puppet one which they would control. Yet the whole of British policy is based upon the hope, if not the expectation, that this won't happen and that some kind of compromise is possible. Isn't that what Katyn represents?

GILBERT: It does and I think your phrase, the whole of British policy, is the key. Churchill had, I think, one overriding understanding of world affairs and the word 'priority' is his word and concept. He was always saying that basically everything in this world is evil; and in the Nazi– Soviet story this is very well borne out. But then we have quarrels with every government. He, for example, had a deep quarrel with the Poles for their seizing of Teschen from Czechoslovakia at the time of the Munich crisis. He regarded that as an absolutely terrible betrayal of everything; it aligned Poland with Hitler, it aligned Poland with the 'grabbing' nations who were breaking international law.

But you see we have to have these priorities. It does not mean that because we say Hitler is evil, Stalin is good. It means that we have limited resources and at the moment we are trying to destroy Hitler, and Hitler is on many fronts.

CHARLTON: What do we know that he actually said to Roosevelt about Katyn, in coming to the subsequent conclusion that 'the issue should be avoided'?

GILBERT: He decided to send Roosevelt O'Malley's despatch, the en-quiry he himself had called for. Now again, to try to recapture the perspective of this: the message which he sends Roosevelt is in fact primarily a message about Yugoslavia, but it happens to begin with the O'Malley despatch. 'Mr President, the first of these two papers is a grim, well-written story, but perhaps a little too well written. Nevertheless if you have time to read it, it would repay the trouble. I should like to have it back when you have finished with it as we are not circulating it officially in any way.' Then he goes on to discuss the then more serious issues of Tito v. Mihailovich, and the whole future of Yugoslavia.

CHARLTON: But it is also an invitation to Roosevelt to say nothing about it either, and confirming that 'we should none of us ever speak a word about it'?

GILBERT: Yes.

CHARLTON: One more thing. The famous episode at Teheran in November 1943, when Stalin cynically talked and joked about executing the officers of the German army (something he subsequently repeats at Yalta). At Teheran, Churchill stalks out of the meeting, actually gets up to leave the room. Roosevelt laughs and smiles genially, and it all blows over. But, it seems to me that that incident is only really intelligible in the light of the knowledge which all three men in that room had – of what really had happened at Katyn, and with Churchill realising that Stalin was proposing to do it again.

GILBERT: And that as far as Stalin was concerned there was nothing unusual about this, this was a way you did behave. I have always felt that. I mean that it was Churchill's sense of revulsion at Katyn and the realisation that this was exactly the order which this man could give.

At the time of Katyn Churchill did say – and this has been repeated by a number of people in their memoirs (Macmillan deals with it) – he said it on many occasions, that it began to obsess him. I found it in a telegram to Smuts, who monitored the Soviet situation very carefully and who was very suspicious of what Katyn implied for the post-war world. Churchill said, 'Will it be said of me that I was so obsessed with the destruction of Hitlerism that I neglected to see the enemy rising in the East? Will this somehow be my epitaph on everything that I have done from the Blitz, the Battle of Britain and onwards?'

BUT CHURCHILL'S SOMBRE self-questioning was overlaid with those more demanding priorities and considerations before which the rights and interests of the small states began to retreat.

A paper of fundamental importance for the understanding of British foreign policy during the Second World War was drawn up by the Northern Department of the Foreign Office, by C. A. Warner and Sir Orme Sargent for Anthony Eden, and went to the Cabinet for its approval in January 1942.

It included this, as part of an examination by Eden of 'the foundations on which cooperation between Great Britain and the USSR can be built during the post-war period':

> On the assumption that Germany is defeated, and German military strength is destroyed and that France remains, for a long time at least, a weak power, there will be no counterweight to Russia in Europe. But it may yet be necessary to maintain cooperation with Russia (a) because she might otherwise be tempted to collaborate with Germany in view of the historical tendency to, and economic urge for, these two Powers to work together; (b) in order to recreate in our own interest the balance of power in Europe against the possibility of a revived Germany, which balance has been destroyed by the collapse of France; (c) in order that, militarily speaking Germany may be encircled. . . . Common prudence requires that we should lay our plans on the assumption that if we want Russia's collaboration after the war we shall have to be prepared to make such a policy advantageous to her. Moreover the application of this policy is going to be a lengthy process. If we are to adopt it, we must therefore start on it now and not wait until the war is over.

Eden's memorandum also included this:

> Soviet policy is amoral; United States policy is exaggeratedly moral, at least where non-American interests are concerned. . . . As United States opinion, however, becomes more realistically-minded under the stress of war, this feeling may be gradually modified, especially as Russian assistance would be invaluable to the United States of America in preventing a revival of Japanese militarism in the Far East.

And so it was, now, that following upon the muted murmurs of the discovery in the Katyn Forest in 1943 there came the victories of the Red Army in the East. The consequences of those victories were being pulled more sharply into focus. With Hitler's presumed defeat, the Soviet Union led by Stalin would soon become the only military and political force on a continent of Europe which would be reduced to military and politicial impotence. Sir Frank Roberts again.

ROBERTS: We and the Americans were thinking basically in terms of – well, to put it flippantly, if you could only treat Stalin like a member of the club he will behave possibly one day like a member of the club; and we will get him into the United Nations, and we will somehow get this Russia as a responsible part of the post-war structure. This was the overriding thing.

But Stalin did not want to be a member of that kind of club. He much preferred to be the Director-General of *his* club, which was a quite different club, which he would not have had us in either. And this is where I think we were wrong. Churchill, I think, saw that he was wrong earlier than Roosevelt.

IT WAS TO FORESTALL the possibility of a 'different kind of club' (which carried, of course, the implication of a divided Europe) that Churchill and his advisers decided that some of Stalin's presumed demands over Poland should be accommodated. One of the crucial conferences of the war was approaching, that at Teheran in November 1943. The attitudes which influenced the Prime Minister's thinking at this time are recalled by Martin Gilbert.

GILBERT: His whole deep involvement with Poland had begun after the First World War, when he was of course excited that Warsaw resisted the arrival of the Red Army and drove it back. But he was then deeply suspicious of the new Poland that emerged through the Treaty of Riga, with its extended eastern frontiers taking in Lwów and Vilna and so on. He felt that this was some sort of distortion. Small nations, yes, he had great sympathy for them. He understood their dilemma: he was always thankful that Britain was not a small nation halfway between Germany and Russia. But he regarded the whole Polish concern with their eastern frontier as an obsession born of something unnatural in 1921. It wasn't as if defending the independence of Poland meant defending frontiers which were somehow a challenge to Russia. It was an approach he had held very seriously, historically.

Poland, I think, in his mind was always slightly beyond the pale, not one of the countries to which he was emotionally drawn. He was of course a great champion of the Czechs because, he said, they were the only democracy in Europe; and he was greatly involved in Yugoslavia's 1920s' and 1930s' struggle between, as it were, the democratic and the anti-democratic forces. At one point he wanted to go to Yugoslavia as an emissary of democracy.

But with Poland, once Hitler came to power, he then saw the thing, as it were, in reverse: that now Poland represented not a bulwark against Communism, but one of the non-Nazi, non-totalitarian states. And therefore he did begin to open contacts with the Poles, and tried to find out what made them tick, how strong they were. He remained suspicious of this Eastern Poland, with these massive minorities, these millions of people who were not Poles and towards whom the Russians would always hold ambitions.

In the West he had always supported Poland – the Polish Corridor and Poland's position between the wars. And he was often asked, of course, to subscribe to statements of defence of the borders of Poland. This he wouldn't do, and curiously, in this had a sort of link with Neville Chamberlain. Chamberlain, when he gave his guarantee to Poland in 1939, made it clear privately (and Churchill supported this) that it was a guarantee to maintain the independence of Poland.

But 'independence' did not mean territorial integrity. So that Poland, yes, must not be crushed; it must still have the sort of government in which there would be all the things which Yalta apparently promised, free elections, and yet no sympathy for this *exaggerated* Polish view. Now when the Poles came to him, he had long discussions with them, and, as you say, he put great pressure on them. At one point in one of these talks the Poles, losing their tempers, said, 'But surely we have the right to resist this?' Then there was no reply from him for a moment. So everybody looked on, and all the officials – what is he going to answer? And they found that he was blubbing, he was actually in tears and shaken. This was conscience you might say, and then he looked up and said, 'Gentlemen, the right to resist, that cannot be denied even to the weakest.' Now this was his true feeling.

Of course you can challenge what he saw as the reality of what the Soviets would demand, and that all you could really hope to do was to obtain some sort of assurance for a reduced area for Poland, but an area which would be compensated for in the West. But this is what we must come back to in the end really, the mystery – the Yalta pledge. He did believe that it could work.

But Yalta was still to come, and over a year away. Taking the 'exaggerated' Polish view with him as a bargaining concession, Churchill proposed to Stalin at Teheran in November 1943 that Poland as a state should be moved bodily westwards: in the hope, it was clear, that the further west her frontiers were drawn, the less Stalin would insist on dominating Poland as a buffer state.

Churchill and Roosevelt were trying to grope their way towards a fundamental understanding with one of the world's most powerful leaders. But Stalin was also among the least known of them. The arts of the yielding compromise, openly acknowledged, and that respect for the opponent's contribution which characterises the British and American political tradition, were wholly alien to him. He had shown himself, in all the uses of power to be pitilessly realistic. The British official minutes of the Teheran Conference distil, in a few laconic exchanges on blue Foreign Office paper, how the British Prime Minister, and his Foreign Secretary, Anthony Eden, tried to probe Stalin's intentions over Poland.

> THE PRIME MINISTER suggested that they should discuss the Polish question.
> MARSHAL STALIN agreed and invited the Prime Minister to begin.
> THE PRIME MINISTER said we had declared war on account of Poland. Poland was therefore important to us. Nothing was more important than the security of the Russian western frontier. But he had given no pledges about frontiers. He wanted heart to heart talks with the Russians about this. When the Marshal felt like telling us what he thought about it, the matter could be discussed and they could reach some agreement, and the Marshal should tell him what was necessary for the defence of the western frontiers of Russia.
> MARSHAL STALIN said he did not feel the need to ask himself how to act. So far his heart did not feel stimulated.
> (He meant that the Prime Minister should become more precise)
> THE PRIME MINISTER said that after this war in Europe, which might end in 1944, the Soviet Union would be overwhelmingly strong and Russia would have a great responsibility for hundreds of years in any decision she took with regard to Poland. Personally, he thought Poland might move westwards like soldiers taking two steps, left close. If Poland trod on some German toes, that could not be helped, but there must be a strong Poland. This instrument was needed in the orchestra of Europe.
> MARSHAL STALIN asked whether we thought he was going to swallow Poland up.
> MR EDEN said he did not know how much the Russians were going to eat. How much would they leave undigested?
> MARSHAL STALIN said the Russians did not want anything belonging to other people, although they might have a bite at Germany.
> MR EDEN said what Poland lost in the East she might gain in the West.
> MARSHAL STALIN said possibly they might, but he did not know.
> THE PRIME MINISTER demonstrated with the help of three matches his idea of moving Poland westwards, which pleased Marshal Stalin.

ROBERTS: This was the way Churchill did conduct those kind of talks, and it was what was being done. I mean, the Poles were being asked to say, 'Well, you can't keep that territory because, after all, it's the Russian armies that are all-powerful in that part of the world, and we will try and compensate you by putting the matches over there.'

CHARLTON: But would you agree that we did rather seem, during this period, to grasp at the hope and the possibility that, by giving back to Stalin these eastern territories, with a large non-Polish population, he would somehow be deterred from intervening in the internal life of Poland? As we now know, with the benefit of hindsight, he wished and was determined to do so.

ROBERTS: But could I just take issue with the words 'giving back to Stalin'? We didn't have them to give back. Stalin was either in occupation of them or about to take them – I mean, not from us, but with the Red Army. The problem was whether we, in treaty form, accepted the situation. The only choice we had, at that time, was either to make the best deal we could, and I am going on to Yalta now; or to say, 'No, we won't make a deal.'

Then you say, 'Why was the deal made?' Well, partly because we did honestly think it was the best deal that could be made.

CHARLTON: On the other hand, the British policy long antedated the Soviet military successes, as seems clear from Eden's belief, as early as 1941, that concessions should be made to the Russian point of view. One can understand Churchill's pressure on the Poles at a time when it was becoming obvious (after Kursk and Stalingrad) that the Russians were going to *take* the greater part of Eastern Europe. But what was the objective of the Foreign Office and Eden's view that we ought to try and *give* Stalin what he'd got in Poland as the result of the pact with Hitler?

ROBERTS: I think that is going a bit too far. I mean, in discussions with the Russians, it was a little bit difficult to deny to them what was obviously a fact, that in 1919 we had considered that the right ethnical frontier was the Curzon Line, and therefore we still did. And in 1942, a little later than the time you're talking about, when we were negotiating the Anglo-Soviet Treaty with the Russians – and the Russians *did* want to make it part of that treaty that we accepted the Curzon Line frontier, or something very like it, in Poland – we refused. We were not giving it away at that time.

CHARLTON: But would you not agree that Eden was working on the War Cabinet in 1942, and on the Americans, to bring them round to this position? Because the record shows clearly that when he was urging this on Churchill (who was in America at the time) and advocating 'stark realism', Churchill, if I may quote it to you, sent this reply to Eden, and a rather frosty one it was!

> Your telegram surprised me. We never recognised the 1941 frontiers. They were acquired by acts of aggression in shameful collusion with Hitler. There must be no mistake about the opinion of any British Government of which I am the head; that it adheres to the principles of the Atlantic Charter and that these principles must become especially active whenever any question of transferring territory is concerned.

ROBERTS: It does not, of course, alter the fact that Churchill in 1943 and 1944 was bringing pressure to bear on the Foreign Office to see reality.

CHARLTON: I quite agree, but what fascinates me is why the Foreign Office is anticipating Soviet demands which the Soviet Union was not then, in 1942, in a position to insist upon.

ROBERTS: Perhaps the Foreign Office at that time were all doing something they were accused of never doing – showing some foresight. Eden was saying, 'This is probably what we will have to settle for in the end, and we had better be ready for it.'

CHARLTON: The record shows that, in the months preceding the Teheran Conference of November 1943, episodes like Katyn, revealed in the middle of that year, were very fresh in your memory – and it shows that you took up personally with Eden the Polish issue. In the context of Teheran, and of Churchill's signal there to Stalin, we were to agree to the Curzon Line. After Katyn you talk about the 'de facto abandonment of the Poles'. And you get this reply from Eden: 'Assuredly,' he says to you, 'I don't want to throw the poor Poles to the Russian wolves.' It seems, obviously, to suggest that you thought that's what British policy *was* doing?

ROBERTS: Well, memory is fallible and I don't remember that particular exchange. But I think our Ministers, after Sikorski had gone, found the Polish government more traditionally nationalistic, less inclined to try and do a deal with the Russians, and therefore a more difficult partner or client. They used to get rather irritated with what they regarded as the unrealism of the London Poles' policies.

On the other hand, we – Churchill more than anyone – were very conscious of the bravery of the Polish airmen (who'd fought in the Battle of Britain) and of the Anders Army (who'd after all contributed enormously to the victory at Monte Cassino), and – don't let's forget it – they had a jolly good navy too, which they'd built up. So there were these two conflicting views. I mean, these splendid Poles who were fighting with us, to whom we owe a lot – and, to put it a little bit unfairly, this damn silly Government-in-Exile who don't see the facts of life. Obviously, I was in the middle of this. And you had sort of specific issues . . . I'm talking about this particular exchange, when I appeared to be thinking that we were throwing the Poles to the wolves.

CHARLTON: It was December 1943 . . . Boxing Day.

ROBERTS: Yes, that's right, and all the time, you see, the Russian armies were advancing. The Russian military position was getting stronger, and therefore, naturally, Churchill was saying, 'It is getting increasingly difficult to argue the Polish case effectively with the Russians, so let's for God's sake get settled on something now, because it'll be worse later on.' And of course he was right.

CHURCHILL HAD ASKED, in return for this concession, that Poland should be free to choose its own form of government. However, he had the ground shot from beneath his feet at Teheran by Roosevelt. The record shows that the American President made no real effort to get anything in return for the Poles. Stalin was undoubtedly free to draw the inference that the Americans had no serious interest in the Balkans or Eastern Europe. Furthermore, it was at Teheran that Churchill's long-argued preference for an Anglo-American invasion into the Balkans, into 'the soft underbelly of Europe', was finally dismissed by the American Chiefs of Staff in favour of the Second Front in Normandy. With it went a favourite topic of speculation for armchair strategists, namely the chance for the West to play a greater role in Eastern Europe. Stalin had seen also that the British were forced to back down.

The issue of territorial concessions broke the ranks of the Polish government in London, with some of them believing that such a device would destroy, not preserve, the unity of the Polish nation. They could not agree. Unable to align themselves with the imperatives of either Anglo-American or Soviet policy, the relevance of the Polish government in London was quickly fading.

Jan Nowak was the courier at the time between the Polish underground resistance in Warsaw, the Home Army, and the Polish government in London.

NOWAK: What they asked Poland to do could not save Poland. And, every Pole knew about this, that concessions would not save Poland. It was quite understandable that when the war was in progress, neither Britain nor the United States could risk an open conflict with the Soviet Union over the Polish issue because it would weaken the war effort. That is understandable. But what I saw was that Britain and the United States *helped* the Soviet Union.

The Poles were asking, 'If you cannot do anything for us, please do not do anything against us; do not weaken our position. At least do not say openly that there will be no resistance, no conflict over Poland.'

I read the document where Bierut, the Polish Communist leader, asked Stalin, 'Will there be any conflict over Poland with the West?' and Stalin says there will be no conflict whatsoever. He just dismissed the idea. You know, this is what the Anglo-Saxons did: they removed the element of doubt. They really offered, in advance, an assurance that 'there will be no resistance over the Polish issue'.

BY THE BEGINNING OF 1944 Anthony Eden was minuting to Churchill, 'The truth is that in the present atmosphere of overwhelming Russian victories there is a public impatience with the Poles. This may not be just, but it is the truth.' Yet it is in the Polish government's lack of agreement and their refusal to give way to the pressure Churchill and Roosevelt applied to win their consent that we must look for the deeply rooted origins of the contemporary upheavals in Poland, according to Jan Nowak.

NOWAK: I feel they were right not to do it. The problem was (and this was said – if I remember – by Raczynski to Eden) that if we really accept the kind of concession you try to impose on us, the unity of the Polish nation will be ruined. This 'Union Sacrée', he used this word, will be destroyed. All right, the cause was lost, the war was lost – but we have to think in terms of the future and to preserve unity. And this unity was preserved. I think that Solidarity has really been in existence in a latent form since the last war. It was forged in the Polish resistance movement and, to the end, thanks to what you call the 'intransigence' of the Poles, it was preserved. Otherwise we would not have Solidarity today.

The government and the system imposed from outside were legitimised in Yalta and Teheran and Potsdam. But Poles never legalised this government. They have never forgotten that the birth-certificate of this government is not Polish. It was born in Moscow, not in Warsaw. It never represented a Polish continuity. It was imposed from outside. And now, until this day, it is a common expression in Poland. 'We and They.' They, the Ruling Group; We, the Society. That is the remnant of the last war.

THE ARCHIVES YIELD a remarkable glimpse of Churchill at this time. Early in 1944 he was writing to Eden.

> Undoubtedly, my own views have changed in the years that have passed. The tremendous victories of the Russian armies, the great changes which have taken place in the character of the Russian state and government and the new confidence which has grown in our hearts towards Stalin, these have all had their effect.

Such uncharacteristic optimism from Churchill concerning Stalin and the Russians was a contrast to his more usual wary pessimism. Within five months of going to Yalta he was confronted by one of the most tragic episodes of the war. The Polish Underground Army rose in Warsaw, as the advancing Russians arrived. Stalin then kept the Red Army in calculated inactivity on the other side of the Vistula opposite Warsaw.

On 14 August 1944, Churchill (in Italy) telegraphed to Eden: 'It certainly is very curious that the Russian armies have ceased their attack on Warsaw and withdrawn some distance at the moment when the Polish Underground Army revolted.' Two German SS divisions which had been retreating thereupon returned to Warsaw and in six weeks of savage fighting – there were 200,000 Polish dead – wiped out the Polish Resistance.

The sinister import of Stalin's decision was compounded, for Churchill particularly, by his refusal to allow British and American aircraft to use Soviet airfields after their dropping missions to Warsaw. It meant a restriction on the already few missions, which involved a 1750-mile round trip and were carried out with conspicuous bravery and heavy casualties.

Churchill had wanted to present Stalin with a *fait accompli* and land on Soviet bases anyway. But Roosevelt, in Churchill's words, 'could not bring himself to make a decision'. More than Katyn in 1943, the fate of the Warsaw Uprising in 1944 brought the West face to face with the reality of Stalin's design for Poland. He had made it clear that he considered those Poles who were not prepared to accept Communist authority as no better than the German enemy.

Throughout this vital year of 1944, preoccupied with the Presidential Election in November, determined to leave the political settlement until the Peace Conference at the end of the war, no clear signals were sent by Roosevelt to Stalin indicating the limits of American tolerance. Churchill had said on his return from Teheran in 1943 that it was there he realised for the first time what a small nation Britain had become, and he fretted impatiently that the Red Army was 'not waiting for the outcome of the American Election'. It was, therefore in the absence of a solid under-standing between the British and the Americans – a consciousness of British military impotence and of American indifference – that Churchill and Roosevelt went to Yalta to meet Stalin in February 1945.

Yalta is often portrayed as a sell-out of Eastern Europe to the Soviet Union. It was in fact an attempt to reopen issues which had already been decided, or were being decided, by the advance of the Red Army.

With Winston Churchill at Yalta was one of his senior advisers, the Military Secretary to the War Cabinet, Sir Ian Jacob.

CHARLTON: Is it possible to recall accurately, do you think, in what frame of mind Churchill and Roosevelt went to Yalta?
JACOB: I think Roosevelt wanted to have further talks with Stalin, and wanted to ensure that Stalin was coming into the war against Japan quickly and would make the necessary arrangements in the Far East for American aeroplanes and all that sort of thing. I think that what Churchill wanted to do was to try and arrive at some sensible arrange-ments for Europe with the Russians gradually advancing over it, and taking control of it. And I have no doubt that Roosevelt was pleased to have a further talk with Stalin because he thought that, after the war, he and Stalin would have been the key figures.
CHARLTON: But would you say they went there, did Churchill go there, with a feeling that a crisis was imminent?
JACOB: No, I do not think so. You see Churchill had had what he thought were very successful talks in Moscow in October 1944 where Stalin was much more accommodating than usual and appeared to agree a good deal with some of the things Churchill was saying – although I do not for a moment think that Churchill thought afterwards that added up to anything very much. But still, I think he probably felt that if he and Roosevelt put the pressure on, then Stalin would be more careful about what he did in Eastern Europe.

There was the famous 'percentages' he drew up in October with Stalin, and Stalin said he agreed with. That was when we had a very difficult period with the Communists in Greece – their irregular forces had been a great danger to everybody – and he knew that Tito was a Communist and that Russia would get into Hungary, Bulgaria and of course Austria before we would. So he wanted to ensure that the thoroughgoing Russian domination of these countries would be limited. He thought that if Stalin agreed to having a fifty-fifty influence, as he put it down for example in Yugoslavia, there would then be legitimate grounds for us holding the Russians to sensible courses and pretty well keeping them out of any idea of controlling Greece. That, Churchill was very keen on.

CHARLTON: While we are, for the moment, digressing, that 'percentages' agreement is one of the most famous documents of the Second World War and has been much criticised since hasn't it? I think the view is that it was a curious diplomacy. Can you say why it took the form it did?

JACOB: Because I think that, curiously enough, Churchill was a practical man, in the sense that he thought if he could demonstrate that sort of thing in simple terms it would be more effective than any other means of doing so. Now it does not mean, of course, any exact figure. But it does mean that you recognise that the influence of the Russians in those countries would, to that extent, be limited.

People who criticise these things, I suppose, criticise any idea of spheres of influence. You see, that is all rot. Spheres of influence exist, and always will exist, and it is no good imagining that they won't exist. So, if you can limit them in some way – the ones you do not like – so much the better. Establish the fact that you are entitled to a full share of your interest in Greece, for example.

CHARLTON: But had Churchill already made up his mind, do you feel, that what happened at Yalta, a few months later – the 'Declaration on Liberated Europe', with its provision for free elections – was not really capable of enforcement? He later agrees, does he not, that the 'percentages' agreement had hampered British protest over what Stalin proposed to do in Poland. One wonders whether Churchill had already made up his mind that Poland had gone by then.

JACOB: I think he had. After all, one has to remember the one big fact at that time was that, there was the Russian army rolling forward in these countries and nothing, nothing you could do – other than starting a war against Russia – would stop them.

CHARLTON: Can I put two Churchill statements to you and ask whether you think Churchill was consistent or, rather, erratic in his attitude to what it was possible to achieve with the Russians?

After Yalta he says, in the House of Commons: 'The impression I brought back is that, so far as Stalin is concerned, I am quite sure that he means to do well to the world and to Poland and I feel no doubt whatsoever in saying that Stalin had been sincere.' Now, that is just after Yalta. Yet only a few months before, in the middle of 1944, he says this to Eden in a minute from Prime Minister to Foreign Secretary:

> Although I have tried in every way to put myself in sympathy with these Communist leaders, I cannot feel the slightest trust or confidence in them. Force and facts are the only realities they understand and every effort should now be concentrated on close relations with the United States of America.

JACOB: Well, I cannot help feeling that he was using what I can only describe as romantic language in the House of Commons. I do not believe for one minute that he felt that.

CHARLTON: Did he take that view because, in your opinion, a break with the Russians was unthinkable in terms of public opinion on the eve of victory?

JACOB: Not only public opinion. There was absolutely nothing you could do. Even if you were signing things that you knew, in your heart, the Russians would never carry out as we would understand 'carrying out', you signed them because there was nothing else you could sign. I was in no doubt that Churchill saw through the Russians at a very early date. He knew perfectly well that they were implacable, Communist imperialists. When he first saw the proposals for the occupation of Germany, and the Zones, he was absolutely horrified. He said: 'Are we going to let these barbarians right into the heart of Europe?' And he wanted to avoid that if he possibly could. Oh no, he was under no illusions about Stalin and . . .

CHARLTON: But 'barbarians' he said?

JACOB: Barbarians, yes. But, I tell you, my overall impression of Yalta is this. That sort of conference is very good for deciding the strategy, the conduct of the war for the next three months or six months. They are admirable for that. But, when you come on to these important diplomatic questions which require settlement they are most *un*suitable. You see, the thing right from the beginning was wrong, because the President arrived and said he must leave on Saturday. Well, the moment he'd said that, the game was in the Russian hands. Stalin knew something had got to be signed, there'd have to be some agreement – and if the President was going to leave on a certain date, they'd have to sign before that and this was only a week, I think.

CHARLTON: Yes . . . six days.

JACOB: Well, that's no length of time for drawing up these frightfully important documents and getting them examined, and so on.

CHARLTON: As Churchill said, even the Almighty took seven.

JACOB: Well, that's right. You see it was a ludicrous way of doing high diplomatic matters. Of course, a great deal of discussion was going on all that time, too, about the shape of the United Nations Organisation and so on – the veto and all those questions were coming up – so that it seemed to me to be a perfectly futile way of conducting foreign policy.

CHARLTON: There's a much-quoted and authentic exchange between Stalin and Milovan Djilas, the Yugoslav leader. In 1945, immediately after Yalta, Stalin said to Djilas, 'This war is not as wars in the past; whoever occupies a territory in *this* war also imposes his own system as far as his army can reach.' Do you think Churchill, do you think Roosevelt, perceived that?

JACOB: Roosevelt I don't think minded anyway. He wasn't interested in the Poles in the least. He had his mind fixed on the idea he wasn't going to annoy Stalin, and he wasn't going to gang up with Churchill. At the end of the war the two great powers would have to decide things between them and therefore he wanted to be quite free for that, and he really wasn't terribly interested in the internal affairs of Europe. Added to that, of course, Roosevelt was a dying man. I got a terrible shock when I saw him – his neck was sunken in, and when he finally initialled the last report of the conference his little squiggle didn't mean anything. Terrible.

THERE WAS ANOTHER aspect of the conduct of the conference which has had critical attention ever since. From the time early in the war when Roosevelt wrote to Churchill telling the Prime Minister, 'Stalin hates the guts of all your top people, but I think I can get along with him,' the President had made this hope and expectation his guiding star. Roosevelt had adopted what quickly came to rankle with the British as a deplorable negotiating technique. This was to exaggerate the differences between the British and Americans in Stalin's presence. 'You'll find us ganging up with the Russians,' Roosevelt's aide Harry Hopkins had said to the British at Teheran. Now, at Yalta, as Stalin was about to swallow up half of Europe, Roosevelt – with all his formidable charm and genial personality reaching out for understanding with Stalin – dwelt on the issues of 'colonialism' and 'imperialism' at Britain's expense. Lord Gladwyn was a first-hand witness at Yalta.

GLADWYN: I had a most deplorable impression of Roosevelt. His one idea was to play up to Stalin, and oil up to him as much as he possibly could. He did everything he could to appease the Russian dictator – 'Uncle Joe' and all that. It was hotted up particularly by Harry Hopkins, who was a charming man, you know, and couldn't be nicer and the inspirer of the New Deal and a social reformer of great merit. But on foreign policy really Hopkins was the champion appeaser of the Russians and he was always, behind the scenes, hotting up Roosevelt in that direction, I think.

ROOSEVELT OPENED THE CONFERENCE at Yalta by volunteering that, while he would like the Russians to make concessions, he would not

insist on any. He also reiterated what he had said at Teheran: that the
Americans would withdraw their forces from continental Europe within
eighteen months of the end of the war. The only obstacle which could be
presumed to Soviet domination in the East was thus removed. And so,
whether an exhausted Eastern Europe would prove a constituency from
which the objectives of Stalin alone could be moulded now depended on
moral exhortation, embodied in the high-sounding manifesto which
emerged from Yalta.

GLADWYN: I was partly responsible for negotiating a thing called the
'Declaration on Liberated Europe'. We and the Americans – some of the
Americans anyhow – thought it was a very good thing to get the Russians
to sign a document whereby they would, in effect, say that when they
reoccupied or, as they called it, 'liberated', these lands occupied by the
Nazis, a reasonable form of democracy would be installed. There would
be suitably democratic elections.

This was all agreed. The exiled governments would in principle return.
All that was put in a document. We had difficulty with Harry Hopkins, I
remember, going and seeing him when he was in bed (and he was always
ill) in the Livadia Palace at Yalta. 'Chip' Bohlen and I and one or two
others went there and argued with him. He wanted to water it all down
so that it was practically nothing. But we resisted that; and the document
on liberated Europe as such – what it says – is quite a good document. It
did get the Russians to agree to do all these things. The only trouble was,
of course, when they got there, into Poland and then to Romania, it was
evident that they were tearing up the Declaration on Liberated Europe.

I never thought that Russians would necessarily abide by it, but I did
think it was very useful to have it as a sort of card to play, if nothing else.

BUT THAT IS NOT the way the Declaration on Liberated Europe,
which was greeted with considerable popular hopes and enthusiasm, was
presented or argued in the forums of the Western democracies. From the
outset, it appears to have been disingenuous.

In addition to Harry Hopkins, ill in bed in the Livadia Palace as Lord
Gladwyn recalled, there was another crucially important aide on the
American side at Yalta. He had helped to draft the Declaration on
Liberated Europe in the State Department. Subsequently he became a
famous symbol of the breakdown in East–West relations as the wartime
alliance fell to pieces in the aftermath of Yalta. Alger Hiss was accused at
his trials in the 1950s of having been a member of a Communist spy ring
passing secret information to the Russians, was convicted of perjury, and
in the end sent to prison. He was assistant to the American Secretary of
State, Edward Stettinius. Stettinius is commonly thought to have been
among the least experienced and weakest of appointments to that office.
Hiss formed the bridge of contact between Hopkins, ill in bed at Yalta,

and Stettinius at the conference table.

Alger Hiss is one of the two senior surviving Americans (Averell Harriman the other) of the Yalta Conference.

HISS: As you know, there was, in the State Department, a division of views between what have been called the 'Yalta group' and the 'Riga group'. The 'Riga group' felt very strongly that all sorts of attempts must be made to prevent any extension of Soviet interests.

The 'Yalta group', which was really the United Nations group (where I was most concerned) took a quite definite position that, if Stalin was to come in to the United Nations he would have to be assured of something very close to a sphere of influence in Eastern Europe; that the *entente cordiale*, which had followed Versailles, was a *bête noire* with the Soviets; and that, if there was to be any kind of, let us say, goodwill on which the United Nations would be dependent, this would have to be accepted.

I have never known just what Roosevelt's personal view was, as between the two groups. Certainly Truman opted hard, after Roosevelt's death, for the Riga group. The Riga group got its name, as you know, from the place where our Foreign Service officers being trained for Russian work – like 'Chip' Bohlen and George Kennan – had their first experience with the Russian language, along the borders of Russia, in Riga which was then part of independent Latvia.

CHARLTON: What were your perceptions of likely Soviet behaviour in Eastern Europe – in the light of what you have just said – when the Declaration on Liberated Europe was being drawn up?

HISS: I would rather speak of that as it appeared at Yalta. The drawing-up beforehand was, let us say, our maximum position. At Yalta the emphasis changed. Far more important was the situation in Japan. Our own Joint Chiefs of Staff were constantly telling us, in the State Department, that unless the Soviets agreed to come into the war in the Far East against Japan we – the Americans alone – would have to count on a million casualties. The bitterness with which the Japanese had resisted each American advance up until then was assumed as 'a given' – and that it would be even more vigorous and more suicidal on the home islands.

When we left Yalta, I happened to be standing with Mr Stettinius, waiting for our car, and General Marshall, Chief of Staff of the United States in those days – who was quite close to Stettinius personally – was waiting for his car. They were chatting casually, and Stettinius said, 'General, you must be very eager to get back to your desk, you've been away for ten days to two weeks.' And Marshall said, very seriously and with that composure he usually had, 'Ed, for what we have gained here I would gladly have stayed a whole month.' I've not seen that in the history books, incidentally. Now obviously he was talking about the military agreement which was reached: that the Russians would attack the Japanese ninety days after the end of the war in Europe.

That meant that it was a political – I was going to use a strong word like 'impossibility'. It was a political necessity that we agree – I was going to say an impossibility that we disagree.

The three major powers *had* to be in basic agreement when we left the Crimea. That meant that some of the language was rubber language, it was stretchable. All diplomats deal in uncertainties, ambiguities. The fact that the language was stretchable and could mean something to one side that it did not quite mean to the other was hardly a novelty in diplomacy. That was clearly so especially with respect to Poland, and, I think, the Eastern bloc, but particularly Poland.

The impression I got, and that Admiral Leahy got, was that the Russians assumed that we were accepting very close to – tantamount to – suzerainty on their part over Eastern Europe other than Poland. Now, it did not work out that way. In fact the 'Riga group' never intended that the Russians be given that kind of a free hand.

CHARLTON: Which brings me to what George Kennan said, writing from Moscow to Bohlen on the eve of Yalta, referring to the Declaration on Liberated Europe and calling it a 'shabby equivocation'. Was that a view you held yourself?

HISS: I never had as strong a position as Kennan on issues of that sort. As a young man he was not an enthusiastic 'New Dealer' as I had been. I thought that the Declaration on Liberated Europe was as far as we could hope to go, and that it was an important statement of principle. Whether it was going to be carried out adequately was another matter. The language which seemed to represent our point of view we thought they would be likely to object to. We made it, we thought, strong, not shabby, because we realised what they had been through.

CHARLTON: But you took part in the working parties which drafted it and, as you have said before, the draft was very close to what was finally accepted. To what extent did you address yourself to the question of Communist ideology and how it would interpret an agreement like this?

HISS: That is a very hard question for me to recall with specificity. Certainly we – after all Mr Harriman had been reporting regularly on Soviet ideology – we had no 'blinders' from that point of view.

CHARLTON: You are a sophisticated diplomat and you know how Communist ideology works. When you worked on the draft, did you work on it in the knowledge that if you *did* try to make it specific, agreement would be impossible?

HISS: Yes, it was a political necessity that we agree.

CHARLTON: When you, with Stettinius, met Eden at Malta immediately before the Yalta conference the evidence, I think, from the British side is that Eden was trying to get this declaration of principles toughened up. What is your recollection of that?

HISS: I think that is true. But I think our position was that this was as far as was reasonable to think we could get agreement. I have to emphasise again that we paid far more attention to the Pacific.

CHARLTON: But Eden, it seems clear, was trying to prevent the relegation of the Polish question to a lesser priority than that of Roosevelt's ideal of the world body: the United Nations, with which work you were closely connected. Now to what extent was he successful in trying to get Stettinius to concentrate on the Polish question at Malta, before the Yalta agreement?

HISS: Not successful. In the first place Stettinius' great interest was the United Nations. He thought of that as his great contribution as a public servant; and it was also terribly important to Roosevelt.

BUT, AS EDEN SAID at Yalta, without a satisfactory agreement on Poland the proposed world body would not be worth much.

In the American archives there is that revealing exchange between Kennan, the American adviser in Moscow, and 'Chip' Bohlen, the principal foreign policy adviser in the State Department to Roosevelt. It shows Kennan declaring in his plea to Bohlen that unless the USA was prepared 'to go the whole hog and oppose with all the physical resources at American disposal the domination of Eastern Europe by a single power . . . we should write it off, frankly acknowledge the division of Europe into spheres of influence, and have nothing to do with the Declaration on Liberated Europe'; which, as already mentioned, Kennan believed to be the 'shabbiest sort of equivocation'.

Bohlen's reply to Kennan was this: 'Either our pals intend to limit themselves or they do not. I submit, as the British say, the answer is not yet clear. What *is* clear is that Soyuz, the Soviet Union, is here to stay as one of the major factors in the world. Quarrel? Yes, but we can always come to that.' But what *was* clear is that doubts were submerged in the hope that Yalta would freeze the territorial stability of Europe. Sir Ian Jacob:

JACOB: I think what happened overall is this: clearly we wanted a close relationship with the Russians, who were our allies in the war and who were having a hell of a time, and if they could survive would be of vital importance in helping to win the war. Therefore every step that could be taken to help them, or to reach some kind of accommodation with them on this or that, would be worth doing. The extent to which we thought that this could be effective varied from time to time, I think.

Occasionally we seemed to have had some successful result with the Russians, but generally speaking we did not. I suppose this is all very much coloured by what I thought at that time. But it did seem to me that we were trying to make friends with a python which is what, I see, I said in my diary in August 1942. It is impossible. A python does not speak your language, you know. It wants to strangle you in the end.

CHARLTON: What stays in your own mind as the most convincing evidence of Roosevelt's view of these old nation-states in Eastern Europe, and of what might happen to them?

JACOB: Well the worst thing of all – and the thing which always stuck in my mind – was his refusal to take any serious action over Poland, and particularly over the Warsaw affair.

CHARLTON: The uprising by the Home Army?

JACOB: Yes: and the Russians sitting there a few miles away and doing absolutely nothing. I thought to myself, this is a really marvellous illustration of something said by an American staff officer (who wrote a book just after the war): that the American attitude to war is that it was like a game of football. You think out a lot of plays, and you win the match and go home and put your feet up, and have a bath. With that you are not creating a political situation.

The other thing that indicated this very clearly was that Roosevelt refused ever to give any instructions to General Eisenhower to bring about any kind of result in Europe which would be important from a political point of view. He could not see any point in occupying Berlin, or Prague or any of these things. He simply was not interested in that: 'Now we have got to win the war and go home.'

CHARLTON: It was stronger than that was it not? I mean, the orders were that American military operations were *not* to be conducted so as to bring about political results.

JACOB: Well, that's right. And what is the point of a war? That seemed to me to be an extraordinarily short-sighted view of the Americans.

'THE BIG THREE' of the wartime Alliance were treading on eggshells at Yalta, in the sense that they clearly intended to make the relationship between East and West, however tense, a manageable one. An analysis of the agreement shows how, in the amendments put forward by the Soviet Union, the Russians sought to make sure that they would not be liable technically for any violations of the agreements once they began to put their intentions for Eastern Europe into practice. Stalin repeatedly made it obvious that he baulked at 'free elections'. He and his foreign minister Molotov spent a good deal of time reformulating the term 'fascist', so it could be stretched to justify the limitations he intended to enforce on freedom of choice for the Poles. Alger Hiss again:

HISS: The tension over Poland was palpable. It did not result in a feeling of crisis, but this was the sticking point, this was the rocky road that somehow had to be smoothed if there was to be eventual agreement. And that, in my opinion, is where the rubber language was used – much more than in the Declaration on Liberated Europe, which was not as specific.

CHARLTON: Yes, it's interesting going back through those exchanges:

Stettinius giving in over the final sentence of the Polish formula, Eden disagreeing with it. But Stettinius later tells us this: Roosevelt was 'so anxious to reach agreement that he was willing to make this concession'. Can you elaborate on that? There's an obvious moment where, if there was going to be a sticking point about Poland, if we were going to dig our heels in against Stalin, that must have been it.

HISS: I have been asked substantially the same question, not with quite such subtle understanding of the situation as you have shown. I've been asked, 'Why the hell didn't we just say: You can't have Poland, because pretty clearly this meant Russian control.' And my answer has always been that we were quite aware that the only way to disagree over Poland was to shatter the Alliance, that we certainly could not fight the Russians militarily at that stage, and that they already possessed half, maybe two-thirds, of Poland militarily. So that the question asked in retrospect now is very different from the question then. What we were doing was arguing largely for phrases, and the particular phrase you're referring to now did not seem too different from other phrases.

CHARLTON: This is the pledge to free and unfettered elections?

HISS: Yes. At Teheran, Roosevelt had said to Stalin that some of his fellow citizens, particularly of Baltic descent, were very disturbed over the incorporation of Lithuania, Estonia, Latvia. Couldn't Stalin have a plebiscite to make this more regular? Stalin was supposed to have said very casually, 'You want a plebiscite? Of course!'

So that the emphasis on 'free elections', where some of the language (we later insisted) was being violated, I'm sure was to Stalin like a 'plebiscite' over Lithuania, Latvia and Estonia. And again I emphasise: from his point of view, not necessarily from ours, that seemed rubbery.

SO IT WAS THAT STALIN could leave Yalta with the conclusion that he had more freedom of action in Eastern Europe than, in the event, the West was willing to concede. Stalin's insistence that all states in Eastern Europe must have governments friendly to the Soviet Union was enshrined at Yalta in a hazy formula which was taken to mean 'governments which could never again provide facilities for German aggression', but which quickly came to mean governments which would be reliably hostile to the West. Given Roosevelt's generosity of spirit towards the Soviet Union, and America's rooted disinclination to adopt or even threaten the pressure of a strong diplomacy against a state which was still an ally in war, the outcome of 'Liberation' for Eastern Europe was inevitable.

GLADWYN: If there hadn't been any Yalta conference at all, the result would have been much the same. I think history would have fulfilled itself, Yalta or no Yalta.

CHARLTON: Should we see Yalta as a stage in Soviet imperial expansion, as some claim it was?

GLADWYN: If you like, yes; you can put it that way. But, as I say, I think it would have happened anyhow. It was an inevitable result of the Hitler war.

CHARLTON: Do you agree that those who influenced our policy (and perhaps yourself included) were on the whole too optimistic?

GLADWYN: Possibly, yes. But I think in view of public opinion, particularly in America, but also in England, it was difficult to be anything else. If you'd given the impression that you were not trying to come to some kind of agreement of a reasonable nature with the Russians there'd have been a revolt in the House of Commons and in the nation generally – certainly in the army.

CHARLTON: Why do you say that: '. . . certainly in the army'?

GLADWYN: Well the army, after all, was very left-wing on the whole, as was shown by the elections in 1945. I think they thought that we were fighting for democracy, and they had certain illusions about the Russians – 'the gallant ally'.

CHARLTON: But surely those illusions were fostered by those who influenced our policy with the constant suppression, or covering up, of information which might have led public opinion to a different conclusion?

GLADWYN: It may have been. But, on the other hand, if we hadn't done something to foster the idea of 'the gallant ally' some people would have said that the Russians might have made a separate deal with Hitler. You see, that was the idea.

YALTA THEN WAS NOT a conspiracy to divide Europe. No such agreement was made. The modern indictment of Yalta is that nothing happened there to deter Stalin from going ahead with what, by that time, he had clearly shown he wished to do: to establish puppet governments throughout Eastern Europe. Roosevelt and Churchill clung to the hope that Stalin would find it in his interest not to do in Poland what he had so often shown he would. Winston Churchill's biographer, Martin Gilbert:

GILBERT: After the war Churchill kept looking back and there was some sort of, perhaps you could say, fatal flaw in his relationship with Stalin over Poland – that he did believe that there was an area where he could make progress. Now here, if I could just read from one of these documents, is a little jotting of his:

> I've been thinking about how I was on Poland and how we fought for Poland at Yalta, and reached agreement, and how these agreements were broken in succeeding months. This possibly was due not to bad faith on the part of Stalin and Molotov, but that when they got home they were held up by their colleagues – is this possible?

In other words he was brooding over it. 'Was this possible?' Was there a possibility, in other words, that he had not been totally naive in accepting the Yalta agreement, the Yalta protocol.

CHURCHILL'S TROUBLED RELUCTANCE to believe that Stalin alone, of all the men he had had to deal with in a long political life, was incapable of being persuaded, was dispelled before the ink was dry on the Yalta agreements. The West was not able to secure for Poland the promise of a government of their choice and free elections. Ever since, at intervals, not just the Poles, but Hungarians, Czechs and Balts have tried to take steps to secure it for themselves.

Yalta did not break down because of any Western action or dereliction. It broke down because Stalin began imposing governments, and the ideology of Marx and Lenin on the peoples concerned, against their wishes and their will. Given the nature of the political system which Stalin had established in the Soviet Union, it was difficult, if not impossible, for him to exercise tolerantly, subtly or with moderation the kind of control he felt he had to have.

The shock of his actions in Eastern Europe, culminating in the political Show Trials and executions of the 1950s, was the crucible in which a naive idealism dissolved and fatal resentments crystallised.

2
FATAL RESENTMENTS

PRESIDENT ROOSEVELT'S expectation of a world restored by the Good Neighbourly visions of the New Deal was not sustained. Within a month of his return from the Yalta Conference, the President's particular vanity, his belief that – after the war – Stalin could be persuaded into the intimate collaboration for which Roosevelt longed, quickly proved false.

On 24 March 1945, while he was at lunch in the White House, the President was handed a cable from Averell Harriman, his Ambassador to Stalin in Moscow. Roosevelt read it with mounting anger and agitation, then said loudly, 'Averell is right. We can't do business with Stalin. He's broken all the promises he made at Yalta.' In his final communications to the Soviet leader the President wrote of his 'bitter resentments' and of Stalin's 'vile misrepresentations'. A week later Roosevelt was dead.

Over the next three years 'the Spirit of Yalta' was snuffed out, and the most pessimistic forecasts of how Stalin would choose to interpret those famously ambiguous accords were confirmed. As the Soviet Commissar took over from the Nazi Gauleiter in command of the old capitals of Central Europe, the uneasy hopes of the West at Yalta – that if the new men fulfilled Stalin's demand for governments 'friendly' to the Soviet Union they could also pose as patriotic, independent leaders – proved illusory. In these years both the nature and the exercise of Soviet power created the fundamental resentments, which must be seen as fatal to reconciling the peoples concerned to the long-term continuation of Russian domination.

By 1948, Czechoslovakia – a parliamentary democracy since the First World War – had been subverted. By 1949 a shuffling procession of tormented 'enemies of the people' crowded the courtrooms of Eastern Europe. The 'new purges' culminated in the 'Show Trials' – ceremonies conforming to the Moscow precedent, which demanded blood sacrifices.

Among the victims of the trial in Prague of Rudolf Slansky, which began in 1952 – following three years of arrests, interrogations and 'preparations' – was a Czech Communist, Eugen Loebl, the Assistant Minister for Foreign Trade.

LOEBL: I was told that, apart from Slansky, nobody would be sentenced to death. And I think the interrogators believed that as well. As a matter of fact, when I was not sentenced to death, but others were, I envied them – how better off they are! I was still in solitary confinement: they do not suffer any more. I was interested in whether my ideas of the trial were right. One, that it is a kind of Soviet occupation of Czechoslovakia, without the army; and the other, whether my analysis is right that it was anti-Semitic. You see, once one is in solitary confinement one lives in a world of ideas. Ideas are important because you don't live with anything else. I was more interested in following what they said – whether it was exactly in contradiction or not. So the actual sentence, the death sentence (I was prepared for either life or death), is really better than to be sentenced to life under those conditions.

CHARLTON: I have here the words of the Prosecutor summing up at the trial.

> I demand the death sentence for all the accused. Let your verdicts become an iron fist, without the slightest pity. Let it be a fire which burns out the roots of this shameful abscess of treason. Let it be a bell ringing through the whole of our beautiful country, for new victories on the march to the sunshine of Socialism.'

Do you remember that?

LOEBL: I remember that, and on top of it all there was fantastic applause. It took three years, from the beginning of my imprisonment to the trial, so to be treated that I confessed to being a traitor. And then I knew at that time that Socialism – what they think is Socialism – is an evil. I should have fought against it, but I did not.

THE SHOW TRIALS which ushered in the 1950s were the culmination of the disciplined ruthlessness with which, step by step, as opportunity afforded, Stalin imposed his power on Eastern Europe after Yalta.

It stood revealed as a jealous power resting on the elimination of all other rival opinions, influences, and connections. These ceremonies of confession falsely obtained by fear and by physical coercion, purges and trials, served the final consolidation of Stalin's empire. Another Communist, in another country, who was made a victim of that ambition and a means to its end, was a Hungarian arraigned for heresy in Budapest in the trial of Laszlo Rajk, Bela Szasz.

SZASZ: Then I was brought to the chief of the Russian Secret Police, which operated in conjunction with the Hungarian Secret Police. That was Major-General Belkin. He was Chief in Eastern Europe of the Russian Secret Police.

CHARLTON: Over the whole area?

SZASZ: For the whole area, yes. He directed this show trial in Hungary. He also directed the Show Trials in Czechoslovakia, in Bulgaria, in Albania, and so on . . .

CHARLTON: Can you see him now, as you talk to me?

SZASZ: Oh very, very well. Yes. He was a rather small, fat man with a big nose (a big red nose which showed that he was a drunkard). And he smoked American cigarettes, which he once offered me. The Russians when they questioned me (because they questioned me as well) told me, 'We are here from the Russian Communist Party, and our sister Party, the Hungarian Communist Party, asked us to intervene in this trial, so now tell the truth and nothing but the truth.' And through an interpreter they questioned me for very long – for about a week, every day eight, nine, ten hours. And, meanwhile, Belkin came in. He wore a tunic made from a fabric which normally women would wear, a silver-grey, shiny tunic. He went to my interpreter and to the Russian colonel who was interrogating me, and asked how it was going. And in the moment when he entered the room, the Russian colonel, who spoke German, shouted at me in German: 'Stand up! Stand up! Stand up!'

I stood up. And when he went, then the Russian colonel said, 'You know who this was?' I said 'No.' And he said, 'He is a much, much greater man than your governor Horthy was! Because he is not only Governor of Hungary, like Horthy was, but he is Governor of Austria, and of Romania, and of Yugoslavia and of Czechoslovakia and of Albania. Because you know Comrade Belkin is the Chief of the Secret Police for Eastern Europe.'

So that was the Governor. I had this very unpleasant interview with the Governor before the Show Trial started.

THE SECRET POLICE. who had their apotheosis in the Show Trials and who followed in the wake of the Red Army, proved not just ancillary to the establishment of Communist power, but were indispensable to it. We have Stalin's own word for that. Today we know that, early in 1945, as the Red Army rolled westwards into the uncharted ambiguities of Yalta, Stalin made what has become his celebrated remark to the Yugoslav Communist leader, Milovan Djilas: 'This war is not as other wars. Whoever occupies a territory in this war imposes his own system as far as his army can reach.'

In contrast, the Americans set their faces determinedly against military operations for political objectives. With Poland already a lost cause from the Western viewpoint early in 1945, Churchill urged upon the Americans the need for an allied advance into Central Europe. Pointing

out that, while it had been designated a Soviet sphere of *military* operations, there was no political agreement with Moscow over Czechoslovakia, he pressed the Americans to liberate Prague while their armies
stood poised to enter it. Despite Churchill's bitter protests, the Allied
commander, General Eisenhower, replied for Washington, 'Why should
we endanger the life of a single American or Briton to capture areas
which we will soon be handing over to the Russians?'

This decision effectively put Czechoslovakia into Russia's exclusive
sphere of influence. In the democratic republic which had been called into
existence under Thomas Masaryk as President after the First World War,
in accordance with the principles of President Woodrow Wilson, it had
an immediate and powerful impact. It was experienced at first hand by a
Czech Foreign Ministry official with the Government-in-Exile in London,
who was made liaison officer to the American army under General
Patton, then advancing on Prague: Ivo Duchacek.

DUCHACEK: I think we were all prisoners of the general atmosphere
during World War II. If Roosevelt and Churchill could cooperate with
Stalin the murderer, the purger, with a system against which the British
Government and Churchill had preached a crusade in 1920, who were
we Czechs to tell Roosevelt and Churchill that this was a wrong calculation? The atmosphere was, I think, that the war had *done* something
to the Soviet Union and to the Communist Party, and that what we
would be facing in 1945 would not be the Communist Party of the Purges
but the Communist Party which ran what they called the Great Patriotic
War, a nationalised Communism, the 'Russian way', with a 'Czech
way' becoming part of the national tradition. To put it very briefly, we
thought that the Communist Party of 1945, or whenever the war would
end (we did not know when it would end), would be a somewhat more
disagreeable Social Democratic Party of 1920. I do not try to shift the
blame from the Czechs to England or France or the United States, but I
would like to place it in the context of illusions which were not ours
alone.

CHARLTON: How important a factor was the perception held by the
Czech people and politicians of the whole Western position over
Czechoslovakia at the time when the Allied armies were only a few miles
from Prague, were being urged by Churchill to take Prague, but with the
Americans refusing to support it?

DUCHACEK: There was a kind of general attitude about the West which
was shattered by Munich in 1938.

CHARLTON: 'A far-away country of which we know nothing?'

DUCHACEK: That's right. Chamberlain's words were sort of floating
above the Czechs. Now I think the Churchill period, plus the Czechoslovak
broadcasts from the BBC, changed that picture. Great Britain was much
more part of Czech thinking in 1945 than at any time before in Czech

history. However, then comes 1945 – and Churchill is gone. Attlee, from the point of view of the Czechs a nondescript person, appearing in the middle of the Potsdam Conference, therefore an unknown. The United States – we are discussing 1945 – also unreliable, a chivalrous knight who comes to save Europe, usually five minutes after midnight – not even before midnight.

CHARLTON: Take one particular episode. The withdrawal by Eisenhower of the American armies from in front of Prague at the request of the Russians.

DUCHACEK: Well, even before that – this is very personal, but I think you might be interested because this is not a story which I think was told. In 1944 the Soviet army reached the Czechoslovak boundary. We immediately offered the Soviet government to negotiate a treaty for the administration of the liberated territories – a kind of technical treaty which the UK and the USA had with other Western allies. That is, what happens after the country is liberated, what is the rate of exchange between local and the imported currency, at what time the civil authorities take over. We had this treaty, I think, just after Easter 1944.

I remember, at that time, I was in the Ministry of Foreign Affairs, which was located in London in George Street. I went to the American Chargé d'Affaires, and asked him whether we could not also have such a treaty when the American and British army would come to Eastern Europe. The answer from both allies – we also asked the British government – was: 'There is no need to make any treaty on the administration of the liberated territories of Czechoslovakia, because the Western armies would never come there. 'This is not our zone of operations.' For us, this information was additional proof that the West was not going to be part of Central European destinies. A well-wisher – but not influential, not interested in Eastern Europe.

Then, however, comes early 1945 when General Patton, after his astonishing sweep down through southern Germany, suddenly liberated a very small portion of western Bohemia. So there I go again to the American Embassy, appointed to the Allied Governments, not to the Court of St James's, and I asked, Well, how come? You told me you would never be there! So what will be the rate of exchange between the US dollar and the Czech crown and so on. The answer was that there were despatches going back and forth between Washington and London. The final answer was that it was too late to conclude any treaty on the administration of the liberated territory by the American army and the American government suggests that an ambassador, with full powers, be appointed to General Patton's army. I was selected to be this ambassador. An answer came from General Patton's HQ, which at the time of this negotiation was in Regensburg, that he would welcome a military mission. To cut a long story short I was changed from a Foreign Service officer into a major. I bought a uniform at Selfridges, put the thing on

me, was flown to Eisenhower's HQ (at Versailles at the time) then immediately flown to Regensburg. General Patton welcomed me in a kind
of icy way: 'Why didn't you come a week before?' It was as if he did not
know. And so it was in an American jeep that I returned to my native
country six years later from London, in this English uniform with Czech
insignia on it, first to western Bohemia and then finally to Pilsen. Now
you asked me about reactions and what they were. You know, it was a
walk to Prague. We could have liberated Prague in six hours. Here was
the crack army of General Patton in Pilsen and the forward elements
were, let us say, twenty miles from Prague. Therefore it was easy. As you
know, the order came that Patton cannot advance to Prague. Your question was what was the reaction? I think it was a feeling of frustration. It
had a devastating effect.

I passed the lines into Prague – the Soviet/American demarcation line –
and I met an older friend of mine who was a jeweller and watchmaker in
Prague. He saw me in the uniform with V Corps, the American insignia
on it, and he put it in one sentence, the answer to your question. He said,
'If General Eisenhower and General Patton don't dare to displease the
Russians, why should I?' And he told me that he was going to join the
Communist Party. He had been a member of my Catholic Democratic
Party. But he was joining the Communist Party. 'This is where the East
wind is going to blow over Prague.' An opportunist? Sure! But I think
that sentence, which I have not forgotten since I met him in June 1945, I
will never forget, because it expressed what this move had done.

As STALIN SURVEYED the extent of the Red Army's penetration into
Europe early in 1945, how he weighed the opportunities offered to him is
still a subject for speculation. The Soviet archives have never been available to Western historians and only in rare, and then usually in censored
instances, to those of the Communist bloc.

'The only realities these Communist leaders understand are facts and
force,' Churchill had said of Stalin and his satraps the year before. Therefore the tragic opening gambit of Roosevelt at Yalta, that all American
forces would be withdrawn from Europe within two years of the war
ending, must surely have been deeply etched in Stalin's mind. He could
afford to wait two years! His concern, after Roosevelt's death, must have
been to see if that Presidential forecast would be fulfilled. It was. The
troops were brought home by President Truman. Stalin could see that he
had got away with the installation of a Communist government in
Poland, following elections whose fraudulence was at once denounced.

Nonetheless, he moved with caution. The Americans, who had paid a
high price at Teheran and at Yalta for Soviet collaboration in the war
against Japan, suddenly had no need of it. The atomic bomb had become
the new determinant of power relationships between nations.

In the satellite countries of Eastern Europe, where the final outcome was not already politically determined, as with Hungary and Czechoslovakia, elections went forward which seemed to lend, at first, some credence to the Yalta declarations. A close study has been made of this early period – before the Communist suppression of democratically-elected representatives in Hungary – by the historian Charles Gati, of Columbia University.

GATI: The old political class had all but disappeared. In that sense there was an administrative and political renewal and reorganisation, quite aside from what the Russians had in mind. The old regime had discredited itself and most of its members had, in point of fact, left Hungary, most of them with the retreating German army. So therefore a new political order did come into being in Hungary, just as it did everywhere else in Europe. There was a lack of continuity everywhere, and in Hungary even more so perhaps than in the West European countries.

The war years and the destruction of the country made economic change of a radical type quite appealing. When you have a war-torn country – Hungary was devastated considerably during the war – then the people become quite ready to look for short cuts. So I would say that there was considerable appeal, among the population at large, in radical, perhaps socialist or social-democratic, transformation. In that sense one could talk about one of two possibilities: either a populist, agrarian, radical transformation or a socialist, industrial transformation. Which one would prevail was, I think, in the end determined by the Soviet Union, but in that sense Hungary was in a radical mood.

Now, when it comes to politics, that is a different story altogether. In politics, whatever other issues existed at the time, there was only one that ultimately determined the political outlook of most voters, and that was the relationship with the Soviet Union. The country was practically unanimously anti-Soviet then, as it is even today. There was no chance for the Communist Party to prevail under free circumstances, because it was linked to the Soviet Union.

CHARLTON: What was the immediate aftermath, in Hungary, of the Yalta agreements? There was a generalised statement to the effect that there will be free elections, and there was something called the Allied Control Commission which was supposed to have jurisdiction in seeing that this broad ideal was everywhere discharged. What actually happened?

GATI: Most Hungarians assumed that Hungary would be in the Soviet sphere, but what that Soviet sphere would signify was something that few people, at that time, could properly understand. A sphere can mean control – becoming in effect the satellite of the Soviet Union – and there were some people who even assumed that, sooner or later, Hungary would be incorporated into the Soviet Union. There was a widespread fear that this would happen. On the other hand, there were those who believed that the West would not tolerate such a development, that Hungary might end up in the Soviet sphere of influence but not in the Soviet sphere of control. Influence would have meant that Hungary's domestic development could be pluralistic, while on foreign policy matters the Soviet Union would insist on Hungary following the Soviet example – what we would understand today, perhaps, as Hungary being 'Finlandised'. So those were the two alternatives that people drew from Yalta – either that Hungary would become a sphere of Soviet control, or that it would be assigned to a Soviet sphere of influence.

CHARLTON: In the immediate aftermath of Yalta, violations of the 'spirit' of the agreements were apparent almost at once in, for example, Romania. What was the reaction to the Western responses to this?

GATI: Disappointment. It made politicians, non-Communist politicians, feel that they were alone, that they could not count on British or American support. Some of these politicians, we now know, visited the American, British and French Embassies in Budapest asking for some small support – for example, prior to elections – and they were invariably told, often in not particularly polite language, that the three Western powers did not believe in interfering in the internal affairs of Hungary and thus assisting these non-Communist parties. It helped divide the non-Communist parties, because some politicians began to make their adjustments to what they sensed was the inevitable Sovietisation of Hungary, while others continued to fight.

CHARLTON: Of the forces which were eligible to contest political life in Hungary, as it began to revive, some were proscribed by the various interpretations of the Yalta agreements. Within those limits of eligibility, what was the political balance in Hungary at the war's end?

GATI: At the war's end it was the Communist Party and the Soviet Union which established the provisional government, and in effect assigned seats and made agreements. I think the elections in November 1945, which were free elections, pretty much reflected those initial choices. What were they? In the elections, the Smallholders' Party, which was a broker-party and quite non-ideological except that it was for Hungary's independence – received 57 per cent of the vote. The Social Democrats, a kind of centralist social-democratic party by European standards, received over 17 per cent of the vote. All in all the Communists could gain only 17 per cent of the vote and I think that was the height of their popularity in Hungary. Never before and never since were the Communists as popular as in November 1945.

IF IN HUNGARY the Communists were relatively few, in Czechoslovakia they were suddenly legion. Among the broad mass of the population there was, again, the general expectation of something better to follow the failures which had led to the war.

In December 1945 both the Americans and the Russians had withdrawn their forces from Czechoslovakia. Unlike the other satellites, there was no Red Army presence to dictate political results. It has been a question of lasting interest why it was that, in what had been the one successful experiment in parliamentary democracy in Eastern and Central Europe, so many of the Czech population shifted their allegiance from subservience to the German occupation to a further subservience to the newly dominant power, the Soviet Union.

Jacques Rupnik, one of the young Czech historians living in the West, has published an important study of the rise of the Czech Communist Party.

RUPNIK: I think what distinguished Czechoslovakia from the rest of Eastern Europe was the existence of a strong, indigenously-rooted Communist Party. Together with Yugoslavia it was the only East European country where the Communist Party in 1945 was an indigenous, strong force which did represent something in domestic politics. Elsewhere – in Bulgaria and Romania – the Communists were a mere handful. There you had no power whatsoever without the backing of the Soviet military. That is why the Communist takeover had to take place immediately, after the Russian liberation. There was no real period of national democracy, or national-democratic road to Socialism and all that stuff we have seen in Czechoslovakia. In Czechoslovakia you do have a strong Communist Party. That is one factor.

CHARLTON: But numerically quite weak. At the end of the war there were only 40,000 members of the Communist Party and within a matter of weeks it was half a million!

RUPNIK: Ah, but this is it! This is the answer: that there was this fantastic radical tide from below, great aspirations that were suddenly expressed after six years of Occupation. People wanted change. And of course one temptation in these situations is to switch as far to the other extreme as possible. And there were the Communists, with what appeared then as their clean wartime record, and their identification with the Soviet Union, the Liberator of Czechoslovakia, the country that stood behind Czechoslovakia.

All that played in favour of the Communists. The second thing I should add is that of course the non-Communist forces were not in conflict with the Communists. The democratic political parties were working in agreement and cooperation with the Communists. You do not have the Polish situation, with a Government-in-Exile which is anti-Communist, and then a Communist-sponsored Lublin government, with the two fighting for legitimacy.

And the third factor one should add – and this is a very touchy subject, and one has to be careful in phrasing it – is really the relative weakness of the domestic resistance during the war. For people who did not overtly resist, the situation was not too bad. The majority of the Czech workers during the war had full employment. I am not talking about the heroic minority which fought throughout, often at very heavy cost. The bulk of the population did not really resist, one should say, and after the war was compensating for that by giving allegiance to the new force in the area – the Soviet Union.

AT YALTA THE RUSSIANS had insisted on an amendment to the agreement about holding 'free elections' which forbade those considered to be 'Fascist' organisations or individuals to take part. It was a category to which they were able to give a wide and arbitrary interpretation, as Churchill said to Stalin at the time. However, the first elections held after the war, in Hungary and Czechoslovakia, returned clear non-Communist majorities. But the result was, from the outset, a deceptive pluralism. The reality was that government and the Communist opposition were permitted to exist only side by side and in coalition, as in Hungary.

GATI: The Communists could not be excluded. Their place in the coalition was a 'given' – the Soviet Union would not have tolerated it otherwise. They could have mobilised mass demonstrations, and stopped some of the factories and, of course, don't forget the Secret Police were already in their hands, so they could have caused a good deal of trouble.
CHARLTON: Isn't this the ambiguity in the Yalta accords? Yalta promises free elections. You have free elections, and they return a non-Communist majority which really cannot operate without the Communists?
GATI: Absolutely true. One way to explain this is that you should understand the political system on two levels. One level was the parliamentary system – and that was pluralistic; not generally free, but pluralistic and dominated by non-Communists. On the other hand, below that parliamentary level – and below the level of an essentially free press (which existed in Hungary for three years) and a free economy (the Stock Market closed in Hungary only in the winter of 1947–8) – the Communist Party was making a determined and successful effort to capture the key positions of coercion in the country, and particularly the dreaded Secret Police. So, in some ways you have two political systems co-existing, side by side, perhaps as a result of Yalta.

FROM THE BEGINNING, therefore, democracy was being reduced, particularly so in Czechoslovakia.
    An important ingredient in the cement which bound the Communist parties of Eastern and Central Europe to Stalin was their enthusiastic promotion, at his insistence, of huge transfers of population. To add to the eight million Germans expelled from the East (in what is now mostly Polish territory), three million Sudeten Germans were expelled from Czechoslovakia. The Communists moved adroitly to exploit the empty

spaces this created for land reform. The vigour and discipline of Marxist–Leninist methods and organisation, unmatched by any effective responses from the democratic parties, show up dramatically in all accounts of their path to power in Czechoslovakia, both before and after withdrawal of the Red Army.

Professor Edward Taborsky was Private Secretary to the ill-fated President of Czechoslovakia, Edward Beneš, and was also his biographer.

TABORSKY: When the Red Army moved in they contacted the local Communists, and arranged a sort of a meeting in a public hall where already they had a prepared list of people who should be on that People's Committee. They were either Communists or pro-Communists. There were quick trials. There was no *habeas corpus* or anything. If you opposed them, and they wanted to get rid of you, they would either denounce you to the Soviet NKVD who would deport you, or they would put you in jail. They would say, 'We saw you with the Gestapo.' So there was simply a lawlessness, and that's how they flourished.

CHARLTON: But there was an extra ingredient in Czechoslovakia with the armed militias. People in the factories were armed.

TABORSKY: That was also part of it, because they organised those People's Militias – as they called them – supposedly guarding the factories against roving 'enemies'. Then of course when the time came they brought them by buses to Prague, and paraded them through the streets with rifles, so they had a sort of private army of sorts. Another thing was the question of 'land reform', because, after all, there was plenty of land from the Sudeten Germans. So you had a number of peasants who, at least temporarily, gave support to the Communists simply in order to get that land.

Let me add one more thing. You know, most intellectuals – I mean artists and writers – were left-leaning of course. Not necessarily Marxist–Leninists but a good many of them were Communist Party members. And now the Communists came, with a Minister of Information controlling everything for publishing and with the slogan that 'under Communism' they would be free to write and publish without any financial worry, and so on. And they enjoyed it. They bitterly resented it after 1948. Some of them said, 'We did not expect that.' But at this time they supported the Communists.

And so you had the organised labour, you had a good many peasants – even though they did not believe in Communism – supporting the Party. And you had this group of intellectuals, especially artists and writers and so on. So it was not merely just a coup by a minority. It was really what helped them to build their position and get away with it.

THE PERIOD FROM 1944 to 1948 is regarded by the Communist

parties of Eastern Europe as the period of revolution, thus justifying 'revolutionary coercion'.

For example, while the Communist Party in Hungary was the real possessor of power, it had suffered a humiliating defeat at the elections. The Hungarian Communist leader, Matyas Rakosi, contributed to the dictionary of politics an epithet for this period which has stuck – his description of Communist methods used against the parliamentary forces as 'salami tactics'. Here is a disarming admission of how the Party in Hungary proceeded to demolish the elected majority against it. Zoltan Vas, the former mayor of Budapest, was one of the Hungarian Communist hierarchy centrally involved. Between 1940 and 1943 he had worked for the Comintern, after that he was posted to the Soviet army and given the rank of Colonel. He was in charge of the psychological warfare waged against the opposing Hungarian army before he became concerned, after the war in Hungary, with 'salami tactics'.

VAS: We had democratic parties – the Smallholders' Party, the Democratic Party, the Social Democratic Party, and about twenty other different kinds of parties. We could not finish them all off at the same time. So we started with the weakest ones. We applied such enormous pressure on them – partly through arrests, since we controlled the police, and partly through economic and all other kinds of pressure – that they were forced to dissolve voluntarily. In other words we 'liquidated' them. Take, for example, the Smallholders' Party, which was the biggest party in Hungary. We organised a Communist-influenced left wing inside that party; then we threw all kinds of accusations at their leaders. We accused their most popular leader, Bela Kovacs, the Secretary-General of their party, of being a traitor to the cause of the Hungarian people. We decided to arrest the Smallholders' leaders. I am using the plural because no matter what my thoughts were in those days (and even then I was more of a humanitarian than the others) I cannot say that in my capacity as a member of the government and of the Politburo I was not responsible for the policies of the Party.
CHARLTON: Can you give me specific examples of the way the 'salami tactics' worked against the Smallholders' Party?
VAS: I've started by relating the Bela Kovacs affair for this very reason. He proved so popular that we could not – I am using the plural once more – we could not take him to court because of his popularity. There was no court in Hungary that would have convicted Bela Kovacs. Then we turned to the Soviet army, requesting that they should arrest him. They snatched him from Hungary, accusing him of 'spying on the Soviet army' for 'the imperialists'. He was sentenced to ten years, and he spent ten years in the Soviet Union.

Another example that illustrates the way we conducted the salami tactic is that of the leader of the Smallholders' Party, the Prime Minister,

Ferenc Nagy. At the time he was on holiday in Switzerland. They sent him a copy of Bela Kovacs' confession, according to which Nagy was also a party to Kovacs' treasonable acts. Nagy wanted to return immediately to protest his innocence, but Rakosi sent him the following reply: 'Come home, come if you like, but there is no telling what the courts will do to you. You might be arrested at the border for your crime, but come anyway.' And so, following Bela Kovacs, the salami tactics took care of the second most important leader of the Smallholders too.

Next on the list was the President of the Republic, Zoltan Tildy, another Smallholder. His son-in-law, the Hungarian Ambassador to Egypt, was arrested and charged with espionage, with betraying state secrets to the enemy. Tildy had no option but to resign immediately. So the real leaders of the Smallholders' Party were put out of action. They were replaced by the so-called leftists of that party – most of whom, of course, had secretly joined the Communist Party.

THESE WERE NOT ISOLATED examples. They had their counterparts throughout Eastern and Central Europe. In the specific, intriguing instance of Hungary, after the 1956 Uprising was put down by the Soviet invasion, the Party has found it expedient to acknowledge some of the truth about the past in order to win greater acceptance of its rule. So it is that, over the years, fragments of authentic history have emerged from the silt of Party secrecy and changes in the Party line. They do not get published in the journals of the Communist Party. However it is evidently permissible for a senior Party figure like Zoltan Vas to concede openly now what the Party always denied. Which is to say that, after their ignominious defeat at the first elections after the war in 1945, those of 1947 in Hungary were rigged by the Communists.

VAS: In the election regulations there was a paragraph according to which anyone who was not staying at his permanent address at the time of the election could go to the Election Committee and ask for a document to enable him to vote in another constituency. The document was printed on a blue card. The blue card stated that although such-and-such a person had been registered to vote in such-and-such a constituency, he would cast his vote, say, not in Budapest but near Lake Balaton instead. There were about 22,000 such voters at the time. But what we did was to forge blue cards and give them to the Communists, thus creating about 80,000 fake ballot papers. Altogether there were 22,000 legitimate ballot papers out of 100,000 blue cards. The rest were fake.

The elections were unfairly conducted in another respect too. Before the election each voter had to appear before a committee to prove he had never been a fascist or a member of certain parties. On this basis a lot of people were disqualified from voting. They never even got as far as to cast either a genuine or a fake vote.

WITHIN THE COMMUNIST PARTIES which Stalin and the Red Army assisted to power, it was quickly demonstrated that there were to be several levels of 'reliability'. Those members who had been trained or educated in Moscow took precedence over all others, including Communists of long standing. A significant discrimination was established between these 'Easterners', or Muscovites, and the 'Westerners', those who had largely had their political education in contact with Western culture and influence.

As the various bridgeheads were seized from the democratic parties by 'salami tactics', those who were considered most reliable of all, the Secret Police, who had a direct chain of command to Moscow, formed sections inside the relevant Ministries, as with Foreign Affairs and Agriculture. This 'Party within the Party' duplicated the Party's own bureaucracy – indeed the whole apparatus of the State. Above the heads of the Communists themselves there hovered an unresolved, hazy and elusive concept: the issue of 'separate roads to Socialism' or the degree of independence to be enjoyed by the states of Eastern Europe once Utopia had been installed in power.

'Salami tactics' were soon to begin devouring Communists also. Bela Szasz was a Communist official in both the Hungarian Foreign and Agricultural Ministries when the anatomy of this future struggle being waged by Stalin stood revealed.

SZASZ: The Muscovites who came home from Moscow told us other Communists that they hoped it would not be in our country like it was in Moscow. And things did not start like in Moscow. Hungary started as a multi-party system, a democracy even in the Western sense. And we, who were Communists, wanted to participate in that democracy. When we saw the so-called 'salami tactics' of Rakosi, who, one by one, killed the democratic parties, then we got suspicious that it would not be different from Russia, but that it would be like in Russia. And the majority of those who came back from Russia and suffered shorter or longer prison sentences there did not want that.

CHARLTON: But what was it that led you to that belief? After all, the formation of a national front which the Communist Party alone will dominate in the end is a fundamental tenet of Marxist–Leninist ideology.

SZASZ: Retrospectively, it looks like that. But Stalin invented this phrase, 'People's Democracy' – which is in itself a tautology, because democracy means the people in power. We thought, 'Our country is not ripe for a Communist takeover, a Communist revolution.' And we thought, 'We will go the democratic way.' For instance the later Prime Minister during the Hungarian Revolution, Imre Nagy, did not want quick collectivisation. He thought it should take at least twenty to twenty-five years. We thought that in this time we could educate the people or win the people for this idea. It was absolutely different than in the Soviet Union. There were several parties in Hungary and the Communists were not in a majority – neither in the Parliament nor in the Ministries. What we did not realise was that it was not important, really. The Communists had the Secret Police in their hands, and the Secret Police had its chain of command to Moscow. The Secret Police was the most reliable group of the Communist Party and formally under the supervision of the Party chief, Rakosi.

I can give my personal experience, for instance. I was then in the Ministry of the Exterior – the Foreign Office, in English – and a colonel of the Secret Police was put in my place. I went over, in the same Ministry, to the department for Press and Culture – and I was head then of this department, but there was a great difference. He had reorganised the Foreign Office completely. In the section where I'd been earlier, the personnel department, that all came into the power of the AVH, the Hungarian Secret Police. It was directed not just by this man but by the Centre of the Secret Police. In my presence this man once phoned to the Secret Police for money: he got not only the money which was his due in the Foreign Office but also some supplement from the Secret Police.

CHARLTON: And who were these people?

SZASZ: These people were trained Secret Policemen – partly trained in Russia, partly not. But the Russians had a completely separate contact and chain of command, through the Hungarian Secret Police. So without the knowledge of the Hungarian government the Russians could initiate things inside the Hungarian Secret Police itself. There was the Ministry of Agriculture and there was a section of Agriculture in the Secret Police. And so on.

CHARLTON: In the memoirs you've written about this you say that for those who had come back from Moscow and been trained in Moscow, 'the Party was not just an abstract idea', a theoretical and practical framework of ideas, as it was for the faithful Party members (in whose ranks I take it you included yourself). For them, these others trained in Moscow, 'it was a collective term embracing notions of power, *our* power, *our* authority, *our* career'.

SZASZ: Yes, sure. Because, for instance, the people of the Secret Police and the people who came to leading positions, mainly educated and trained in Moscow, had a lot of material and other advantages. For instance, leaders of the Hungarian Communist Party could write any cheque for any sum and the National Bank would honour these cheques. A simple detective of the Secret Police earned about eight times as much as a manual worker.

CHARLTON: I'd like to press the point with you why, as a loyal member of the Party, you were surprised by all this. In fact you're saying you trusted Stalin – either that, or you believed that Russia had somehow changed during the course of the war, and that things were going to be different.

SZASZ: Russia changed for a while during the war and after the war, but then changed back again.

CHARLTON: Yes, but your hope or belief or expectation that things in Hungary would not follow the Moscow experience was based upon what?

SZASZ: It was not only *my* expectation, but the expectation of even the most Stalinist leader, like Revai. I remember he published a pamphlet about 'The Real Hungarian Socialism', and this was taught in seminars. Suddenly they withdrew this pamphlet, but the general opinion in Hungary, and not only in Communist circles, was that the way of Hungary could not be the way of Russia. You see, it was a different country with different traditions and different people.

CHARLTON: But this is the sort of naive delusion for which people like Roosevelt are reproached in hindsight by many historians. It seems less understandable among the ranks of you Communists. Why did you think the nature of the Soviet Union had fundamentally changed?

SZASZ: We did not think the Soviet Union had changed fundamentally. But we thought in general that we would not follow the Soviet way.

CHARLTON: But what was going to guarantee that?

SZASZ: Nothing. Nothing, in retrospect. But I am absolutely sure the policy of the Soviet Union was not certain at this moment. Stalin was really a man close to paranoia. Such a man cannot be counted as normal. His fear of the Western influence in Hungary and everywhere else was so strong that the trials, the Show Trials – like our trial, the Rajk trial – were part of this fear, and whose aim therefore was to eliminate the people who had some Western connections.

ONCE AGAIN IT WAS the significance of the situation in Poland which was to provide the key to the next events in Central Europe. Today we know, from disclosures which have come from within the Communist parties of the Eastern bloc, that Stalin did not see the countries of Eastern Europe as a single unit, but made a distinction. The countries along the border of the Soviet Union – particularly Poland, but also Romania and Bulgaria, which were the strategic highways leading to Germany and the Balkans – were not negotiable, and he had taken effective power in them almost immediately. That first step had been followed by a pause, and the time had come for another advance. Czechoslovakia and Hungary were targets of opportunity in the hands of Stalin's satraps, Gottwald and Rakosi, who would prove obedient to his will.

GATI: Rakosi in Hungary and Gottwald in Czechoslovakia were told to 'go slow'. Specifically, they were told that the takeovers in those two countries should not take place in less than ten to fifteen years. Now the reason for that is very revealing and very important. For Stalin the reason was to accommodate the West, in those two countries, in order to divert attention from Poland. Indeed among the top leaders of the Hungarian Communist Party – the very few leaders who knew about this – the slow road was called 'The Polish Trade-off'. So that if the West were to protest about what was happening in Poland, Stalin would be in the position to point to Czechoslovakia and Hungary, and claim that what was happening in Poland was indigenous domestic development. He had nothing to do with it, the Soviet Union had nothing to do with it. After all, take a look at Czechoslovakia and Hungary – the Soviet army could have effected a takeover there, but it didn't happen. Therefore he was innocent.

AND WHEN NO CHALLENGE, beyond protest, came from the West, Stalin's hands were untied. An inevitable casualty of the Soviet leader's perception of an opportunity renewed was the parliamentary democracy in Czechoslovakia. Offered up as a sacrifice by the West to Hitler at Munich, the Czechs had sought a new relationship with the Russians.

The Czech President, Edward Beneš, was the incarnation of the optimistic interpretation of Yalta. That is, 'cooperation' between East and West, as allies, and with a role for Czechoslovakia to play as 'a useful bridge' between them. The President, who was the political heir to Thomas Masaryk, the founder of the Czech parliamentary democracy, proved to be a fateful instrument of its eventual domination by the Communists.

President Beneš's secretary, and his adviser at the time, was Edward Taborsky.

TABORSKY: One main asset they got was the unbelievable behaviour of the President at that time. I talked to him many times about the situation, especially when it was obvious the Communists had begun their push, and that the only obstacle would be him. He must act firmly, not as a man above the parties, but simply to take control, and whenever they would go to excess, he must stop them. And he agreed with that. But when he came back, he did nothing about it – partly, probably, because he was not physically well but I think it was mostly his own attitude. He was a parliamentarian, used to manoeuvre, and he hoped that in this way he would be able to manoeuvre indefinitely.

But the Communists began to fill the vacancies with their people, especially in the Police and so on, and he did nothing about it. After we returned I remember how, time and again, several times, I mentioned to him – because I was also a legal adviser – 'Mr President, this is not right legally. You should not sign it.' And he said, 'No, I won't sign it.' But when Gottwald came to see him, he did sign it, you see. He instructed me several times, for instance: 'You phone the Minister of the Interior' – who was a Communist. They had arrested Vaclav Talich, the

Philharmonic Orchestra conductor. 'You phone him. That is intolerable. It should not be done.' I phoned the Minister. But Beneš did nothing about it. So he simply began to yield you see. It was unbelievable to me. So, obviously the Communists came to the conclusion that he could be pushed around. And he was.

THE SHADOW OF MUNICH darkened all Beneš's considerations. Against, at first, the strong objections of Churchill and Eden, who wanted to keep Czechoslovakia out of the Soviet orbit, Beneš went to Moscow during the war determined to base post-war policy on a close understanding and alliance with the Soviet Union, and in effect reverse Thomas Masaryk's historical policy of looking westwards. In Moscow in December 1943 Beneš prepared the ground for a far-reaching treaty and received (and believed) Stalin's assurances about non-interference in Czech affairs. Edward Taborsky accompanied President Beneš on this visit to the Kremlin.

TABORSKY: At 8 o'clock we arrived. We were ushered into a sort of reception room on the second floor somewhere of the Kremlin, and we waited there. And, all of a sudden, the door opened and there Stalin walked in, flanked by Molotov, I remember, and walked towards us. We moved towards him, and my first impression was, well, what a small-sized fellow! I imagined him, seeing him from his portraits, as having dark hair and a fine face. Now I saw him as an elderly gentleman, with thinning hair and a lot of wrinkles. He came towards us, walking really like an old man walks, shook our hands, and immediately started joking, you see. And so it was a sort of pleasant impression. It was quite different from what I expected – the man of iron will, the dictator. Here was an old uncle of sorts, shaking hands with you, patting the President on the shoulder, and starting talking. It did not look like an iron-fisted dictator who was responsible for so many things at home and so on.

You know that one reason for this trip to Moscow was the conclusion of the alliance treaty between the Soviet Union and Czechoslovakia. It was negotiated before, but on the Russian initiative while there, they included that Article that Czechoslovakia and the Soviet Union 'Would not interfere in one another's internal affairs'. They stressed that all along. Whenever Beneš wanted to explain to the Soviets, as a good friend, 'Now, this is what we propose to do in Czechoslovakia,' Stalin and Molotov would almost close their ears! 'All that's your affair,' and, 'We don't want to interfere, you know. And if we go on like that, maybe the West would feel that we want to interfere, so don't tell us about it.' Something like that, you see.

CHARLTON: Of course with the benefit of hindsight . . .

TABORSKY: Yes, they were not sincere. We know that now, of course. Beneš learnt that very shortly thereafter. He came back from Moscow in January 1944, quite jubilant about it. Everything seemed OK. 'Everything is settled, we have no problems.' And then by the autumn of 1944 it all began to collapse.

CHARLTON: Can you remember Beneš's immediate reactions as he came away from that meeting in December 1943 with Stalin?

TABORSKY: I remember that we were in the villa, waiting for him to come back. It was a long meeting in the evening. Stalin always operated late in the evening. Beneš came back and he was all jubilant. 'We have settled everything, we agreed on everything.' That was it. Then he sat at the table and began to tell us about the details and so on. And he was quite convinced that there would be no problem over the next years, and that the Soviets would respect Czechoslovakia's independence. He assumed that the Soviet Union would simply be exhausted at the end of the war, and would need a lot of Western aid, especially American aid, to subsidise the development of the Soviet Union. He felt that Czechoslovakia was a test case of goodwill. He felt that the Russians would want to prove to the West that they could be trusted by leaving Czechoslovakia alone.

THE TRANSCRIPTS OF BENEŠ's conversations with Stalin have only recently been published.* They contain remarkable disclosures. They show that as early as 1943 Czechoslovakia offered itself as an instrument of Russian expansion into Central Europe, Beneš telling Stalin that Czechoslovakia would always speak and act in a manner agreeable to the Soviet government. This posture of unsolicited subordination to Stalin reveals the personal tragedy of a man who, in trying to rehabilitate himself and his country from the disaster of Munich and appeasement, proceeded to make essentially the same miscalculation about Stalin's intentions. The Czech historian, Jacques Rupnik.

RUPNIK: Beneš promised to the Russians in domestic policy things that were far beyond anything that the Russians themselves were asking for. The Slovaks were to be politically written off as far as he was concerned.

CHARLTON: And punished?

RUPNIK: And punished. Secondly, transfer of the Sudeten Germans: they were to be expelled.

CHARLTON: Three million people.

RUPNIK: Three million people. Then, a widespread programme of nationalisation of industry, and a transition to Socialism, again far beyond what the Russians were expecting from him. This is an absolutely devastating document for Beneš's standing in history.

---

* The Beneš–Stalin–Molotov Conversations in December 1943: New Documents, tr. Wojtech Mastny, Columbia University Press.

WHILE PRESIDENT BENEŠ, as the man who stood for continuity with the past and the link with parliamentary democracy and its restoration, was shaping with Stalin the new post-war Czechoslovakia the record of his Moscow conversations shows how he had come to embody the breach with that past.

His acquiescence in the reduction of democracy, and his enthusiasm for the expulsion and transfer of the German population of the Sudentenland, have assumed a particular significance for a later generation of historians like Jacques Rupnik.

RUPNIK: He is the stepping-stone, really, for the Communist transition to power. We can say, perhaps, that there was not much scope for a genuine Western-type parliamentary democracy. What is astonishing is that Beneš was not prepared to stand up for that and to fight for that. Let's recall that the two main political parties from pre-war Czechoslovakia, the Agrarian Party and the People's Party in Slovakia (the big Catholic party) are being banned, so that the whole political spectrum of the country is being shrunk and moved from right to left. Then you have the German question. That is the essential breach. This is why this question is being so eagerly debated today among Czechoslovak intellectuals, especially the dissident historians. What was the meaning of that transfer? Was it simply an easy way to compensate for what happened in the 1930s when the Germans sided with Hitler to destroy Czechoslovakia? Or wasn't it to have deeper significance for the country, which has really been based since the thirteenth century on a coexistence of Czechs and Germans in Bohemia? That historical breach has left enormous consequences.

I mean the fact that the first labour camps in May 1945 were set up for the Sudeten Germans, considered to be collectively guilty because of their association with Hitler's Germany, is of course meagre consolation to the people who ended up in those *same* labour camps after the Communists took power in 1948 because they were Catholics, or nationalists, or simply opposed to Communist rule. The fact is that Beneš and all the non-Communist parties accepted that people should be deprived of their civil rights, including the right to vote, on the basis of their nationality. That is, the Germans and the Hungarians in Czechoslovakia are written off for all practical purposes. That is an essential breach that only prepares the way for many similar breaches. In 1945 it is done on national grounds: you cannot vote because you are German or Hungarian. After 1948 you will be deprived of your civil rights because you are an opponent of Communism, or because you are a religious believer, or any other reason. And of course, for historians looking back at the formation of a totalitarian system in Czechoslovakia after 1948, this is a vital turning point.

THE CZECH PRESIDENT'S jubilation at his treaty with Stalin was short-lived. He watched with alarm the fate meted out to the Poles in the Warsaw Uprising and then, as the Soviet army arrived at the Czech border, he saw the Russians promptly announce the annexation of Ruthenia, a part of Czechoslovakia itself. By the time of his second meeting with Stalin in Moscow just before the return of the Czech Government-in-Exile at the time of Liberation, Stalin's earlier assurances were being rapidly discounted. But still Beneš sounded no public alarm, and refused to allow his misgivings to become a matter for any public controversy.

Edward Taborsky once more.

TABORSKY: The basic reason is that he felt that if he would suddenly change around and do what the Poles were doing, then he would be even worse off. He trusted Stalin: his trust was betrayed. What do you do now? Do you turn around and fight them? So he thought now he could salvage most by still continuing to say: 'Well, we will not make it any problem.' He always stressed about Ruthenia for instance – 'We will never make it any matter of public controversy.'

CHARLTON: Can I refresh your mind about what Stalin actually said at that second meeting – at the well-known dinner speech in March 1945, with Beneš sitting there? This is Stalin, I think, at his most cynically guileful, in view of what subsequently happened. He says this: 'The Soviet Union wants nothing other than to gain allies who will always be prepared to resist the German danger. The Soviet Union will not interfere in the internal affairs of its allies.' And then he turns to Beneš and says, 'I know that even among you there are some who doubt it, perhaps even you are a little dubious, but I give you the assurance that we will never interfere in the internal affairs of our allies. Such is Lenin's neo-Slavism, which we Bolshevik Communists are following, that there can be no talk of a hegemony of the Soviet Union.' Now, was Beneš reassured by that? He must have known that this was nonsense, otherwise why was Stalin asking for Communists in the government?

TABORSKY: Well, I think Beneš was not 100 per cent reassured. But again he tried to cling to that hope that at least Stalin will not go overboard. The hope that if he saw that the Communists in Czechoslovakia have a strong position in government, that nothing really can be decided against them, that that would be some sort of an assurance to Stalin, that Czechoslovakia will not turn around internally. It was sheer desperation, really. He wouldn't reveal it to anybody, including myself. No, he was always trying to be optimistic, as optimistic as he could be – though you could see somehow in his face he was bitterly disappointed.

THE CZECH AND HUNGARIAN Communists had returned to Prague and Budapest at the war's end with instructions to await the appropriate time for the final seizure of power. 'The appropriate time', it was clear, would conform to Stalin's interests and nothing else. That time had come. These disciplined, unscrupulous minorities showed themselves pledged to the service of the political interests of the Soviet Union. With a brilliant blatancy, Stalin ordered the changes which finally settled the question of power for the Czech and Hungarian nations. Today, it is known when and why the parties switched their tactics, as Charles Gati says.

GATI: They changed in the autumn of 1947. To explain this in Hungarian terms: at the very end of August 1947 there were still elections in Hungary. The Communist Party, cheating a little bit at the elections, could still get only 22 per cent of the vote. So you still had a 78 per cent non-Communist majority in the country. Now, why would the Communists have wanted an election that they knew they couldn't win, except that they were still told by the Soviet Union not to seize power? But then, the next month something happened. The Communist Information Bureau (Cominform) was created – a small organisation of European Communist parties. It was formed in Poland, and it was there that Soviet leaders such as Zhdanov and Malenkov made their speeches.

What the West came to understand at the time was that this was the beginning of the 'Cold War', because Zhdanov made his famous speech about 'two camps' prevailing in the world, the end of 'cooperation' among the three major allies, and so on. But in point of fact there was a second theme at this conference, and that had to do with the behaviour of Communist parties both in Eastern and Western Europe. The two parties that were criticised most bluntly at that meeting, behind the scenes, were the French and the Italian Communist parties. They were criticised for having allowed themselves to be kicked out of the coalition governments of those two countries.

There were other developments, I think, as important or even more important to Stalin. One was the American policy of 'Containment', expressed in the Truman Doctrine and the Marshall Plan. The other one, I think, was this incipient diversity in international Communism after the war. There were too many roads to power. Stalin was losing control. He was concerned about the Yugoslavs, who were going too fast by his standards, and he was concerned about the Italians and the French, the Czechs and the Hungarians, who were going a bit too slow. All in all, I think the meeting in Poland was intended to accomplish at least two things. First, to mobilise the Communist parties behind a tough Soviet foreign policy, aimed at the isolation of the United States in the world; and secondly, the meeting intended to re-establish Soviet control over international Communism.

THE CZECH COMMUNIST PARTY archives which were briefly opened during the 'Prague Spring' of 1968 showed that it *was* the failure of the big Italian and French parties which led Stalin to dismiss the option for the Czechs of the parliamentary path to power. The Cominform meeting instructed the Czech Communists to seize it. The Communist coup d'état came in February 1948.

Shortly afterwards President Beneš died, a broken man. A few days before his death he said, 'My greatest mistake was that I refused to believe that Stalin lied to me cynically, and that his assurances were an intentional deceit.' And yet, it was Beneš himself who defined that mutual relationship in such submissively deferential terms at their meeting in Moscow in December 1943.

The claim of the Czech Communists that they achieved power by constitutional means cannot be sustained. The critical move in a constitutional battle with President Beneš, which went on for six days, was the creation overnight throughout Czechoslovakia of so-called 'Action Committees', outside the normal organs of power. They had orders to use revolutionary methods to wrest for themselves as much authority as possible.

The non-Communist parties had made no preparations in the event that Beneš would fail, as he did, to hold out against such pressures. During the six days of the crisis the Communist Prime Minister, Klement Gottwald, and the Trade Union leader, Zapotocky, saw Beneš every day, demanding his approval of a new government. In the end they backed that demand with threats. The record survives of President Beneš's last conversation with them in his office on 25 February 1948, here recalled by Jacques Rupnik.

RUPNIK: This is a transcript of what was actually said: 'You only need one stone to start the avalanche. In the factories the avalanche is already on the move.' And Zapotocky finally adds, 'A single man cannot oppose an avalanche.' Indeed Beneš felt very much the same way, that there was no chance of resisting that avalanche, and this is what he replied to Zapotocky at that crucial moment: 'I don't want to complicate things for you. What matters for me is to be able to save not the appearances, that's not the word, but a decent, honest position, and to create a situation which would leave the way open for you. I don't want to create any unnecessary difficulties for you. It's not in my nature.'

THE THREAT OF VIOLENCE, rather than violence itself, had proved sufficient. As thousands of Communists from the Action Committees paraded the streets of Prague in blue overalls with guns in their belts, so passed the Czech parliamentary democracy.

All important Cabinet posts went to the Communists with the exception of Foreign Affairs, which stayed in the hands of one of the best known of European politicians, Jan Masaryk, the son of Thomas Masaryk, the republic's founder. A year before, Jan Masaryk had said to an American correspondent, 'If I have to choose between East and West,

I would have to go with the East, but it would kill me.'

Three weeks after the coup of 1948, Masaryk's body was found beneath the window of his office in the Foreign Ministry. Officially it was called suicide. But the strong presumption that Masaryk was murdered is another of those undiscussable resentments buried in the minds of a nation, another symbol of the extinction of the democratic tradition in Czech Socialism. The sudden availability in 1968 of the archives of the Czech Communist Party to paths of enquiry formerly barred, and today barred once more, naturally renewed interest in the manner of Jan Masaryk's death, as Edward Taborsky relates.

TABORSKY: I think probably the final outcome, when they finally reveal everything (although many things will probably be lost meanwhile), will probably conclude by saying that Masaryk was disposed of by the Soviet Secret Police. There is some evidence for it. There was disorder in Masaryk's room. The argument is that, had he wanted to commit suicide, he would have taken pills and certainly would not have jumped from a window in his bathroom which was so hard to have access to. I talked to Dr Klinger, who was his personal physician, and he brought some evidence about this. He noted for instance that Masaryk's clothing was soiled – which is an indication that he was in fear of his life, and might have had some struggle. There were plenty of cigarettes in his room which seemed to have been smoked not only by Masaryk but by other people. And the doorman in the building where Masaryk had his apartment saw some people coming in. And so I think that when they began to examine all that in 1968, they were obviously coming to the conclusion that he did not commit suicide but was simply disposed of. But before they could do it, of course, it was stopped, and the Soviet invasion came. Then they produced something which is also indicative of guilt. They said it was neither suicide nor anything else: it was just sheer accident. He just fell from the window by accident – which is the least likely explanation.

CHARLTON: You know that room and that window?

TABORSKY: I know that apartment, yes. I was there several times.

THE CZECH COUP, following the promulgation of the Marshall Plan and the formation of Cominform, was among the last milestones on the road to the protracted period of the Cold War.

Stalin's decision to refuse the American offer of the Marshall Plan, originally intended for the economic salvation of all of Europe, was on the grounds that it was aimed at the political and economic system of the Soviet Union. This was the final notice from him that Europe was to be divided into two implacably hostile camps, ideologically opposed. That settled the argument for the countries of Eastern and Central Europe who had hoped to keep bridges open between the two. What would today be called 'Finlandisation' was henceforth for them a dead issue.

Within the Soviet bloc the next five years were devoted to the vilifica-tion of heresies. Greatest among them was held to be 'Titoism' in Yugo-slavia. The Marshall Plan and the Tito heresy set the stage for the coercive parables of the Show Trials, which settled the fate of the so-called 'Westerners' in the Communist parties. One of these 'Westerners' was the Czech Deputy Minister for Foreign Trade in the Communist government led by Gottwald, Eugen Loebl.

LOEBL: Even Gottwald was afraid of Moscow because, don't forget, this was at the same time as the Yugoslav events. I was asked by Gottwald to work out an analysis of our future economic development; I advocated close cooperation with the West and Gottwald was very, very much in favour of that. As far as the Marshall Plan is concerned, there were two views in our Politburo and also in the Polish Politburo. At that time by chance Mr Minc (who was the economic dictator of Poland) was in Czechoslovakia, and he was all for the Marshall Plan being accepted. I wrote a paper for Gottwald: I thought we could be better off if we remained in between. I figured out that with our uranium ore, if we were to go on to the open market we could be the most developed country in Europe at that time.

CHARLTON: If Czechoslovakia maintained control of its uranium mines?

LOEBL: Yes. Just to sell it at world prices, you see. When Mikoyan asked us to orient the majority of our foreign trade towards the East, he wanted to pay a very low price for uranium ore. I refused, I broke up the negotiations. Stalin interfered, and accepted actually all that I asked for. So we thought, well, each country's entitled to fight for its own interests – and I thought I had won a great victory, and so did Gottwald.

CHARLTON: But in ideological terms, it perhaps sealed your fate. Your position on that particular issue was a direct challenge to the Soviet Union, a violation of 'fraternal ties'.

LOEBL: But, you see, there is where I was wrong. I simply believed that a Marxist country can't do what a Marxist country does. It was just a belief that a Marxist country cannot be an imperialist country.

IN THE SAME MONTH of the Czech coup, February 1948, Tito was summoned to Moscow by Stalin. But he refused to go, sending Edward Kardelj, a member of his Politburo, instead. Kardelj's memoirs were pub-lished in 1982, and he recalls that when he arrived in Moscow, Molotov threw a document in front of him and said: 'Sign this!' 'I picked it up,' said Kardelj, 'and read that our two countries, the Soviet Union and Yugoslavia, would be obliged to consult each other on all matters of foreign policy. My blood boiled, and I felt that, not only I was being insulted and humiliated, but also the whole of Yugoslavia.'

Tito refused to come to heel. Among the more remarkable information now available at first hand is the knowledge of how Stalin then prepared to invade Yugoslavia – and why he stopped short. One of those involved in planning this undertaking was the Hungarian general, Bela Kiraly.

KIRALY: I was the designated commander of the army which was supposed to invade Yugoslavia. The Hungarian army was supposed to break through between the Danube and the Tisza river, create a bridgehead on the Danube, and stop there. The privilege to invade the heretic capital, Belgrade, was reserved for the Soviet Union. In other words everything was prepared. What saved Tito against the military invasion was the Korean War. America stood up. Consequently, they assumed that if they invaded Yugoslavia, America would stand up again. I'm absolutely convinced of that. Because what we did was not a war *manoeuvre*, it was a systematic build-up, a systematic preparation for the war which was supposed to come sometime in '51 or something like that.

CHARLTON: Do you think the Soviet acquisition of the atomic bomb in 1949 accelerated Stalin's schedule?

KIRALY: Absolutely sure. I mean, in the sense that it gave Stalin a kind of security that the Soviet Union was no longer a target which could not reciprocate in kind, you know.

CHARLTON: Therefore, how influential was the fact the Soviet Union did not possess the atomic weapon between 1945 and '49, and was in that sense strategically weak? How far does that, to you, explain Stalin's much-discussed and often-remarked essential caution in his exploitation of the situation in Eastern Europe?

KIRALY: What you ask in that question is really, I would say, a statement which absolutely justifies what I'm saying. He was preparing the war against Tito. But when he saw that his war – because after all the Korean War was Stalin's war through proxies – when he saw that even in Korea the Russian advance, the Soviet advance, met a very determined American resistance, he expected that too in Yugoslavia. Stalin did not want to have his soldiers shoot on Americans, no.

FOLLOWING YUGOSLAVIA'S 'Declaration of Independence', Stalin's Cold War against Tito meant that, within the pale, any sympathisers or rival influences, real or imagined, had to be eliminated.

In Hungary in 1949, Laszlo Rajk, the Minister for the Interior (who had supervised the rigged elections and been the chief surgeon of 'salami tactics'), was arrested. He became the chief accused, and Tito's chief accuser, at a major political trial indistinguishable from the numbing audacity of the Moscow trials of the 1930s where, as has been said, 'everything was true but the facts'.

Laszlo Rajk was in the hands of the interrogators for three months, duly confessed, and was in the end hanged. Bela Szasz was a principal witness and himself a victim of the Rajk trial.

Szasz: Laszlo Rajk was one of the few Hungarian Communists who were never in Moscow – except for a three-day visit. They could not choose for trial 'Muscovites' who were Hungarian leaders, because then they would have said abroad that British and American intelligence were so strong that they could penetrate even the lines of the Russians and organise spies in Moscow itself. But they had to choose a Hungarian leader, and Matyas Rakosi always regarded Rajk as one of his greatest rivals. Rajk was a very good-looking young man. Rakosi was not. And Rajk had a certain power-base among the peasants, among those young intellectuals who came from the peasantry. Because in Hungary there was a so-called People's Colleges organisation, and Rajk was patron of this. He had a certain power-base of which Rakosi was very jealous.

Charlton: And the real reason for the Rajk trial?

Szasz: I think there were several reasons. First of all Stalin wanted to hold these satellite countries on a shorter rein. Secondly, he wanted to eliminate everybody who he suspected could organise, or could resist. Thirdly he wanted to hit Tito, who had left the Moscow Camp. Fourthly, maybe this idea of human sacrifice.

Charlton: Blood sacrifice?

Szasz: Blood sacrifice, yes. Sufficient for him to drive into the whole people the fear that no deviation will be tolerated.

Stalin's unleashing of this modern inquisition began in Budapest with the Rajk trial, and marched on to Prague.

In Czechoslovakia, Stalin enlarged the categories of those who were now considered 'dangerous' and therefore disposable. Eugen Loebl was one of the Communists who confessed at the Slansky Show Trials in Prague in 1952.

Loebl: It was, first of all, Tito. There were very good ties between Czechoslovakia and Tito. Gottwald's daughter was married to a high official in the Yugoslav Ministry of Foreign Affairs – it went even so far. It had been a great love affair during the war in Moscow. So the Soviets were afraid that Czechoslovakia might choose the road of Tito. My interrogators – Czech, Slovak, and Soviet interrogators – took part in the preparation and direction of the Rajk trial. They made witnesses there say that there was a very strong Tito movement in Hungary, but that the centre of it was in Czechoslovakia. So, with this information, Stalin approached Gottwald and offered him help. The very same Soviet interrogators came to Czechoslovakia to discover all the ties and connections of the Titoist movement between Hungary and Czechoslovakia and between Yugoslavia and Czechoslovakia.

Charlton: So Stalin decided personally?

LOEBL: Stalin decided personally, and Gottwald accepted personally.

CHARLTON: And how and when did Stalin decide, in your view?

LOEBL: It was before the Rajk trial, and I think that one of the tasks of the Rajk trial was to be the overture for this drama.

CHARLTON: Who was it who sorted out the victims for these purges – the Czech authorities or the KGB (then the NKVD), the Soviet Secret Police?

LOEBL: I think the KGB gave the general direction. For instance, at the beginning I was supposed to be sentenced as a 'Slovak bourgeois nationalist', and the heads of it would have been Clementis and Husak. But they changed it. They wanted to have also a *Czech* Titoist movement. I witnessed all that. When I confessed after fourteen months I always had to change the confession – because what was one day a crime, was the next day not a crime. But it was the Soviet political line.

I would say the other cause of the trial has the following political background. The Soviets were all out for Israel. They hoped that the Israeli left-wing government, and left-wing intellectuals, would be the ideal outpost for the Soviets in the Near East. And I remember that I once spoke with Andrej Vyshinsky, the Soviet Deputy Foreign Minister. Egypt wanted to buy a whole factory to produce guns, and Vyshinsky opposed it. He said, 'Nothing to Egypt, only Israel.' When Israel refused to play the Soviet game – and the Soviet strategic goal was to have a foothold in the Near East – the only alternative was to make friends with the Arabs, and in order to make friends with the Arabs they had to prove their anti-semitism and take the anti-Zionist line; and in order to give it credibility and force, they took 'the Jewish intellectual', Slansky, Secretary-General of the Czech Communist Party.

THE OFFERING UP of such raw material for vivisection at the Show Trials produced the terror which effectively bound Eastern Europe to Stalin's command for the time being.

We have, again at first hand from Bela Szasz the evidence of the cruelties by which these bizarre confessions were produced.

SZASZ: We entered an enormous room, where Gabor Peter, then the Chief of the Hungarian Secret Police, sat at a table – a table which was formed like a capital T. I was put at the foot of the T and the first question from Gabor Peter was, '*Who is Wagner?*' I thought of the musician, I thought of different people; and well . . . it occurred to me that we had a Consul in the Foreign Office in Czechoslovakia who was called Wagner. So I told him. Then, '*What did Wagner tell you to tell Szönyi?*'

Szönyi was then a high Party official and Chief of the Cadre Department. I could not understand this. And then, they brought in Szönyi, who looked very tired. Gabor Peter said, '*Did Szasz give you a message from Wagner?*' So he says 'Yes'. '*What message did he give?*' He said something, and slowly I found out that this Wagner in their story was nobody else but Allen Dulles, who was (at the time when Szönyi was in Switzerland) the US representative of Intelligence who was supposed to organise this group of Szönyi's into a spy group.

CHARLTON: 'Wagner' was the code name for Allen Dulles, the head of the CIA?

SZASZ: Yes, that's it. I absolutely denied it, and then Gabor Peter said, 'Well, *bastinado* to him.' And then I got the first *bastinado*. Later I got more.

CHARLTON: What happens in a *bastinado*?

SZASZ: Well, you have to lie on your stomach. Two or three people sit on you, and your feet are naked. They hold your feet and they get rubber truncheons . . . they hit your feet, the soles of your feet. And so much so. About twenty-five times each. I got twenty-five each on thirty-six times. And my skin was really completely – it was like beefsteak, my feet. And I had to stand on these feet for nine days and nine nights without food, and without water, to make a confession. But I denied them this pleasure.

CHARLTON: Then what happened?

SZASZ: When I came to the Chief first, into his anteroom, there was a Hungarian who served in the NKVD, and who was Colonel Szucs. And there he made a great speech, that I have to 'help the Party'. They know very well that I am not a criminal. When I make my confession they will take me away, in a few months' time, and I will have a beautiful time in the Crimea. Then I will come back and they will let me do whatever I want, and so on and so on. But you have to confess. You have to help the Party. You have to help to strike a blow at the imperialist circle and their servant Tito.

CHARLTON: In the account you've written of this, you say that at one stage 'to incriminate others I scribbled for several nights' after the NKVD man had said that 'for the time being it's enough for you to write down who could have been a spy, later we shall see who was.' The point is, your interrogators don't really know what it is they wish you to confess to, and you don't know what it is that you're being asked to agree took place?

SZASZ: Yes. The Secret Policeman told me that 'for the time being it is enough you write down on that paper who could have been a spy'. I wrote down names, mainly people who were abroad. He wasn't pleased, and I got beaten again. This very hard beating, and this standing for nine days and so on, it went on for nearly two months. We got very little food. Soup, or two slices of bread every day. That is one method to break people, to underfeed them. Break them physically, break them psychologically, then they will be ready to sign anything to get rid of the tortures; accept everything, only to get rid of the torture.

THOSE WHO HAD DEDICATED themselves to the Party were required to be immune to the call of pity, to ignore truth and deny justice. What mattered was to be objectively right. And all that was objective, and all that was right, was laid down by the Party.

The interrogations and 'confessions' were the ultimate revelation of 'means and ends' – the exacting of obedience to the Party, which was, in the end, one man – Stalin. Eugen Loebl went through something of the same ordeal as Szasz.

LOEBL: They had all the material on my life. The only thing they wanted me to say was that whatever I did, I did it as an enemy of the Party, or mankind, and Czechoslovakia and the Soviet Union.
CHARLTON: It was made clear to you right from the beginning that this deposition you wrote out – this story of your life – was going to form the basis of an indictment?
LOEBL: At that time I had an illusion. I thought it was also the basis of my rehabilitation, because I could prove that I had not done anything which was in conflict with any law, or with the interests of the Party or with any order of the Party. So at the beginning I thought that, well, I was a rather successful Minister, that enemies wanted to eliminate me and give false testimony. Only when after two weeks, the Soviet interrogators started interrogating me, then I knew that this was the end.
CHARLTON: Can you tell me how a deposition, as in your own case, is converted into an indictment which provides the basis for a Show Trial?
LOEBL: I was not supposed to sit down. I had to stand or walk sixteen hours a day, in the cell. They did not bring me at all to the fresh air, so I was always in the cell. For interrogation I could not sit down, I had to stand. During the night they woke me up each five or six minutes to get up from my bed and report. 'Prisoner 1473 reports. One Prisoner, everything is in order.' After two, three or four nights I fell asleep always immediately after such a report. Being wakened up out of a deep sleep played havoc with the nerves. I was not allowed to read, not allowed to write, not allowed to smoke. I was always hungry, but it was not a starvation diet.

And the greatest force and the greatest pain was caused by time. The day had no end. Just to walk after a few days, each step was painful. And each minute was endless. So the combination of physical pain and tremendous boredom creates a situation where you yourself feel, and try to persuade yourself, to give up all values. Forget about what is right and wrong. The only thing is that you may have the right to sit down, smoke a cigarette, read something. Even if you are sentenced to life, as long as you can sit – this seemed to be the greatest desire and dream. What they achieve is to demoralise. They have time, you see. If they had beaten me up – and if I had given in, under pain – well, one day pain disappears and I would deny it all again. But here I had to convince myself, and in this demoralised state of affairs (and this *is* a process of demoralisation) I confessed to whatever they wanted.

I did not even dream, at the trial, of telling the truth. In a sense I was afraid that somebody else (say, Slansky) could deny it, and then I would have to choose between the alternatives again, to be honest or dishonest. I could sit down; I could smoke; I could read. And I knew that if I were to do something in accordance with my values, I would be exposed again to such a situation, and would end up with giving in again. So it was definitely not a brainwashing. Nothing like Koestler assumes. It was brutal force combined with a sophisticated method: how to demoralise you. This happened to all the defendants, and that is why we all became very willing tools of the interrogators.

CHARLTON: How long did this take?

LOEBL: Being a fool, it took me fourteen months. I should have given in after two months. There were many times I just wanted to give in and confess everything. But then I saw my interrogators, and had such a feeling of hatred, such a feeling that they should not triumph over me – so again I denied everything. But it took fourteen months. But I would like to say very frankly it is a process of demoralisation; and I think this is also the policy of the Soviets with regard to all oppressed nations. They put the emphasis on the process of demoralisation, because dictatorship needs demoralised people. Democracy dies, and goes to pieces, if people have no moral values.

LIKE FERMENTATION BUBBLING UP, the trials brought to the surface the inner character of the political system Lenin and Stalin had created and which produced (in Bela Szasz's description) 'volunteers for the gallows'.

SZASZ: I suppose one could distinguish three different stages of an interrogation. The first stage was to break this man, or this woman (there were a few women) – to make a prefabricated element out of him, which will be part of a building, the whole Show Trial. The second stage was to bring these prefabricated elements into some relation and make of it a kind of basic edifice. The third was to beautify this edifice, to make the Show Trial complete and whole as a story, and to file down the contradictions. Which they didn't do, of course. Even in print I am named once as an English, once as an American agent. They were full of contradictions.

CHARLTON: In your account of this trial, you are brought face to face with Rajk as somebody who's provided some of the evidence at the trial which is to lead to Rajk's condemnation and sentence to death. When you are brought face to face with him, your former friend, you say this: 'Looking into Rajk's tired eyes, I realised that he knew he had come to the end of the road, and that he was doomed.'

SZASZ: Yes. And to show me that he did not mind whatever I said – because I did not make a confession against him – he signed every page of the protocol, even those pages which he should not have signed. He signed at least fifty, maybe a hundred. The interrogator told him, 'Ah, you know very well how one has to do it!' And he signed every page. He wanted to show me he did not mind whatever I said about him. I should not suffer therefore; I could say whatever I wanted. He did it with a look. Signing every page and looking at me.

CHARLTON: You say this also: 'In the end, Rajk accepted the Golden Bridge offered to his self-respect.' What do you mean by that?

SZASZ: In the beginning Rajk definitely was extremely strongly tortured. And they told him the same thing as they told me, and others who did not confess – that he should help the Communist Party, and that with his sacrifice, with his political and moral suicide, he helps the Communist Party. He accepted this Golden Bridge. That is what I said. And perhaps he regarded it really as a sacrifice, for the Communist Party. Maybe he was no longer a believer. Maybe he simply gave up everything after the deceptions he suffered.

CHARLTON: The Rajk trial took place in 1949. It wasn't until seven years afterwards that the evidence of the secret tapes of a conversation between János Kádár, Hungary's present leader, and Rajk were revealed. What can you tell us about that?

SZASZ: The taped conversation discloses that Kádár said to Rajk, 'Comrade Rakosi sends me to you. We know very well that you are not a spy, not a conspirator, but you have to make this sacrifice for the Communist Party because we are in such-and-such a situation.' And Rajk discussed the whole thing with him in a very angry way. But, in the end, apparently Kádár convinced him, or at least – we never know what happens inside a man – he accepted. Maybe because he wanted to build a bridge for his self-esteem.

THESE EVENTS, and their many victims of thirty years ago and more, have no special claim upon us because of pain and suffering. These were men who had taken up the cause of a creed which in the end devoured them. They were in many instances men who had forfeited the right to protest against torture, or secret prisons, or organised lying, for they had helped to procure them and inflict them upon others. They were not apostles of independence or nationalism. They were indeed rather shadowy and obscure heroes.

It was in prison that men like Eugen Loebl were forced to confront the consequences of their own beliefs.

LOEBL: I had to kill the time somehow in those endless days, so I started to think. I wanted to know whether all that I saw, all that I heard, people crying who had been beaten and so on, whether this is a deviation of Marxism or whether it is inbuilt in Marxism. I wanted to know whether I was co-responsible for what happened, or whether I was an innocent victim. And I was hoping only that my conclusion would be that I was an innocent victim, that with all great ideologies it happens that, once applied, it could be misused.

CHARLTON: What conclusion did you come to? Were you as guilty of your situation as those who inflicted it upon you?

LOEBL: Well, if my answer is that these dehumanised and inhumane activities or features are inbuilt in Marxism, then I am co-responsible. Because I advocated Marxism, I persuaded many people to become Marxists; I fought for Marxism.

But if Marxism is an ideology that leads towards, or is an avenue to, a humane society, then I am just an innocent victim and it is just my personal tragedy. It took a few months until I came to the conclusion that Marxism, and everything I believed in, is a most inhumane philosophy, and in whatever form it is applied will result in an inhumane society. Consequently, I am co-responsible for my fate as well. I cannot blame anybody but me. And if they had not imprisoned me, I would have been instrumental in bringing other people to the situation in which I was.

CHARLTON: Can you put a figure to the number of people, the number of individuals, who were directly affected in your view by the Purge Trials?

LOEBL: There were many thousands, I think. Many thousands. Not all were in prison, naturally, but dismissed from work – and then there were the families. Thousands were imprisoned.

UTOPIA IN POWER STOOD symbolised in the Show Trials as a quintessential mendacity. A pervasive cynicism took hold, and began to heighten and widen and deepen throughout Eastern Europe.

Today, if one looks at the political geology of Stalin's fracturing monolith, one can see there the rising, expanding seam of intellectual challenge to the basic tenets of the Communist faith. This critique has come from within the ranks of Communism – ranging from Milovan Djilas and his political assault on the New Class, to the devastating historical and philosophical examination by one of the most formidable of contemporary minds, Leszek Kolakowski. It points in one direction only: to the decline of that hold on the mind once exercised by the Soviet Union, which has accompanied the eclipse of its ideology.

3
THE ECLIPSE OF IDEOLOGY

THE YEASTS OF DISCONTENT with Soviet colonial rule over Eastern Europe have been at their most restless in attacking and breaking down the 'certainties' of the Marxist–Leninist ideology. As with every system of thought and ideas, the strength of Communism has depended to a large extent on its power to attract and to hold the minds of intelligent people. Today it is almost palpable that on the battlefield of ideas in Eastern Europe since the death of Stalin, the 'Ideology' which was once a heady propellant has now lost virtually all impulsion.

The crushing by the Red Army of the Hungarian Uprising in 1956; the Soviet invasion of Czechoslovakia in 1968 which sought to prevent the evolution in Prague of what was deemed to be 'Communism with a human face'; and in the present day the smothering of Solidarity, the cot death of a free trade union movement in Poland: all these have shown that when it comes to ways of thinking about past, present or future, the Soviet Union has not been able to sustain any fundamental ideological loyalties.

It is time to look more closely now at the formidable critique of Communism which has come from within the ranks of its ruling caste in Eastern Europe over the years, a contribution which discloses that same pattern of development which marks the recurring cycle of social disturbances there. It is one of gathering, cumulative opposition. What began as a challenge to Soviet orthodoxy on a relatively narrow front, exemplified by the Yugoslav leader Milovan Djilas and his book *The New Class* (published in 1957), then broadened out in the attempts and failures to revise the faith in the 1950s and 1960s, has reached a significant new plateau in the magisterial studies of Communism, root and branch, by the Polish philosopher, Leszek Kolakowski. With Kolakowski one is left to conclude that if ideology is dead it still appears indispensable. In this judgement, Eastern Europe forty years after the Second World War is chained to an ideological corpse. What, then, is left?

Leonard Schapiro, a distinguished elder among those British political scientists who have specialised in Soviet studies, offered this reply as the distilled essence of Soviet ideology today. It was among his last public reflections on a subject to which he devoted an academic life.

SCHAPIRO: What this ideology has come to mean is a method of control. There are two elements in Soviet ideology which are absolutely indestructible, and any amount of force will be applied to preserve them. One is the doctrine of 'proletarian internationalism', which means that the Soviet Union comes first, and that in order to preserve 'the centre of world Socialism' everything has to be subordinated in other countries to the interests of the Soviet Union. This is the basis of the Soviet Union's domination over the satellites, and remains fundamental. Now, that is really 'ideology'. Secondly, there is the doctrine that the Party has got an inalienable right to rule, because this can only derive from ideology. Nobody has ever elected the Party, no Communist Party has ever come to power on the basis of popular acclaim (except, perhaps, by accident or misunderstanding); and therefore the foundation of the Party's pre-dominance has to be ideological.

Now, in that sense ideology is very real, so I think it is wrong to talk about the 'death' of ideology. If you mean by the death of ideology the fact that the tenets of Marxism have been discredited, the unity of Marxism has been shattered, the practical success of Marxist-type governments has been demonstrated to be non-existent – in that sense of course, the death of ideology *has* got a meaning. It is true, I am sure, in the Soviet Union (and I should think in most of the satellites, except perhaps Bulgaria) that nobody believes any more in any of the tenets of the system. But when one talks about the 'death' one has to remember, I think, those two pillars which survive. They are of course the pillars of 'Control' which is what Communism has become and has come to mean. All the deviations from it have not, I think, been so much matters of theory: they have been struggles for liberation from what has been felt to be an alien straitjacket.

LEONARD SCHAPIRO DEFINES the one sense in which Kolakowski seems prepared to acknowledge that ideology is indispensable. 'Faith in Communism' in Eastern Europe (according to Kolakowski) came to an end with the failure of the considerable efforts to reform Communism and the Communist parties after Stalin's death in 1953.

The contrast between the visions of a society which was 'socially just' (if rigidly organised) and the reality of one in which human rights have been cynically trampled down was the revelation which put an end to Communism's greatest allure for anyone but the truest believer. Here is that inherent magnetism described by Kolakowski himself, one of the younger generation of Communists in Poland after the war.

KOLAKOWSKI: We were perfectly aware at the time that we were a small minority in a country which was essentially hostile to Communism and to the Soviet Union. Nevertheless, we were of course convinced that Communism is not only the best but the *only* solution for the continuous progress of mankind. There were many illusions and errors behind this judgement. Of course there were the sort of normal illusions of young intellectuals who want to have a universal key, so to say, an all-embracing perfect system, explaining past history and giving a prescription for a glorious future. Marxism seemed to us attractive because it has this apparent power of supplying explanations for virtually everything, and at the same time offering an intellectual instrument to the cause of people oppressed and exploited.

However, there were other reasons for it. We somehow saw Communism as a continuation of the revolutionary, humanist, socialist tradition – of the spirit of the enlightenment which Marxism to some extent used to be. We were very hostile to a certain kind of cultural tradition that had dominated Polish life in past decades, the clerical, somewhat obscurantist tradition – a tradition of bigotry. We believed Marxism to be an intellectual instrument to oppose this tradition, and one which would give us a large, internationalist, rationalist view of the world. These were illusions, to be sure. But they were not absolutely foolish, I would say.

Polish culture was really torn between various tendencies, as all national cultures are. We believed that by identifying ourselves with Communism we could continue this tradition of enlightenment and of rationalism and internationalism as represented by the left-orientated intelligentsia before the war, and earlier, in fact, in the nineteenth century.

Another reason was that we believed that, after the unspeakable horrors of the war and the Nazi occupation of Poland, Communism proved to be the most effective force in opposing the barbarity to which Europe had fallen prey. The democratic establishments of pre-war Europe seemed to us to be utterly discredited. So there it is. There were various motives which led both me and many of my colleagues to Communism.

THE OLDER GENERATION of 'believers' who came to power in Eastern Europe after the last war were a highly resistant strain who had proved their immunity to the moral and intellectual doubts which had, in the 1920s and '30s, driven others out of the Communist fold and out of Communist parties all around the world – as with Stalin's bloody purges. These were hardened souls, who had maintained their loyalty to the

Party throughout both its vegetarian and its carnivorous times.

Among them was Eduard Goldstücker, a Czech Communist who kept the faith for thirty-seven years, and who was imprisoned himself in the purges of the 1950s in Eastern Europe, later playing a leading part in the events which led up to what became known as the 'Prague Spring' of 1968.

GOLDSTÜCKER: If you embrace a set of ideas, or a creed, as whole-heartedly as I did, then you need a tremendous lot of hammering, of counter-arguments, of experience, to shatter that creed. It takes a very long time and is a very complicated development. That was our case, my case and the case of many of my generation in Central Europe at that time. You see: it is the problem of the conflict of rational criticism and belief. The stronger you believe, the weaker becomes your rational criticism or your critical faculties and your readiness to apply them.

Although you flatter yourself you are an intellectual, based on reason and the critical analysis of problems, your capacity to apply that criticism is weakened, even nullified by the strength of your creed, of your belief. And Stalin built up (or rather Lenin built up) so-called Marxism–Leninism as a creed, as a religion.

Now the problem, the eternal problem, was the same with the Nazis in Germany. There were many people who, out of pure motives, joined the Nazi regime and stayed with it to the bitter end, in spite of everything that happened and that should have indicated to them that they were on the wrong path. That happened to us. The problem is the conflict between Belief and Reason. It is a tragic conflict, really.

CHARLTON: There must have been particular moments, though, when you did have to fight off the mounting evidence . . .

GOLDSTÜCKER: Oh yes, of course.

CHARLTON: . . . in order to sustain this belief. Let me put to you, for example, something that I saw that Michael Foot, in a book review, had written quite recently about Koestler's *Darkness at Noon*. He said that, with it, 'a terrifying shaft of darkness was cast over the past as well as the future'. It was an indelible moment for him. Now I assume you read Koestler's novel. It made no such impact?

GOLDSTÜCKER: Yes, I read the book in very dramatic circumstances – in 1941 in Oxford during Hitler's march into the heart of Russia. And I read at the same time Hemingway's *For Whom the Bell Tolls*, which contained criticism of Stalinist policies in Spain. I read *Darkness at Noon* against Stalin's boast, shortly before the war, that 'whoever dares to put his pig's snout in the Soviet garden will be ejected, annihilated'. And now I saw that, instead, Hitler's armies are marching towards Moscow. Every day. Total collapse of the Soviet army. There was a joke floating around London at the time. It said the Czechs and Poles are the best experts on

Russian affairs, but you have to know who you are talking to! If the Russians are advancing and you ask the Poles they will say, 'Yes they're advancing, but wait till the end!' And if the Russians are retreating, ask the Czechs and they will say, 'Yes they're retreating but in the end they'll advance!' That was my situation.

I'll give you a better example of that onslaught of counter-arguments which I brushed aside. In 1936, as you remember, André Gide went to the Soviet Union and he published his little booklet *Retour de l'URSS*. I was a student of German and French literature, and Gide's booklet created a tremendous wave of discussion, a heated, passionate debate thoughout Europe. I took part in those discussions. But, by that time we had so accommodated, become so adapted, that we simply rejected and eliminated anything that criticised the Soviet Union. We even refused to read it, because that was the voice of 'the enemy' – at that time the 'Trotskyite enemy'. And if it is an enemy, then he has an evil motive which should be rejected without examining it in detail. That was our answer to it. And that, again, is the situation of a believer who does not want his belief to be undermined.

THE QUALITY AND ALSO the significance of the defection from Communism has to be assessed in the light of such, typically, lengthy devotion. Slowly eroded, it led on from disenchantment to rejection.

The Yugoslav Communist Milovan Djilas spent nine years in prison in Yugoslavia, and today, living in one of the greystone, heavy-set streets in the centre of Belgrade, is consigned officially to the Orwellian category of 'Unperson', ostracised from normal political or social contacts. One of the leading personalities in Tito's partisan war, Djilas was among the first to represent and articulate feelings and attitudes which were to emerge as a fundamental post-war heresy. Now aged seventy-one, he is still a compelling figure. Imprisoned by Tito in the 1950s, he spent the time learning English, translating Milton's *Paradise Lost*, and reading the works of Sir Thomas More.

In his subsequent writing, which followed the famous *Conversations with Stalin* and *The New Class*, Djilas has evoked the practical effects of ideology by recalling life under the absolute authority of Stalin, where even the wife of the persecuted Russian poet Boris Pasternak felt constrained to say, 'Most of all my children love Stalin, and after that they love me.' It is witness, Djilas feels, that Communists like himself lived in a state close to hypnotic trance; in which they were not quite ill or unbalanced, but not quite normal either.

DJILAS: Communism is not a religion, but the feelings of believers in Communism are very close to religious beliefs, to some Puritan beliefs or maybe extreme Catholic beliefs in the Middle Ages.

CHARLTON: It is not a matter of analysis or reason, then, but of faith?

DJILAS: For Communism the beginning is in Marx. For Marx, and for all Communists, it is characteristic that Communism has two essential sides to it. One is really scientific – in its analysis. The approach to the facts is scientific: to collect the facts and analyse them rationally. But the *aim* is irrational. The aim is *not* analytic. In the aim you *must* believe: that means a future perfect society, a classless society – in that you must believe. Let me underline that this is the essential trait or characteristic of Communism – this unification, this synthesis of absolute belief and scientific or, better, rational analysis.

CHARLTON: Can those two elements, in your view, still be reconciled?

DJILAS: Well, I came to change my opinion through praxis. I saw, for example (and even by the end of the war), the practices of the Soviet Union. At the same time the conflict with Stalin was very important in my mind, to protect Yugoslavia and the Yugoslav Party. That was in the beginning. And later I started to think about what *we* were; because the origins of Yugoslav Communism were very similar and very strongly connected with the Soviet Union. I started to see, in the similarity of the system, some similar problems and similar 'cults' as in the Soviet Union.

CHARLTON: But when a historian looks at these two periods in your life, which take you from rapture with Stalin to a profound disillusion and rejection of all that he stood for, what are they to make of, say, two old statements of yours. I'd like to remind you of what you said in 1942:

> Can there be any greater honour and happiness than to feel that one's closest and most beloved friend is Stalin. Stalin is the bitterest enemy of all that is inhumane, before whose eyes are unravelled future centuries. There are no riddles in the world that Stalin cannot solve.

DJILAS: This is typical for the believer.

CHARLTON: And you really believed that?

DJILAS: Yes, absolutely.

CHARLTON: You really believed that Stalin could solve 'all the riddles'?

DJILAS: It is a literary expression, and the style is romantic. But, essentially, I believed it. Stalin was not only the person but also a symbol, an incarnation of the Idea for us.

CHARLTON: And then, twenty years later, at the time of your renunciation of Communist doctrine, we find you saying this:

> Stalin was the greatest criminal of all time. In him was joined the criminal senselessness of a Caligula, with the refinement of a Borgia and the brutality of Ivan the Terrible.

DJILAS: In this I also believed. I am now a believer in freedom, as I believed once in Communism. In youth Communism for me was freedom; but I came to see that it was not so in practice.

CHARLTON: What was the key to this spell that Stalin cast over you? Elsewhere you have said, 'I loved him.' And now you tell me it was a matter of faith – you really did. But, again, in what sense? How would you explain to somebody who has not had the experience at all – how you 'loved' Stalin?

DJILAS: Well, first of all being a young Communist I really was Leninist (or Stalinist), and that was the teaching and the only teaching which existed in the Party in Yugoslavia. And later there was struggle in Yugoslavia – brutalities – and then especially the war reinforced our belief. My belief. I mean that reality itself helped us to reinforce those feelings and beliefs.

Even, for example, at the time of the trials in Moscow: many, many Communists thought that there was something wrong – that they were incorrect. I very easily convinced myself (I was one of the leaders in Yugoslavia) that while everything might have been wrong in some details, everything must be true.

Then there was Spain and the struggle there. Then, Hitlerism – and the false policy of the Western countries in the period of Munich. They forced such a belief in Stalin and in the Soviet Union. Without a sufficient 'reality', that belief could not have been so strong and successful. Only when the reality began to separate, and to come into conflict with my own thinking, did I start to see Stalin more critically.

CHARLTON: In trying to understand how you came to reassess your whole intellectual position about Communism, how much importance should be put down to the personality of Stalin himself? When you first met him in Moscow he was, to you, man made God. You ended up seeing him very differently. I remember vividly the description you give in your *Conversations with Stalin* about the wrinkled skin crawling on the back of his neck, when you sat behind him in the car at night on the way to his dacha outside Moscow. It embodied for me the change in your perception of him from adulation to revulsion. One can almost feel your revulsion growing, yet at the time there was no explanation for me of what produced it.

DJILAS: His physical traits and qualities I saw from the beginning. And in my first publication the Russians insisted on correcting some of my description of him – that he had long arms, that he was quite small, and so on. And his pock-marks: they had to be eliminated. But I think I described him from the first correctly, physically. About his head, I said that it was relatively beautiful – like the peasants from Montenegro. And this is true. He had some attraction. He was a very alive person, with very alive, fast reactions – with fast nerves. You could do nothing in the presence of Stalin he did not notice. Smile or make some movement – he at once remarked it and its meaning. In his sphere he was, I think, a very intelligent man.

CHARLTON: The wrinkled skin on the back of his neck?

DJILAS: It was my second description of Stalin. When I was with him for the last time in January 1948, he was physically ruined, old and tired and a little senile. When I first met him during the war, in the Soviet Union, I did not see really either Stalin, or the Soviet Union, as a whole. It was a very poor and dirty country at this period. But I had come from the war where conditions were even worse. I explained this to myself as the consequence of the war. So I did not *see*, really. And Stalin, I saw through my idolatry.

But the last time I saw the man and not the God. By then I was more mature in politics, and some disagreements with the Soviet Union had started. Then I began to see Stalin not as the incarnation of the absolute Idea but as a strong, political but ordinary mortal. Talented, but not without faults. But I have to say that the illusions, connected with the ideology, are stronger than any reality.

WHILE THEIR COMMITMENT lasted, these men could not be shaken from their conviction that mankind had entered a new era under Stalin, the genius who could do no wrong. As Leszek Kolakowski has put it recently, 'The unity and loyalty of even a guilty Party was a thousand times more important than frivolous considerations of morality and the like.'

This acceptance of and evangelism for the 'historical inevitability' of what was happening around them led on, naturally, to the feeling that there could be no turning back.

The force of such convictions enabled them to laugh, for a time, in the face of the Cassandra-like cries from fellow intellectuals like Arthur Koestler.

GOLDSTÜCKER: It is not a question of individual psychology or, if it is, it applied to very very many individuals. Communism is something more than an individual psychological programme.

CHARLTON: But can I put to you Arthur Koestler's famous indictment at the West Berlin Cultural Congress in 1950. He said this, of the intellectuals:

> Faced with Destiny's challenge they preached neutrality towards the Bubonic Plague. Mostly they are the victims of a professional disease, the intellectual's estrangement from reality. Having lost touch with reality, they have acquired a devilish Art. They can prove everything they believe and believe everything they can prove.

Do you recognise yourself in that?

GOLDSTÜCKER: Yes, yes, yes. Only I would add that it takes a very long time to admit that what you embraced, as a young man, with the enthusiasm of your early years, is proving to be false, and that you are clutching to it as long as you can. Even beyond the reasonable time.

CHARLTON: For fear of what?

GOLDSTÜCKER: For fear of losing yourself, really. Of finding yourself deprived of any perspective of the future. The collapse of everything, of your whole world. You see that was the case – I quoted the debate about Gide – that was the case in the Moscow Trials. I was in Moscow in 1935 in a more or less privileged position as a delegate to the last Congress of the Youth Communist International. That was late summer, the beginning of autumn 1935. It was almost a year after the murder of Kirov and the start of the great Stalinist purge and terror. And, although people other than Communists were already sitting in the Lubyanka, I never felt more free in my life than I felt there. I know now that my every step was followed and that we moved in an illusory world that did not exist in reality. But, nevertheless, at that time I felt myself to be a free man, absolutely free as never before. I wrote to my wife, who was my girlfriend at the time, that I never felt as free as I did at that time.

See how far your delusion can take you!

THE YUGOSLAVS WERE the first to demonstrate that ideological illusions were not in all cases strong enough to overcome reality. Tito's partisans had made their own revolution, in imitation of the 'Soviet model' but independently. That fact, and the help of their geography led to a successful challenge to the Kremlin orthodoxy Stalin had been demanding. The most eloquent testimony of the origins of Tito's heresy has come from Milovan Djilas, Tito's Chief of 'Agitation and Propaganda', who saw at first hand the penetration of the Yugoslav Party and Politburo by the Soviet Secret Police. This brought Djilas into direct contact and conflict with Stalin.

As we have seen, in *Conversations with Stalin*, Djilas has recorded the change in his own perceptions from seeing the Soviet leader as God to seeing him as Man. It released in him, he says, everything else. Stalin told Djilas repeatedly that Communism was to be spread by Soviet power alone, as the only reliable or desirable means. For Djilas (who thinks the West has never understood the importance of ideology for any Soviet leadership) it meant that imperialism had to be ideological too, or else it commanded no legitimacy. Djilas was forced therefore to recognise that the ideology was so narrow as to preclude alternative interpretations of the true faith. He came to see Stalin's decisive motivation as Russian nationalism, disguised within Communist ideology.

That, for Djilas, was enough to begin toppling the walls of the secular city of God. His world quickly filled with a plenitude of those 'basic contradictions' which Communists are so fond of diagnosing in others. Marking his own exit from Communism, he underlined some crucial moments.

DJILAS: How to explain to you? First, the Russians started to organise intelligence services inside our Party, and around the Central Committee. We discovered this even during the war. We asked ourselves: why? There is no difference between us and them. That means that they do not believe in us or that they have some intention. In this way Tito was a far-seeing man. The feeling of the power of the State in him was stronger than in any of us, and he felt it from the beginning very strongly. He started to understand better that we must save the autonomy of the Party, of power, from Soviet orders. So really the first substantial differences were connected with Soviet spying methods in Yugoslavia.

The second was connected with my sector of work. I was Chief of Agitation and Propaganda; and there the Russians tried to introduce their own methods in political propaganda and in culture and other fields. They tried to give a different interpretation of the Yugoslav revolution, to underestimate it and *over*estimate the Soviet role in the Yugoslav revolution. This was the new reality for us, and it was so apparent in my sector of the work that I started to be in conflict with the Soviet Union. The first secret attack against Yugoslavia, as is now discovered in new documents, was really against me. They even tried to expel me from the Central Committee. This was the start of a purge in Yugoslavia: first through me (expel me from the Central Committee), and in the second phase there would probably have been a trial.

But, not just Tito, other members of the Central Committee did not agree with this. Tito felt that this was really the beginning of his own dethroning. He understood it. If I had not been a product of the Yugoslav revolution and a participant in it, as with the other leaders in Yugoslavia, there would have been no conflicts with Stalin. Through revolution we really attained self-consciousness. We had created our *own* State and our *own* police apparatus. I think the quarrel between me and Stalin, the disagreements, started in connection with my remark and complaint about the attitudes and behaviour of the Red Army in Yugoslavia.

But, thinking in perspective, I believe that Stalin had the idea to cheat me, to use my idealism until some later period. I think he understood that it is relatively easy to play with those 'idealists' in Communism. And, probably, if I was not a Yugoslav Communist, a man from a different revolutionary experience, and a man with some moral qualities, he would have so treated me. The incident over the Red Army was only one 'visible' incident, but there were many incidents (as I have told you); in the Secret Services, in propaganda, many unknown incidents. At the same time, some Yugoslav Communists, very close to the leadership, were very actively in contact with the Soviet Union, intriguing against Tito and Tito's leadership – and of course against me. Many incidents are not known well. I shall try to explain this in my next book. It is complex.
CHARLTON: You have spoken of the blinding effect which the Communist revelation, its ideology, had for you. In its completeness you had a whole architecture of thought, beautifully arranged in your mind, which holds together until 1948. And suddenly, as it seems to me, it disintegrated. I wonder whether there must not have been some other dimension that you have not really spoken about? Perhaps the burden of guilt for the violence that Communism had produced might have been a factor? What of those mass deportations of people, trials, executions? Was there some sense of repentance growing within you?

DJILAS: No. I have never felt repentance. I think that Westerners over-estimate violence in Communism, and for the Communists, as something very decisive, in the sense of inhuman. Violence is part of any politics and Communism is, of course, strongly connected with such ideas. But I think the essentials are those Utopian conceptions, as I told you. For example, imagine if Stalin had really succeeded in creating a perfect society. Nobody would have reproached him for his crimes – only maybe a small group of humanitarian philosophers: but all of Europe and the left would have been enthusiastic, and said: 'Yes, this might not be a good way or a good manner but it is inevitable – and for such great achievements we must pardon this way.'

CHARLTON: And yet I was struck by something that you wrote when you were reviewing the book by Nadezhda Mandelstam, the wife of the Soviet poet Mandelstam who died in the Gulag. You have this sentence, talking about her, that 'the black depths of immeasurable and unjustified violence calmed her anger and aroused her capacity for thought'. It occurred to me that you were talking here about yourself, that when you looked back on what you had done – on those 'black depths of immeasurable violence' – that you really could not go on with it. In retrospect, you could not face yourself. True?

DJILAS: That was the war, the revolution. I did my duty as did the other Yugoslav leaders. They created a revolutionary army. This isn't easy; it can't be done without some conflict, some cruel methods even. But this is normal in war, and especially one must keep in mind the kind of war we had on our hands. We developed small guerrilla units and there was con-flict with different political groups – with very cruel terror against Com-munists, not only from the German occupiers but from our own domestic police and the counter-revolutionary group – this was civil war connected with national war. It was complicated. I will not say that our revolution was not cruel – it was – but no more, no less, than other revolutions.

CHARLTON: So the real reason for your own disillusionment is the sheer failure of the Communists, and your understanding that you too had failed? The sheer failure to achieve what you set out to do?

DJILAS: Yes, this is true. We see now from Belgrade to Peking there are many variants of this society, but none of them is successful. One might be a little worse than the other, one a little better if you compare them.

CHARLTON: But when was it really apparent to you that nothing was happening as you Communists said it was going to, that none of these scientific predictions was being fulfilled?

DJILAS: Too late. When I was in prison. Even when I wrote *The New Class*, it was (from my point of view) still a Marxist book. But in prison, at the end, I understood that 'science' is not enough to change society. In general I think that science may help in politics, but politics is something different from science. Politics is using the sciences but society cannot be built up, or ruled, by science.

*Top: 'We got down finally, absolutely exhausted, to the coast' – Lord Gladwyn
(p. 12). (Left to right) Secretary of State Stettinius, Molotov, Churchill and
Roosevelt arrive at Yalta, February 1945.
Bottom: 'Why the hell didn't we just say you can't have Poland. . .' – Alger Hiss
(p. 50), here seated, head bowed, behind Roosevelt and Stettinius at Yalta with
Stalin (far left), Molotov and Gromyko, and Churchill (lower right).*

Top: *Alger Hiss testifies at Senator McCarthy's hearings on un-American activities. 'He formed the bridge of contact between Hopkins, ill in bed at Yalta, and Stettinius at the conference table. . .' (p. 45).*
Bottom: *Churchill with General Sikorski. 'Sikorski's death was a major disaster. I took the news to Churchill, who wept' – Sir Frank Roberts (p. 27).*

The Katyn Massacre – the bodies of the Polish officers. 'Churchill and Eden said, really, "For God's sake don't let us talk too much about this"' – Sir Frank Roberts (p. 27).

STALIN STRIDES.

Top: 'Russia would have a great responsibility for hundreds of years in any decision she took with Poland' – Churchill to Stalin at Teheran, 1943 (p. 36). Bottom: Stalin, as seen by Punch *in 1946. 'A python does not speak your language you know. It wants to strangle you in the end' – Sir Ian Jacob (p. 48).*

*Beneš with Patton's army at Pilsen in 1945. 'It was a walk to Prague' –
Ivo Duchacek (p. 58).*

Top: *President Beneš with Edward Taborsky. 'Mr President, this is not right legally. You should not sign it' – Edward Taborsky (p. 69).*
Bottom: *Beneš with Molotov in Moscow, March 1945. 'He is the stepping-stone really for the Communist transition to power' – Jacques Rupnik (p. 72).*

*Top: Broken printing press and rigged elections, Poland 1947. 'We could not
finish them all off at the same time. So we started with the weakest ones.
We applied such enormous pressure on them. . .' – Zoltan Vas (p. 64).
Bottom: Beneš with Gottwald and Trade Union leader Zapotocky (left and
right). 'A single man cannot oppose an avalanche' – Zapotocky to Beneš (p. 75).*

Top: Jan Masaryk dead. 'When they began to examine all that in 1968 they were obviously coming to the conclusion he did not commit suicide. . .' – Edward Taborsky (p. 76).
Bottom: Show Trials and Purges. '. . . they had to prove their anti-semitism, they took "the Jewish intellectual" Slansky' – Eugen Loebl (p. 80). Slansky (third from left), Secretary-General of the Czechoslovak Communist Party, executed in 1952, seen here with (from left) Defence Minister Svobada and President Gottwald.

Top: Milovan Djilas today at home in Belgrade (with Michael Charlton).
'In prison, in the end, I understood that "science" is not enough to change
society. . .' (p. 96).
Bottom: General Bela Kiraly. 'I was the designated commander of the army
which was supposed to invade Yugoslavia. . .' (p. 78).

Top: *Budapest, November 1956. 'Comrade . . . Prime Minister, the Russian tanks are on our square. . .'*
Bottom: *'. . . I can count them, one, two, twenty-five – and they are turning towards the Parliament. . .' – General Bela Kiraly (p. 126).*

Top: *Budapest, November 1956. Stalin's statue pulled down.* 'One single shot could make the revolution. . .'

Bottom: '. . . one single shot did *make the revolution*' – General Bela Kiraly (p. 123). *The body of a Secret Policeman lies in the gutter.*

Top: *Imre Nagy in the Hungarian Parliament. 'I am sorry Shakespeare is not alive, he could have written about the whole Imre Nagy case. It would be better than* Hamlet!' – *General Bela Kiraly (p. 127).*

Bottom: *Brezhnev and Kosygin (fourth and fifth from left) confront Dubček at Cierna, July 1968, before the invasion of Czechoslovakia. 'Sasha! Sasha! what are you doing in chains. . .' (p. 129).*

Top: Soviet troops invade Prague, August 1968. 'We see now after all these experiences that what really came about is a Russian Empire. . .' – Eduard Goldstücker (p. 115).
Bottom: Prague, 1968. 'We became dominated by a regime which is historically backward. . .' – Eduard Goldstücker (p. 119).

Top: *The rise of Solidarity: Lech Walesa. 'I think that Solidarity has really been in existence since the last war. . .' – Jan Nowak (p. 40).*
Bottom: *Leaflets being passed to the crowd from strikers inside the Lenin Shipyard, Gdańsk 1980. '. . . the issues they were principally interested in were all the taboo subjects which nobody could mention before' – Norman Davies (p. 145).*

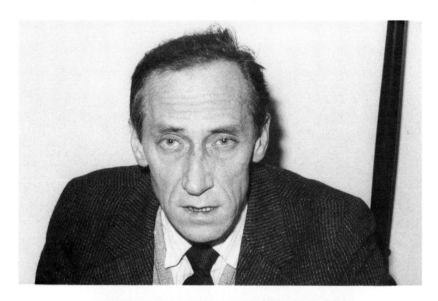

Top: The Polish philosopher Leszek Kolakowski, All Souls College, Oxford.
'Mendacity is the immortal soul of Communism. . .' (p. 133).
Bottom: Professor Richard Pipes, former White House adviser to President
Reagan on Soviet relations. 'Basically the Soviet Union is the last large white
man's empire in the world' (p. 148).

Top: *Arkady Shevchenko, former personal adviser to the Soviet Foreign Minister Gromyko. '. . . I know that it was always painful for him, Gromyko, to meet with all these leaders. . .' (p. 156).*
Bottom: *Zbigniew Brzezinski with Soviet Ambassador Dobrynin and President Carter. 'The moment is extremely ripe for a broad Western initiative' (p. 174).*

CHARLTON: Was it the realisation that the standard of living does not necessarily rise in relation to industrialisation? That collectivisation of agriculture, central planning, public property and industrialisation do not lead to a classless society?

DJILAS: There is no such country! No such country. And I think there is something wrong with the idea as such. By 'scientific method' it is possible to build up a factory, or a town or city, or a street – but not a society. A society is the product of so many unpredictable factors, of human passions, and of different social groups that cannot be built by science. Even the prediction that, with industrialisation, the problems will be resolved, is nonsense. We see from Western countries which are more industrialised than the Soviet Union that they have serious social and economic problems. And this is *not* only the problem of capitalist 'property'. Now we see that even property is less important than Socialist theoreticians, including Marx, taught – that with the liquidation of capitalist property the problems would be solved. Really the problems start *after* this . . . the problems start *after* this.

CHARLTON: Was your belief in Communism justified then?

DJILAS: It was absolutely not justified. But, contrary to my belief, Communism still is a very strong reality. My belief in Communism not only is not justified, everything which in Communism was taught, happened contrary. Take for example the withdrawing of the State. The State is stronger and stronger.

CHARLTON: The 'withering away of the State'. . . .

DJILAS: The withering away of the State. The State is stronger and stronger. The liquidation of oppression? Oppression is relatively stronger and stronger. A classless society? We have really a *class* society, with one privileged group and all the other social groups oppressed. Liquidation of war – a great ideal of Communism? We now have war between Communist states! Not between capitalist states, but between Communist states, and very cruel wars.

Standards of living? Well, standards of living have been going up in the Communist countries, in Eastern Europe especially, but not as absolutely as if the Western system was there. The Western system now, as it is, is a better system. I say this openly, not because I am partisan of the capitalist system; I am not. But this system in the West is better. It is more human. In the West you have everything that you have in the East and you have something more. Political freedoms and greater possibilities. In every way it is better. Communism predicted the end of Imperialism; we have now New Imperialism. The Soviet Union basically is military and imperialist. I compare it with the Turkish Empire.

CHARLTON: Yes. I thought that was a strange analogy to use.

DJILAS: But not completely strange.

CHARLTON: I realise that Turkey of course has a special significance, in historical terms, for your own country, Yugoslavia, but . . .

DJILAS: There are many similarities. It is not the same, of course, because that happened in the Middle Ages and we are now in the Industrial Era. But I think that the Communism of today is industrial feudalism. I think this is very near to the truth. Any such formulation is schematic, not completely accurate and so on, but this is very near to the truth.

See, for example, how the entire apparatus is connected with the centre. You cannot be director of the factory without some approval from the centre. All privileged places, the better paid, are in the hands of the members of the Party. And the Party is hierarchical, just as it was in the Turkish state during the Ottoman Empire. Then central power was united with religion in Turkey, when the Sultan was at the same time the Caliph. And now the Politburo in the Soviet Union is also the owner of the ideology.

THROUGHOUT, I THINK, but in those last thoughts particularly, Djilas illuminates the decisive importance which Stalin's policy of national humiliation for the countries of the Communist bloc assumed. And of course he gives support to the relevance of Churchill's insight concerning the 'small birds', when the British Prime Minister challenged Stalin on the first night at Yalta over the rights of the smaller nations.

When it was made unequivocally apparent to Djilas that 'the small birds' were to be caged and muted by Stalin – first and alone among the post-war Communist hierarchy it was this Yugoslav revolutionary of long and significant standing who felt compelled to signal that 'scientific Socialism', once installed, was a false dawn. The romantic Utopian, fiercely represented in Milovan Djilas, led a first wave of departure from the mind, if not yet the body, of the Communist church. Djilas came to the view that Utopia, in power, had failed to fulfil predictions and transcend the issue of national independence as between Yugoslavia and the Soviet Union. It re-created it. It also failed to transcend 'class', and rather than abolishing it had introduced a 'new class' of unassailable privilege.

At this stage, however, Czechoslovak Communists, like Eduard Goldstücker, were still taking a different view of the possibilities.

GOLDSTÜCKER: I was terribly shocked in 1948 at the breach between the Cominform and Tito. That was already for me a time of sneaking doubts. But, again, we saw that Yugoslavia had two things in her inheritance which made her situation more difficult than ours. First, she inherited a terrible hatred among the smaller nations composing it, which would take generations to overcome. Second, that Yugoslavia had never really had a democratic tradition, as we did. We thought that with that democratic tradition, and the possibility of solving our Czech/ Slovak problem amicably, we stood the chance of creating a European Socialism different from Tito's – and different, of course, from Stalin's.
CHARLTON: But Djilas's dissent went to the very core of belief at this time. What did you think of his critique?

GOLDSTÜCKER: I thought that his New Class – I read it when it was new – was somewhat exaggerated: he went a little too far by calling it a New Class; it was not a 'class' in the real sense of the word. It is not a *constant* class because there the privileges and power begin and end with your function and do not constitute 'class'. Even Ceauşescu's family is not eternal or permanent!

CHARLTON: That is not much comfort, though – it is a distinction without a difference – to those who watch those big black cars, with their blinds drawn, shooting up and down the boulevards.

GOLDSTÜCKER: You know the definition of those cars by the people: 'What is that black Czech car?' Answer: 'It is the modern means of communication of the proletariat used by its representatives!' But you see in Yugoslavia things tend to be much more crudely, or cruelly, done than in our country. In their country the alternative is either consent or mortal enmity. In Czechoslovakia that was never the tradition.

IN SPITE OF HIS first doubts in 1948, Goldstücker maintained his Party loyalty. The evidence was mounting that the only permissible ideological line for the loyal Czech Communists to follow was complicity in Stalin's determination to deprive the nation of its historical and cultural identity.

GOLDSTÜCKER: The 'nationality problem' is the key problem in Central Europe and in Europe altogether. I said at the Kafka Conference in 1963 – and it was quoted against me after 1968 – that in the transition period between Capitalism and Socialism the individual citizen can experience a more acute form of alienation than under Capitalism, even, as our experiences show. What we now see, we, the self-deceived generation, is that, instead of Socialism, the Soviet Revolution brought the Russian Empire. This Russian Empire is proceeding as all other empires have proceeded in the past – building itself as a larger and larger unit of suppressed and oppressed peoples.

Engels says somewhere that the rationalist philosophers firmly believed that they were ushering in the Age of Reason and, he said, that instead of the Age of Reason, the Age of Money came.

We were convinced that we were ushering in the Age of Fraternity or Equality or Liberty – genuinely this time. We see now, after all those experiences, that what really came about is a Russian Empire. There is a direct line between all the dreams about the greatness of Russia and Stalin's actual policy. Read one of the key books in this respect, written in the middle of the nineteenth century, Nicolai Danilevsky's *Russia and Europe*, in 1869. He proposes the creation of a Slav federation there as a means of rejuvenating and re-creating mankind. He lists the territories which should belong to the Slav federation. They are the territories now under the domination of Moscow (with one exception, the district of Constantinople).

Between 1948 and 1951 (when I was arrested) the amount of sur-
reptitious 'Russification' of Czechoslovakia was breathtaking. All the
traditional cultural connections with the West were systematically cut
off. Our children were not allowed to know that radio was invented by
Marconi; they had to believe it was Popov. The electric bulb was not
invented by Edison but by – who was it now? – Zagorchkin! The only
valid biological ideas were those of Michurin and Lysenko. Delegations
of Soviet peasants came to Czechoslovakia to teach our peasants to produce proper agricultural results. They were hailed as 'The Masters of
High Yields'. Later, when I was in prison and after three and a half years
had access to newspapers, I read Khrushchev's report listing the yields.
They were miserable, horrible. The milk yield was ridiculous. Nevertheless, they were hailed as 'The Masters of High Yields'.

And, of course, there was the militarisation of life, which was directly
evolved from the Tsarist system. The policeman as a force, and the non-
commissioned officer wielding a high degree of power. It was the hier-
archisation of our society, something quite alien to us, but which derived
directly from the Tsarist regimes.

CHARLTON: But how can you say the 'Russification' was breathtaking
when you Communists had not only sought it, but exacted it from Beneš?
Beneš made this agreement with the Russians that the Czech army would
be rebuilt on the Russian model, the cultural life would become more
intimate, the trade with the West would be turned round. . . .

GOLDSTÜCKER: There was no such agreement. Trade and so on was
being systematically undermined and destroyed after February 1948.

CHARLTON: But it is there, in the 1943 agreement, in black and white,
the reorientation of Czechoslovakia's trade with the West.

GOLDSTÜCKER: Oh yes, but that did not mean to destroy wilfully and
systematically all trade connections with the West.

CHARLTON: But you have to be almost purblind not to see the implications of it.

GOLDSTÜCKER: No, no. For instance, the destruction of our light
industry, the china and glass and the textile industry where we had great
possibilities of exporting – that was deliberate sabotage, from Stalin's
point of view, to cut off Czechoslovakia's connections with the West.

SUCH FUNDAMENTAL DISENCHANTMENTS in the 'Age of Yearn-
ing', with its earnest, vaulting desire to bring about perfection on Earth,
are understandable when the means – and ends – of that attempt were
forcibly viewed (as in Goldstücker's case) through the judas-holes in the
political prisons. But their origins lay beyond the experience of purges
and Show Trials.

In a remark to the American diplomat Averell Harriman during the
war, Stalin had said at the time of the tremendous sacrifices then being
made by the Russians in the course of the battles in the East: 'We are

under no illusions that they are fighting for us. They are fighting for Mother Russia.'

After the war, Stalin quickly revealed that his object was not merely to restore the authority of the Party, eroded as it had been in the more genuine and patriotic fraternity of the war experience, but to raise that authority, and Party ideology, to new heights. How would a new post-war generation respond?

It was into this particular context that one of the most significant intellects of the present day, Leszek Kolakowski, was introduced. Eighteen when the war finished, Kolakowski soon became a lecturer at the graduate institute for Communist Party members in Warsaw, and was Professor of the History of Philosophy at Warsaw University in 1968 when he was dismissed, for political reasons. He was one of a new generation in Eastern Europe at the war's end, a generation 'hot for certainties' which saw in Communism, as he has told us, not only deliverance from 'an obscurantist tradition' but a body of ideas 'offering a large, internationalist and rational view of the world', 'the most effective instrument against the barbarism in Europe' which had been unleashed by Hitler.

Today Leszek Kolakowski is credited with having opened a new era in Marxist criticism with his profound survey of the crisis through which a great part of the Marxist intelligentsia has been passing. An early, but obviously seminal, experience of Kolakowski's makes it clear that, while the military frontier in Europe, across which the Western NATO Alliance confronts the Warsaw Pact, is one reality, there is another and dramatic divide: the trenches of the mind which separate the 'satellite countries' from the Soviet Union under Communism.

KOLAKOWSKI: I remember very well a visit to Moscow in 1950, still under Stalin, with a small group of colleagues. We were sent to Moscow by the Central Committee of the Polish Party in order to become better acquainted in the Holy Shrine, so to say: with both the philosophical and political ideas of Marxism. It was indeed quite an experience. We spent three months in Moscow having contacts with various Soviet scholars and intellectuals, listening to their lectures and so on. And we were really quite shattered. We were young people – I cannot say that we were learned or wise. Nevertheless we could not fail to notice the absolutely miserable intellectual level of those poeple.

It really was a disaster. We could not fail to notice the destruction of various areas of culture in the Soviet Union, the miserable level of philosopy, of social thought, of painting; and we were disturbed by what we saw. We had not seen much of course; we were not really aware of its extent. We were isolated, and we had no idea of the extent of the repression. Nevertheless, in spite of our political commitment, we had to recognise some extremely unpleasant and alarming aspects of this society. Still, we were trying to explain everything to ourselves, so that

we could, somehow, reconcile what we saw with our political commitment. But it was a general impression of intellectual destruction. All those
people who were supposed to be the luminaries of Soviet intellectual life
proved to be mentally Neanderthals. They were really people of an
incredibly low level of knowledge; and that could only have disturbed us.
CHARLTON: Forgive me for suggesting it, but this is something which
goes far beyond the traditional Polish contempt for the quality of Russian
life and thought – which is, wouldn't you agree, a historical attitude of
the Polish people. It was much more than that?
KOLAKOWSKI: Yes. It is true that, as the result of various historical
experiences and hostilities there developed in Poland a sort of contempt
for what is Russian. It is a contempt which I have always found (and still
do) very regrettable – because I like very many sides of Russian culture.
My father was born in St Petersburg, he was entirely bilingual in Polish
and Russian, and he liked Russian literature. So did I. One can say there
is a certain ambiguity in this attitude of Poles to Russia. On the one hand,
contempt; on the other hand, a certain fascination – especially with
Russian literature. But what I have said had nothing to do with this
tradition. Nothing whatsoever. We came to the Soviet Union full of confidence and without any prejudices against the Russians.

AND SO, IN THE MOST sensitive province of the Soviet empire, Stalin's
attempt to recruit the new generation for a 'clean start' (as he had said at
Yalta), foundered almost at once. The moral and cultural shock which
direct experience of the new Enlightenment in its homeland had upon
men of influence like Kolakowski spelt the certain failure of the attempt
to communise Poland in the Soviet image.

There are echoes of the Polish philosopher's feelings in the testimony
of the Czech Communist Eduard Goldstücker, whose perceptions of the
moral righteousness of the 'Progressive' Soviet state only very slowly dissolved over half a lifetime, and only at the point where he felt no more
excuses could be made.

GOLDSTÜCKER: I saw the Soviet Union in the best of lights, although
there were doubts which I immediately suppressed. In 1935 I was in the
Soviet Union when they had that experiment of a different kind of working week; they wanted to do away with Sundays as a religious holiday
and make every seventh day a free day. When I walked along Moscow's
main road, Gorky Street, on the eve of such a free day, I saw drunken
people lying in the main street of Moscow every few steps. Dead drunk,
lying in the gutter. It was half dark, and you almost stepped on them. It
shocked me horribly. But again the immediate, almost instinctive
reaction was to say: 'Well, this is Russia, the old neglected society of the
Muzhiks. They have not had time to overcome this yet.'
Twenty-seven years later I was in Moscow – in 1962 – and I saw an

elderly man coming out of a shop which sold vodka in that little – at that time three-rouble – vodka bottle. He opened it in front of me outside the shop, and drank it at one go. Then he started walking, and walked straight into a lamppost with his forehead – and started bleeding. That time my reaction was quite different. It was that this is not Tsarism any more, but the great tragedy which happened to us in Central Europe. We became dominated by a regime which is historically backward, much more backward than we are. It has happened very rarely in history that the colonising power was historically backward compared to the colonised.

It was in March 1953 that lightning struck the very top of the Marxist–Leninist mountain. Stalin died. He slowly choked to death over a period of three days, after suffering a stroke at his dacha a few miles outside Moscow. With 'everything inside him desolate' by then, and 'embittered against all the world', he had been found as he lived – alone.

The scene has been graphically described by his daughter, Svetlana. The household was too frightened to approach him closely as he lay dying; the doctors applying leeches to the back of his neck, and a special session of the Academy of Sciences called to sanction unavailing treatment. His life was full of menace to the end – and his death was a release from a burden which had become insupportable to all. The outcome of the power struggles and palace revolutions in the Kremlin over the next three years confirmed the immutability of the *status quo* and the Party's total grip. But the moral ruin of Communism shook for a time the entire edifice of power.

By 1956, Stalin's eventual successor, Khrushchev, was providing the spectacle in the famous Secret Speech to the 20th Party Congress of Stalin's most faithful accomplices denouncing Stalin's crimes. Leonard Schapiro.

SCHAPIRO: It was enormously significant. I think, incidentally, it was very courageous of Khrushchev to agree because, as Tocqueville pointed out a long time ago, the most dangerous time for a bad regime comes when it tries to improve. Here was a definite shift for the better in the Soviet regime and a recognition, anyway, of some of the awful things that had happened. It was fraught with very great danger, and in fact for some years afterwards, perhaps even to the present day, the Soviet Union is faced with certain risks as a result of taking that step. The force of 1956 is not yet spent.

The real significance of it was not so much what was disclosed (because many people must have known) but that it did something that was against the rules. You see, ideology, as the French scholar Alain Besançon points out, is primarily a system which exists on a false framework – but this false framework can never be challenged. In other words, Stalin was wholly good; and the criticism of the Soviet Union was a pure invention of the 'cold warriors'. The moment that is challenged, the moment you talk in relatively truthful terms of something that has happened in the past – even though everybody does know about it – the shock of this happening is tremendous.

I remember myself the sense of absolute shock, not so much at the Secret Speech (which was not very secret, incidentally; it was pushed through all the letter-boxes of Eastern Europe, no doubt by the KGB) but in fact that this was now *openly* talked about had a tremendous effect in Russia and a tremendous effect in Europe. I think the significance of it cannot be overrated. I imagine that it is one of the most powerful effects in the undermining of the strength of Communism. The strength of Communism now is not in its doctrines, but in something else. It is the class struggle, class warfare which attracts many people – the have-nots against the haves, or, as people visualise it, anti-Americanism. This is the very important element in Communism. It is motives of that kind rather than any ideological loyalties.

CHARLTON: How successful have the Communists been, since the Khrushchev speech in 1956, in claiming that Marxism, the great deliverance, was somehow falsified by this one man Joseph Stalin?

SCHAPIRO: I think they have been effective enough for their purposes. They have obviously regained their control, for example, over such an operation as the Fronts, the various Communist Fronts. They do very nicely. There are very many repercussions of the tentacles of Communist overt and covert operations which persist; which goes to show that Communism is not, primarily, a matter of ideology and thought and intellectual ideas, but of *organisation*. This is what Lenin intended it to be.

This is the difference between Marx and Lenin. For Marx it was a 'scientific idea', and Marx is full of outbursts against people who are 'unscientific' and are liars and disregard the evidence. I am sure he really believed that. He was an old-fashioned German scholar in some respects, and the idea that anyone would fiddle evidence he would regard as preposterous. Lenin transformed all that into an organisational system, a system of using anarchy for your own ends, and for controlling power, when once you got it. This is what Communism has been ever since, and to some extent the intellectual covering of it is illusory.

KHRUSHCHEV'S SPEECH put an end to 'the silence of the grave' which Stalin had, for so many years, imposed on open discussion and disagreement. When Stalin died there were estimated to have been fifteen million people in concentration camps in the Soviet Union. The new leadership set out to convince the world that Communist power was intact, while seeking to convey that its condemnation of Stalinism was profound and sincere.

However, it has yet to explain officially what specific elements in the theory of Soviet Communism are assignable to it. The solemn triflings and impenetrable obscurities of the body of ideology began to come to pieces in the hands, not of those who chose to exploit what Professor Leonard Schapiro makes clear was a moment of great and obvious weakness in order to destroy the Communist faith, but of those who were charged with breathing new life into it. Among them was Kolakowski, in Poland.

KOLAKOWSKI: The mid-fifties was a period in Poland (in other countries as well, but particularly in Poland) where there was this movement trying, somehow, to rejuvenate Communist ideology or Marxist ideas — to get rid of the monstrosities of Stalinism, and to make Communism both intellectually respectable and morally worthy. This movement was called 'Revisionism', and was branded with this name by the Party leaders.

CHARLTON: So your purpose was what? To rescue Communism from degeneration? An attempt to start afresh?

KOLAKOWSKI: You see, I am not really able to say exactly what was our thinking in our writing at this period. It was a mixture of genuine desire and genuine belief that Communism *can* somehow be rescued morally and intellectually, and on the other hand a little bit of calculation. We tried to speak, to some extent, in the language of inherited Marxist stereotypes. We looked, in Marx, for ideas which clearly run against the entire Leninist and Stalinist doctrine and practice. We tried to oppose Marxism to Leninism (and to Stalinism), and for a few years we used the language of Marxist clichés.

Revisionism in Poland played a certain role in the disintegration of Communist doctrine precisely because it appealed to the same stereotypes. The Party and the people in the Party apparatus, the Party's ideologists, were insensitive to the arguments coming entirely from the outside; whereas voices coming from the *inside* were more important. Revisionism therefore proved to be, to some extent, effective. Its advocates were Party members and Party activists; and therefore Revisionism cut its own roots, so to speak, by its own effectiveness. By destroying the Party ideology, and so contributing to the process whereby the ideology of Communism really became irrelevant, it somehow made itself useless. After a certain period there was nothing to revise any more!

IN THE TUMULTS WHICH FOLLOWED Stalin's death and denunciation the Soviet Union faced for the first time widespread unrest throughout Eastern Europe.

At this distance, few things seem as eloquent of that precarious time for Communist rule — and of the nature and limits of the Party's efforts to come to terms with Stalin's legacy — than the evidence which has recently emerged from Poland. Some background interviews conducted with the Polish leader Wladyslaw Gomulka in 1971 have come to light in the West. Gomulka, who was at the head of government in Poland for fourteen years, reveals that in the course of a two-hour shouting match (as he calls it) with Khrushchev in 1957, the question of Soviet responsibility for the Katyn massacre was raised between them. The murder of those 15,000 Polish officer prisoners in the Soviet Union during the time of Stalin's Pact with Hitler has always been denied by the Russians and all discussion of it prevented. Katyn remained a central statement in any evaluation of Polish–Soviet relations. Gomulka records Khrushchev as 'obviously blaming Stalin for everything', and saying of Stalin that, 'His account is so loaded with crimes that he can stand one more.'

Gomulka goes on to admit that while he later thought he had been wrong (and regretted he'd done nothing to follow up Khrushchev's cue), 'I simply did not feel strong enough to reverse myself on Katyn.' And so, that lie has been perpetuated.

At the time (in Gomulka's words),

> the nation was like a horse breaking free from its harness. . . . Lots of young people dedicated to the Party came forward to help. They were the dangerous ones. They talked without stop about democracy when what we wanted was discipline and obedience!

But the successful stand of the Polish revisionists and their challenge spread. The spirit of criticism had been fostered, and it flourished. The unexpected climax came in Hungary in the Uprising of October 1956.

A major figure in the events which culminated in the Soviet invasion of Hungary, followed by the overthrow of a Communist government there, was General Bela Kiraly.

KIRALY: In any historical event there are overriding causes and there are immediate causes. The overriding cause was, unquestionably, total disappointment with the totalitarian regime, the total disappointment with Soviet domination, the total disappointment with the exploited economy, the total disappointment with discrimination against people because – I don't know – of their 'origin' or something. In other words, total disappointment with the state of the individual and of the nation. That is the overriding cause. But, out of that, revolution does not come. There must be some little thing which triggers off the whole explosion.

In June 1956, when already pressure forced the Party to make a change in the leadership, the stupid Stalinists, instead of letting Imre Nagy into the leadership, exchanged Matyas Rakosi with Ernö Gerö. That was almost parallel with the Poles, but how much wiser they were! They brought in Gomulka. At the time Gomulka, like Imre Nagy, was thought to have been a 'reformer'. Gomulka at that time symbolised the forces of change. Had Rakosi been replaced in Hungary by Imre Nagy that June, there would not have been a revolution. I am as convinced of that as I am sitting here! The revolution's immediate causes started then with the installation of Gerö, who continued the stubborn Stalinist line and increased the discontent. And the discontent became louder and louder.

Secondly, on the day of 23 October when the Party faced a mass demonstration in Budapest, even then the revolution could have been avoided. But that hot moment was the last historic chance for the Communist Party of Hungary. If they had been wise enough to say, 'All right, Imre Nagy, come and take over the government,' and if at that moment Imre Nagy, on the radio – nice, soft, compromising, soothing – had said, 'All right, Hungarian friends, patriots, I take over the government; we return to the reform programmes of 1953, go home, sleep. We will talk tomorrow,' then no revolution would have occurred.

But instead, Gerö came on the radio with his sharp, arrogant, defiant, Stalinist, suppressive voice and said, 'We will show you!'

That was the last chance for the Party. They missed the chance. And then – one single shot could make the revolution. And one single shot *did* make the revolution.

THE HUNGARIANS TRIED but failed to repeat the limited Polish achievement of October 1956.

What was at stake in both Poland and Hungary was whether the basic nature of a Communist Party could be changed. Against the fulminations of Khrushchev, and the final preparations for invasion of Poland by the Red Army, the Polish Communist Party had stood its ground, united in recalling to the leadership Wladyslaw Gomulka. Gomulka had been deposed and imprisoned at Stalin's command during the campaign to crush Tito and his heresy of 'national Communism'.

The possibility of such a change at the top, even in the face of outright Soviet opposition, prompted similar efforts in Hungary. Against a groundswell of popular discontent, the Hungarian Party – which after years of effective repression had given all the appearances of invincibility – suddenly began to disintegrate.

Early in the morning of 23 October 1956 students at Budapest University adopted a programme which called for the reconstitution of the government under the leadership of another Communist, Imre Nagy, who like Gomulka in Poland had been purged and imprisoned at the time of the Tito heresy. A student march that day turned into a mass demonstration. The same evening, shots were fired (probably by the Hungarian Secret Police) into the crowd, and the mass demonstration turned into an open revolt by the nation.

General Bela Kiraly was released from prison (after the Party purges of the early 1950s) just three weeks before the Hungarian Uprising. He became Commander-in-Chief of the Hungarian National Guard, and emerged as the elected leader of the 'freedom-fighter forces' during the Soviet invasion.

KIRALY: The Hungarian Revolution was not planned. Nobody wanted a revolution. The Hungarians demonstrated for the Poles' successful and peaceful solution. No one planned a revolution. They were drawn into it by violence.

CHARLTON: To what extent was help expected from the West, and what part did that play in the calculations of those who, like you, put themselves at the head of spontaneous events?

KIRALY: It *was* a spontaneous event and it was *not* planned. During the revolution, when the Soviet tanks appeared, of course such thoughts began to emerge.

I have an eyewitness. When I was already elected Commander-in-Chief of the freedom-fighter force, the National Guard of Hungary, the *New York Times* Correspondent in Vienna, John MacCormac, came to my own headquarters with a friend of mine who was a diplomat. Mac-Cormac asked me exactly what you are asking me now. He said: 'Tomorrow it will be on the front page of the *New York Times*. Should I print that you want the Marines?' And I told him: 'No sir, we do not want the Marines. We want peace with the Soviet Union. If you bring in the Marines it will be the Third World War, and after that nothing will be left of Hungary. I do not want to incinerate Hungary.' Now, many young hot-headed freedom-fighters, after they arrived in the West, began to say, 'You let us down. We waited for the British, the French, the Americans – you did not come.' But the political debate during this time was *not* based on the return of the Soviet Union. The hope against hope was that, after all, they would *not* return. The big debate was what kind of neutrality we would like to have – the Austrian or the Finnish kind. No one knew the precise definition of either. But *that* is what was on the mind of the people. If someone is sincerely asking what they thought at home then, it was how to have a neutrality which would not humiliate the Soviet Union and which would be acceptable to the Soviet Union. That was the basic term, *not* armed help from the West.

CHARLTON: On the other hand you are, as you remind us, Commander-in-Chief of forces in a revolution against the ruling Communist power. Where did you think help would come from? Where were you looking for help in sustaining your challenge?

KIRALY: Here, for the first time I have to disagree with your statement buried in that question! We were *not* fighting against the Communist Party. Imre Nagy was a Communist. Imre Nagy remained a member of the Central Committee of the *renewed* Communist Party. They were fighting against 'men of blood', against the Secret Police – but *not* against the Communist Party. The Hungarian Revolution was not an anti-Communist revolution, I must protest that this was so.

CHARLTON: Two hundred thousand people out in the streets . . .

KIRALY: Not against the Communist Party. It was *for* democracy, yes. It was against totalitarianism, yes.

CHARLTON: And therefore against the Communist Party?

KIRALY: No, no, no, no, no! The Hungarian people was wiser than that. Wisdom dictated that you cannot just abolish a Communist Party at the threshold of the Soviet Union, with Soviet garrisons in Hungary. It would be an offence against the wisdom of the Hungarian people. Look at the students' Sixteen Points. They wanted *reform* within the Party. You know what I would say? 'Euro-Communism' started in Budapest: because if you look at the University students' Sixteen Points it is internal democracy in the Communist Party itself, for internal democracy in the government. Euro-Communism, yes.

We did not look for outside help. I have to tell you, it is not a heroic thing that I am saying! For the last twenty-five years I have been a student of history, I acquired a Ph.D. at Columbia University, and being a historian commits me to tell the truth. I cannot picture myself as a hero who stood up at the barricades and looked for armed help from the West. You know what I was looking for? Compromise! I would have gone out of my way to establish a settlement acceptable to the Soviet Union because I knew that Western military power would *not* come at all, and I have dreaded a war on Hungarian soil.

THE FORCES FOR REFORM which, in the Poland of the 1950s, had been contained within the exclusive framework of the Party's authority, went beyond such constraints in Budapest. The new government in Hungary led by Imre Nagy included non-Communist politicians, and Nagy was also pledged to negotiate the withdrawal of Soviet armed forces (for which, of course, he had no mandate from the Russians). The Hungarian Communist Party, however, confirmed Nagy's programme and his leadership. In Moscow, when the Soviet leaders came to the conclusion that Nagy could not limit demands in keeping with a Communist Hungary under Soviet tutelage, they launched an all-out invasion of Hungary by the Red Army. Fighting went on well into November. The Uprising was crushed. Nagy himself was later hanged by the Russians.

The late leader of the Soviet Union, Yuri Andropov, was intimately involved in these events, and their outcome, as the Russian Ambassador to Hungary in 1956, and General Bela Kiraly was the appointed commander of the Hungarian armed forces under this newly-constituted government led by Imre Nagy.

KIRALY: When the Soviet aggression came on 4 November 1956 it was a very dramatic moment. I reported to Imre Nagy every half-hour on the Soviet movements. We called each other 'Comrade', not in the Communist Party sense but in the Hungarian sense. There is a beautiful Hungarian word for that – *Bajtars* – which means comrade-in-arms; but you cannot translate it. I told him that this was the moment when he had to go on the radio and announce that Hungary was being attacked by the Soviet Union and that we were at war with the Soviet Union. As a military man I had to give that advice to him, because the Minister of Defence, General Pal Maleter, was by then out of contact with us in the Soviet headquarters. And Nagy told me, 'No, no, no. I forbid you to go to the radio with any such message. You have to know, as a General Staff Officer, that it is a political decision.'

I said, 'All right, that is what I am asking you. Should I or should *you*? But we are at *war* with the Soviet Union.' And he said, 'No. We will never be at war with the Soviet Union.'

CHARLTON: Even then?

KIRALY: Even then. 'Andropov is with me', said Imre Nagy. And he tried to call Moscow because, 'Andropov assures me there is some misunderstanding here.'

Five minutes later I called Imre Nagy back and told him, 'Comrade, *Bajtars*, Prime Minister, the Russian tanks are on our *square* – I can count them, one, two, twenty-five – and they are turning towards the Parliament.'

We did not have any antitank guns in our headquarters, you know. We just waited to see whether they would attack us. They did not. They turned towards the Parliament. And then Imre Nagy's response was a very dramatic one. He said to me, 'Thank you. I do not need any more reports.' No more reports from the Commander-in-Chief? What is going on?

I then instantly ordered my staff to go over to the other side of the Danube, where we had a more protected headquarters, in Buda, than the one in Pest. On our way there we turned on the radio. Imre Nagy's voice was there, with this dramatic announcement: 'Imre Nagy speaking, the Prime Minister of Hungary. I inform the Hungarian nation and the world that Soviet forces have attacked Hungary with the obvious intention of overthrowing the legally-constituted government. Our troops are fighting . . .' That was his last statement. In other words, my last report, that the tanks were already within shooting distance of the Parliament – only then did Imre Nagy evolve from his somewhat wishful thinking that the Soviet Union would not butcher another Socialist country. He was a Utopian.

CHARLTON: And all the time Andropov, the Soviet Ambassador, was in Nagy's office assuring him this was not going to happen?

KIRALY: I am absolutely sure he got an instruction. He was there to lure the Hungarian government into inactivity when the Soviet troops were already on the move.

CHARLTON: Djilas said subsequently that Nagy (whom he greatly admired, and who, he suggested, would have provided a model of a Socialist state of great importance for the future of Eastern Europe, and a way out of its dilemma for the Soviet Union) had a very narrow understanding of the Soviet Union. He suggests that Nagy was naive. He adduces as evidence for this that Nagy put his fate in the hands of the Yugoslavs when he took refuge in their Legation 'because they were a liberal country', which as Djilas says was nonsense.

KIRALY: Of course, I understand your criticism in an objective way. But with hundreds of tanks invading, here was a man at a dividing point of history. A great power has invaded your country. You are the man whose prestige is such that whatever you say people will follow you. Now, unquestionably he says until the last, 'I hope that the Soviet Union will not be such a beast as to attack a country which is not anti-Communist.' It did *not* want to be a member of Nato.

What can he say? He can say, 'All right, the Soviet Union attacked us. Fight back – to the last cottage.' Or he can say, 'The Soviet Union has attacked us. We will lose the war. Lay down your arms.' There was no other choice for Imre Nagy on the morning of 4 November 1956. He knew that, with war, we were now suppressed. There was no hope. He did not have the heart to say, 'Fight until the last cottage.' He was really an emotional Hungarian patriot, Communist or not. He did not want to inspire any more heroes. We had more than enough heroes. So the other choice was to lay down arms.

In Hungarian history there is a moment which is debated down to the present day. In 1849, Lajos Kossuth decided to leave the country and invested all political power in the Commander-in-Chief of the army, General Gorgey. Gorgey went to Russia and said that he wanted to lay down arms, unconditionally. Ever since, there has been this 'Gorgey question' in the heart and mind of every Hungarian six-year-old. Imre Nagy did not want to be a Gorgey. He did not say, 'Lay down your arms, there is no other hope.' He would have liked to save Hungarian blood without becoming another Gorgey, before he closed the door of his office and – where to go? See?

I can add another footnote to the whole thing. When it was crystal clear, after midnight, that it was a Soviet aggression (I already knew it was war but we did not use the term 'war') I told Imre Nagy that we still had small aeroplanes at Kelenfold, a little airport. It was not occupied by the Russians. He could get out of the country with a few associates. He said, 'I will never leave the country.' He could have flown to Vienna; he could have gone to Frankfurt. He did not want to leave the country. It is a pathetic thing. I am sorry that Shakespeare is not alive. He could have written about the whole Imre Nagy case. It would have been better than *Hamlet*.

THE RUSSIANS HAD SAVED their hegemony in Eastern Europe only by their vast and preponderant military might, and at the moment when freedom *under* Communism was seen by them to be freedom *from* Communism.

Hopes that the Polish 'October' would lead on to a transformation of the totalitarian Communism Stalin had put down like a grid over Eastern Europe proved to be a fantasy. All overt dissent was, once more, ruthlessly extinguished.

The character and ambition of Soviet Communism in power had been amassing a growing body of criticism following Stalin's death, to which '1956 in Budapest' added its considerable weight. In particular the question was whether the innate character of Soviet Communism is the inevitable outcome of such immersion in Marxist political theory and general philosophy.

KOLAKOWSKI: Even now, I would not say that there was a fateful, historical destiny whereby Marxist doctrine must necessarily have led to the Stalinist dictatorship in Russia. No, there were many historical accidents which were at work. I do not mean only, and obviously, that Marx himself did not imagine Communism as a concentration camp. The fact is that a series of historical accidents, none of which was necessary, led to the establishment of the rule of a Party professing Marxist ideology in Russia. One should not underestimate various Russian traditions in this development.

I would phrase the question somewhat differently. How was it possible that this Marxist doctrine, with its ostensibly humanist and internationalist ideas, could have become a pretty efficient ideological instrument to justify, and to glorify, the most oppressive imperialist system of the twentieth century? And to what extent, in order to fulfil this role, had this doctrine to be deformed or distorted?

My argument is that it did not need to be fundamentally distorted, only readjusted. Then it could have played this role quite successfully. In fact it was Marx's (not Stalin's) view that the whole idea of Communism may be summed up in a single phrase – the abolition of private property. So, there is nothing un-Marxist in the claim that, once we abolish private property, mankind is liberated.

It was Marx and not Stalin who believed that Communism consists of centralised rule by the State of the entire economic process, that 'economy' in the old sense would cease to exist and everything would be administered by the State.

Marx took over from Saint-Simon a fine-sounding phrase: that in a Socialist society political government would cease to exist and would be replaced by 'administration of things'. He did not trumpet the fact that you cannot administer 'things' without using people for the purpose. If it is the State which runs everything, which nationalises everything, and if everything is made 'State property' – then people are made State property as well. This was Bakunin's point. He was not comparable to Marx to be sure – Marx was much superior intellectually; nevertheless Bakunin's critique was very penetrating.

He somehow noticed that State socialism, developed by Marx, would lead to State tyranny.

THE STULTIFIED IDEOLOGY and economic fiasco led within a few years to the next full-blown crisis in Central Europe, Czechoslovakia in 1968. Under the nominal leadership of Alexander Dubček, a movement for reform inside the Czech Communist Party set out to lay the corner-stones of a new edifice of theory which would stand on the ruins of Stalin's dictatorship. They adopted the label for it of 'Communism with a Human Face'.

These Czech reformers maintained that the socialised economy could not be revived if Stalin's model stayed in place. The same kind of argu-ments were, by this time, being heard in the Soviet Union itself. Czecho-slovakia thus found itself at the centre of a more profound and dangerous crisis. For, had the Czechs succeeded, they would have challenged the whole direction of Soviet development since Lenin. Moscow came to the conclusion that, once again, events in Eastern and Central Europe were threatening the cohesion of the entire Soviet political and military system.

The Red Army invaded Czechoslovakia. Dubček and the Prague government were arrested and taken to Moscow where, under duress, they submitted.

Mr Brezhnev is recorded as saying mockingly to Dubček, as he stood before him in weakness and in tears, 'Sasha, Sasha, what are you doing in chains?'

One of the principal witnesses for events inside the Czechoslovak Communist Party at the time of the 'Prague Spring' in 1968 is Eduard Goldstücker.

GOLDSTÜCKER: In 1968 our [Czechoslovak] society was obviously developing into some sort of pluralism, but not necessarily a pluralism modelled on the Western democracies, which means several political parties competing for power. My expression at that time was that we wanted to bring about 'enlightened Socialism', that was my expression all the time, 'enlightened Socialism'. (It led to one of our leading carica-turists publishing a cartoon with Socialism personified, surrounded by lamps of various forms.)

My ideas at the beginning of 1968 were optimistic about the future of Czech democracy. I should like to quote to you two sentences of an article I wrote in February 1963, by which I introduced the public dis-cussion of Franz Kafka. It starts from ideas formulated by Jean-Paul Sartre at the Peace Conference in Moscow in July 1962, that it is necessary to 'demilitarise culture'. He quoted Kafka as an example and I said,

> But before this can happen we must fulfil one very important condition –
> to see to it that even the weirdest imagination could not apply any of

Kafka's vision of bureaucratic chicaneries and cruelties to our public affairs. If the history of our time has proved anything beyond a shadow of a doubt, it is that it was fatally wrong to believe that a new and higher social order could be created without benefit of humanity and justice, and that great human achievements in any field could be indefinitely, and loudly advocated in theory while being trampled upon in fact.

CHARLTON: Do you still insist that Socialism can create the chance of society 'at a higher level', as you were telling those students in Prague in 1968?

GOLDSTÜCKER: Oh yes, oh yes, certainly. But a 'higher level' for me means not copying the pre-1938 system but taking into consideration the changes which our society went through in the meantime.

CHARLTON: But where is this rainbow which arcs across the sky for you? It always recedes, it seems. Events in Czechoslovakia have disproved, have they not, your hopes?

GOLDSTÜCKER: Oh they have certainly got worse; of course they got worse after the occupation. Czechoslovakia has been deliberately reduced to the level of a colony.

CHARLTON: Can I ask you then what seems to me to be the fundamental question. Can a Marxist–Leninist Communist Party be democratised?

GOLDSTÜCKER: Look, Marxism–Leninism for me – it is absolutely clear – came to reveal its true substance as the ideology of Moscow, of the Moscow leadership. 'Marxism–Leninism', even in the combination of words, is a creation by Stalin. It means approving everything the Moscow leadership does. No matter how sincere a Socialist, if you do not follow to the last letter, to the last whim, what they call Marxism–Leninism you are, in their eyes, an enemy. Marxism–Leninism is just an ideological cloak to conceal Moscow's domination.

CHARLTON: After all your experiences, why is it that you think it only necessary to adapt the thing and not to reconsider your whole belief, as so many did?

GOLDSTÜCKER: For the simple reason that I did not accept that the horror of Stalinism was the convincing, final argument that what the Soviet Revolution originally stood for was impossible. I said that there were other possibilities; we must follow them up, explore them and try to bring them to fruition.

CHARLTON: Is that still your position?

GOLDSTÜCKER: No, no, of course not. After 1968, and after Poland, there is no productive force to be derived from the Soviet system any longer. It is finished, and sooner or later it has to be destroyed.

CHARLTON: 'Destroyed' is an un-Parliamentary word. How is it to be destroyed?

GOLDSTÜCKER: Either that system will still find some sort of path indicated by the democratisation efforts of Hungary in 1956, of Czechoslovakia in 1968 or Poland now, or it will have to be destroyed in a terrible explosion. Destruction in the sense of old Karl Marx. Marx said that the bourgeois state has to be destroyed and replaced by another. So, destruction – and destruction with an explosion.

None of them will say, 'All right, we will stop being Hungarians, and Poles and Romanians, and we will merge into the Soviet Empire.' And that gives us all the prerequisites of a struggle in the future – in the not very far-off future – against that Empire. That struggle might take various forms up to the ultimate, an armed struggle eventually. Of course, a terrible explosion destroying empires is a terribly dangerous thing for the whole of mankind.

And there is the attitude of the West now. There is a tendency to derive from this situation the lesson that the best thing is to try and influence things in such a way that nothing untoward happens to the Soviet Empire. As Helmut Sonnenfeldt formulated it, that the peoples of Eastern Europe find their natural relationship to Moscow. That means that they submit. We called it the 'Brezh-feldt doctrine'!

It is impossible. It is impossible. The rulers of the Soviet Empire – I will be cynical – are guided by the quotation from Lenin, who said that the capitalists would sell for money even their own mother. That is the guiding principle of Soviet policy towards the West.

IN THIS LITANY OF realities which have accompanied the Communist experience in Eastern Europe, the time has clearly passed when its believers accepted an ideology which daily experience contradicted.

Eduard Goldstücker's prediction of an 'explosive crisis' would seem to lend support to a contention of Kolakowski, who holds that wherever Communism is in power, the ruling class transforms it into an ideology whose real sources are nationalism, racism or imperialism. In this way, he considers, it is producing its own grave-diggers. What then is still 'living', for Kolakowski, in Communist ideology as an idea, and a Utopian scheme for a man-determined future?

KOLAKOWSKI: It is really in an obvious state of decline all over the world. As an intellectual instrument it is completely worthless. It explains nothing. But we can make a distinction between Leninism as a political doctrine – and as a tradition of Marxism – and Socialism on the other hand which was much more differentiated.

I do not believe that Marxism, meaning the theoretical work of Marx, is now able to provide us with clues to historical explanations, let alone give us a recipe for the glorious future. Nevertheless, I would not say Marx is, so to say, a 'dead body'. I think that Marx simply belongs to the heritage of European culture, that he had some important and interesting insights which proved to be of value, that some of his ideas were assimilated in our character but in such a way that one does not have to be a Marxist in order to accept them. But Marxism, as a system, with all-

embracing pretensions is really completely dead. Marxism as a body
of thought which deals with various historical subjects is still interesting
but has very little to do with Marxism as a political force operating
today.

CHARLTON: If, as an explanatory system, it is finished, how do you
explain that it continues to be effective, in the sense that it is used as a
rationale by a superpower in the hands of a small élite who constantly
make use of it? If it is so weak, why is it so strong?

KOLAKOWSKI: Yes, that is the question. But, you see, I think that
Marxism was transformed in such a way that it has become a sort of con-
venient jargon in which all kinds of claims and grievances can be expressed, many of them of a kind which have absolutely nothing to do
with those Marx identifies himself with. Just imagine Marx, with his
strongly 'Eurocentric' orientation, with his total contempt for all non-
European cultures, with his belief that colonisation processes were
'historically progressive', just imagine him when he hears about 'Islamic
Marxists'! It has become really an idiom in which you can express any
sort of claim. The use of Marxist idiom in the Third World is really of no
great importance; if it is replaced by another idiom, nothing in particular
would change.

There is another thing. Marxism as an ideology of the Soviet Empire
proved to be efficient as a self-justifying, legitimising instrument of the
Soviet Empire, and it is still used for this purpose. It is necessary, in fact.
Even so, hardly anybody takes it seriously any more in socialist countries.
In socialist countries the general attitude is that real belief in Marxism–
Leninism is good for West European adolescents – but it is not really
taken seriously. It is necessary because they have no other legitimacy –
neither from democratic elections nor from the inheritance of monarchi-
cal charisma. Ideology is their only form of legitimacy and power. Therefore they are *compelled* to stick to it, even though neither the rulers, nor
those they rule, believe in it. But – and here is a question which I am not
able to answer, of course – how long can a system of power survive of
which the only legitimacy is ideology, in conditions where this ideology is
no longer believed? I do not know.

CHARLTON: Well, that is exactly what I was going to ask you. Surely it
is a question of very great importance for us all?

KOLAKOWSKI: Yes, for all of us. I wish I knew. But you can notice
how, over the years, even this official ideology has changed. Of course
the wooden formulae of Marxism–Leninism are still repeated as an
official doctrine, taught in the universities or repeated in textbooks. But
whenever the government is trying to have a minimal contact with the
population, the ideological slogans and ideas employed are not
'Marxism–Leninism' any more. It is a syncretic mixture. Some Marxist
phrases are mixed with imperialist ideas – the Glory of Empire,
xenophobic, racist and nationalist ideas. What the Germans call an

eklektische Bettlersuppe – a mixed beggar's broth. It is incoherent, not codified, in many ways using only vague hints and allusions for things which cannot be spoken: this is *real* ideology.

It is a far cry from Stalin's time, when everything was so neatly arranged, codified, numerated, so that you could learn the entire ideology in the proper order. Now nobody knows exactly what this ideology is. This is one of the symptoms of its decline.

CHARLTON: In some of your recent writings you put a point which, you say, is not sufficiently appreciated in the West. 'Mendacity,' you say, 'is not an accidental blemish on the body of Communism. It is the absolute condition of its health and its life.' How important is that belief in your critique of Communism? Is it at the core of its failure for you?

KOLAKOWSKI: I would say so. Yes. Mendacity is the immortal soul of Communism. They cannot get rid of it. The gap between reality and the façade is so enormous that the lie has become a sort of normal, and natural, way of life.

CHARLTON: But why is that a necessary and permanent condition of Communist societies?

KOLAKOWSKI: Because Communism lives on inevitably impossible promises. Because its legitimacy is based upon expectations which necessarily will *not* be fulfilled. Because its inherited ideology cannot be dismissed, and at the same time it is in glaring contradiction to reality. So, in order to keep this legitimacy principle alive, they have to keep the mendacious façade without which they would fall apart. It is perhaps the most oppressive part of life under Communism. Not terror, not exploitation, but the all-pervading lie, felt by everybody, known to everybody. It is something which makes life intolerable for people under Communism. You could see it in events which shook Poland in these last years. How important it was – this feeling of people that they eventually can get rid of the lie – how important a factor it was in the movement of Solidarity.

THE POLISH PHILOSOPHER, now a Fellow of All Souls College, Oxford, leaves us with a view of Communism in Eastern Europe increasingly imprisoned in absurdities and with an official ideology neither able to interpret the world nor to change it.

For himself he sees in this general collapse of the Communist faith only that what he calls 'the great fantasy of our time' has ended in the same way as all such attempts, individual or collective. It has revealed itself to him as the 'farcical aspect of human bondage'. He dismissed the prospects of its revival or resuscitation thus:

KOLAKOWSKI: I do not expect any resurrections of the Marxist movement either within the Soviet Empire or in the West. I think the whole system of ideas is collapsing, really. It does not mean that the entire

Soviet Union is about to collapse, but I strongly believe that it is internally corroded by so many disintegrating factors that I do believe that Sovietism and the Soviet Empire is *going* to collapse. But if you ask me when, I can only say, 'I wish I knew.' Communism has been largely exposed as what it has always been – a naked force. Polish events were in this respect very revealing, in that Communist power felt compelled to appear for what it was – the gun.

4

LOOKING BACK TO THE FUTURE

NEARLY FOUR DECADES HAVE PASSED since the Soviet Union emerged from the ordeal of invasion and war to harvest the fruits of its decisive victories over Hitler's armies. Ever since, the peace which the Russians have demanded is an uninterrupted hegemony over the peoples and cultures which constitute the former nation-states of Eastern Europe.

The Soviet conquest of half of Europe satisfied a traditional wish of Russian diplomacy – the creation of a military glacis beyond the Soviet Union's western frontier. It offered another cardinal advantage – the insulation of the mass of Soviet citizens at home from the allurements of the capitalist West, with its material seductions and its individual freedoms, while the heirs of Lenin got on with 'the Building of Communism'.

But the Soviet conquest also brought the moral responsibility for the prosperity and the hopes of an additional one hundred or so million people. And it is this mundane test which, forty years on, the Soviet Union continues to fail. That failure, and the fundamental antipathies which it has bred, are responsible for the evolving challenge to the nature of Soviet control in Eastern and Central Europe, and for the faded appeal of Communist ideology.

At the time of the division of Europe into two camps, there was no shortage of forecasts, Churchill's among them, that it did not contain the essentials of a durable peace. In the aftermath of the breakdown of the Yalta agreement he had warned Stalin of 'the long reproaches of the aftertime', which would follow the imposition of Communist governments, and the ideology of Marx and Lenin, against the will of the peoples concerned.

Forty years on in Eastern Europe, within the 'Cordon Stalinaire', those 'long reproaches of the aftertime' are undiminished and, in the case of Poland, most obviously, gather force. Churchill's forecast has found confirmation in both the occurrence and repetition of events.

It is time to ask, in the context of the present demands and dangers, the attendant economic malaise and political stagnation in Eastern Europe, whether a momentum has been established there which will compel the Russians to make changes they have hitherto always refused. And whether such changes – on these the outer limits of the Soviet Empire – are likely to dictate the necessity for change at its hub, in Moscow and in the Soviet Union itself. How different in quality or character is the situation the Russians face today from the one they have faced, and dealt with effectively, since Yalta?

Seweryn Bialer is a former high-ranking Polish Communist who taught at the Higher Party School, attached to the Central Committee, which trained Poland's senior Party cadres. He is now the Director of the Research Institute for International Change at Columbia University, New York.

BIALER: It is different in many important ways. First of all, those regimes were created illegitimately. They were imposed on the people of Eastern Europe by the Soviet army. The Soviet political leadership hoped that, after a decade or more, when a new generation had grown up under Socialism – or the East European type of Socialism – the question of legitimacy would be solved, and they would accept the regime. Secondly, they hoped that the regimes would attain legitimacy through per-formance – that they would really *perform* so well that, again, the population would accept them.

Neither thing has happened. The primary sin, present at the birth of those regimes, is still plaguing the Soviet Union and there is really no way out of it.

What has changed now, and very dramatically, is that the Soviets themselves see it. They never accepted it after 1956 (when they strangled the Hungarian Revolution) and in 1968 (when they invaded Czecho-slovakia). They still believed that those were exceptions – flukes of specific situations. Now they *do* believe that there is a trend, and they are very worried.

DO THE SOVIET LEADERS see Eastern Europe, as we have known it since 1945, as being in the process of disintegration? Or is Poland judged by them to be like a fire in a furnace: something which can be contained? It is hard to assess. The remarkable degree of secrecy preserved by the innermost councils of the Soviet government continues to prove more or less unassailable. What *is* known is that, even at the higher levels of Soviet policy considerations, the *status* of Eastern Europe is not a subject which qualifies for open discussion or argument.

However, some insights are available. The highest-ranking Soviet diplomat to defect to the West so far (he broke with Soviet Russia in

1978) is Arkady Shevchenko. Shevchenko had twenty-two years in the Soviet Foreign Service, and was a personal political adviser to the Foreign Minister, Mr Gromyko. He was also one of the younger Soviet aides in Khrushchev's entourage when the latter made his celebrated visit to the United States in 1959. Shevchenko confirms the concern in Moscow at the unpredictable drift in Eastern Europe from its early foundations of an effective Soviet domination.

SHEVCHENKO: After the Second World War when the USSR occupied all these countries it was considered, as you might put it, a new acquisition. After the Occupation they established puppet regimes everywhere, which had absolutely nothing to do with the national forces in these countries. They selected all the leaders there, and they established their control – like they have it in East Germany, which they now consider as their property. In my view they will *never* give that up, they will never do anything to withdraw from East Germany. And you know, when I was involved in 'Helsinki' [in the Helsinki agreements], their preoccupation was that the West would not make claims in Eastern Europe. They had no doubts that it was their Empire there, and they wanted the West to recognise their presence there. That was the sole purpose of that.

CHARLTON: Can I read to you these words from a telegram from the British Ambassador in Moscow, Sir Archibald Clark-Kerr, a very long time ago – in 1946. They formed the basis of the Foreign Office advice which went to President Truman: 'We British agree that the satellite regimes are not likely to wither away. We do not minimise powerful domestic resentment against them, particularly in Poland. We do however wish to emphasise that, in our opinion, the Soviet Union is willing to go to almost any lengths, and employ almost any measures to achieve this end . . .' Do you see any reason today to question that opinion, or modify it, from what you know of Moscow's thinking from the 'inside'? Is that still the position?

SHEVCHENCKO: I would say that it would have been much better and wiser if even *after* that period – when the Soviets still needed the help of the United States and the Western countries – not to allow the Soviet Union actually to consolidate and establish regimes in the old East European countries. It is a historical mistake and it was a missed opportunity. If more pressure had been exercised, and a stronger position been taken by the United States and the United Kingdom, perhaps there would have been some chance to establish – or re-establish – nations which would be free.

CHARLTON: What is the evidence for that, from your direct experience?

SHEVCHENKO: The evidence is that the Soviet Union was weak at this time. The war effort had actually almost depleted the resources of the Soviet Union, and politically they needed something – some kind of cooperation with the West. I would say that they would not have dared a military confrontation with the West, had there been a 'strong' diplomacy, and if it had taken strong moves to prevent the Soviets occupying these areas. In my view it was the failure of Western diplomacy to put strong pressure on Stalin, and the Soviet leadership, which actually led to the establishment of the puppet regimes in all these various countries. I've discussed this with the people in Gromyko's entourage, for instance with Ambassador Gusev* (who was the Soviet ambassador to the United Kingdom in wartime), and his opinion coincides with what I said to you – that if the West *had* taken a stronger position, the situation would have probably been a different one. Now, Gusev was no pro-Westerner or anything like that! But he knew a lot about this period.

Gromyko would never discuss these 'historical' circumstances. What was discussed with Gromyko many times (I was personally involved) was that there is some concern in the Soviet leadership at the tendency for independence from the Soviet Union by East European countries. Not only Poland – it started, actually, with Romania. Our preoccupation, in the discussion in which I myself participated, was how to try again to put these countries under more control because, even in foreign policy, sometimes they acted not exactly as the Soviets wished. They made their own initiatives and there were internal developments which, from the Soviet point of view at least, were controversial.

Take Hungary, for example. When the Hungarians started their economic reforms, they were very successful (and I myself had been in Hungary and I saw that the Hungarian economy was good), because they started to get rid of State control as it is in the Soviet Union. And in Moscow now they're looking at all that in the sense that if all this goes on and on, and develops more and more, then it could be a danger that we will *lose* this country – these countries – with the forces gathering in Romania and now again Poland. You know, it's a disaster. It has become a disaster. Even the most loyal country to the Soviet Union – Bulgaria – they also started to introduce some things which the Soviets don't like.

As for the view of the Politburo, the Central Committee of the Soviet Union, pessimistic may be too strong a word. There is certainly concern. Ten or fifteen years ago they would not dare – no East European country would *dare* to come out with some of their own proposals concerning relations with a Western country. They are starting to do that now – not even closely coordinating the position, not even asking permission! But the Soviets are afraid especially in one field where they are very rigid. This is the military one and the insistence they should be in the Warsaw

---

* It was through Ambassador Gusev that Churchill and Roosevelt communicated with Stalin in Moscow. Gusev, an apparently wintry and inaccessible personality, was known to the Prime Minister and the President, in their private correspondence, as 'Frogface'.

Pact. Where military cooperation is concerned, or control over their armies, it is an area where the Soviets will make no concessions at all. Many of the officers of all these countries have been trained in the Soviet Union in the Soviet military schools – and they try to maintain this tradition. They rely on the armies in these countries as a strong force which would support them.

CHARLTON: Were you surprised by the appearance of General Jaruzelski in Poland as a temporary solution to the Soviet Union's difficulties there? The West was caught by surprise.
SHEVCHENKO: I was not surprised at all. And what do you mean by temporary? It might last twenty years.
CHARLTON: Ideologically, surely it is very difficult to explain why you have to turn to the army, and why the Party's authority collapsed there?
SHEVCHENKO: It is true that ideologically it *is* very difficult to explain, but I can tell you one thing. In the Soviet Union itself *everything* can be explained! Unfortunately the Soviet population in general, and the Party, accept what the Party tells them. When I was in Moscow, for several years before the recent events in Poland, in the Central Committee it was believed (and there are even letters to the Soviet Party organisations which said so) that the Party in Poland was not strong, and could not control the situation. I feel they have no problem to explain that in the Soviet Union. They have more difficulty with the French, or with other Communist parties in Europe, but not in the Soviet Union. In the Soviet Union there is great respect for the military in general. For the Soviets it is not something bad, this respect for the army; it is very much respected among the Soviet population.

Therefore it is hard to tell how much time it will take for the situation in Eastern Europe to become unmanageable. As you know, in the past the Soviet government has not hesitated to use crude military measures to remove the leadership and put others in. It happened in Czechoslovakia, and in Hungary, and now in Poland. For the time being the situation is still manageable. But it can come, that moment, when it will get more and more difficult for the Soviet Union to manage the situation. It might well be. But I would not say this time will come soon.

THE POLISH EVENTS, and the still-to-be-determined extent to which their infection is contagious, dispels one of the misconceptions which has coloured the Western view – the often stated belief that, with the passing of time, the countries of Eastern Europe would come to accept that degree of command and conformity the Russians exact.

Developments there give point to a central perception of '*détente*' as it was practised, for example, during the Nixon Presidency. As Henry Kissinger expressed it to President Nixon: 'The major long-term question is whether the Soviets can hold their own bloc together while waiting for the West to succumb to a long period of relaxation. Certainly our chances are as good as Brezhnev's, given the history of dissent in Eastern Europe.'

The endemic strains between the satellite countries and the Soviet Union were seen as a constant threat to the stability of Europe, and therefore at the heart of a stable international relationship. Kissinger's principal aide, Hal Sonnenfeldt, enunciated what became known as the Sonnenfeldt doctrine. It was subsequently disowned by Kissinger as embodying a doctrine of practical action. At the time, nonetheless, it reverberated as evidence that the Nixon Presidency, in reflecting on the dangers at its heart, accepted the division of Europe. Sonnenfeldt's argument called for the states of Eastern Europe to seek their evolution in what he called 'an organic relationship with the Soviet Union'. The corollary of this argument was that only then might the Russians be persuaded to feel more secure, and so relax their hold in order to ward off the recurring crises. Sonnenfeldt was President Nixon's and Henry Kissinger's principal adviser in the National Security Council on policy towards the Soviet bloc.

SONNENFELDT: I have never thought that the recognition of spheres of influence, in the sense of recognising the sensitivity of the Soviet Union to what was happening in Eastern Europe, was an adequate policy in its totality. Obviously, when one is dealing with an enormous power like the Soviet Union, one has to pay attention to its security concerns and above all its capacity to *act* on its security concerns with an enormous military power. But the situation in Eastern Europe, as it emerged at the end of the Second World War, has always been untenable, in my view, over the long run. I have used the word 'unnatural' – and so have many others – because it rested on force. While I have agreed with the notion of respecting – and being careful about – Soviet security concerns, I have never accepted the proposition that we cannot be in favour of change, and rather fundamental change, in Eastern Europe. I think this *has* to happen, or else we will have a constant repetition of Hungarys, Czecho-slovakias and Polands. At some point that is going to mean, not a controlled event, but an *un*controlled event, and one that could have horrendous consequences.

CHARLTON: Do you think what you said in 1975 – 'It should be our policy to strive for an evolution that makes the relationship between the Soviet Union and the East European States *an organic one*' – is still an adequate policy in view of what has happened – in Poland particularly?

SONNENFELDT: I think it is an adequate guideline, provided we understand what I meant to convey by the word 'organic'. I meant a more natural relationship. I used the term 'organic' in its dictionary meaning of 'as between living organisms'. So, I believe it *is* still a sensible guideline for Western policy to seek relationships which will make it less and less likely that the Soviet Union will constantly intervene with force – and constantly resort to repression to hold things together in Eastern Europe. The Soviet Union can do that of course, but the consequences will make the situation worse and worse and less stable in Eastern Europe.

CHARLTON: You went on to say, in that much-discussed formulation of yours during the Kissinger years, that: 'This has worked in Poland. The Poles have been able to overcome their romantic political inclinations which led to their disasters in the past. They have been skilful in developing a policy that is satisfying their needs for a national identity, without arousing Soviet reaction.' Now, surely, your argument has been overtaken by events?

SONNENFELDT: In regard to Poland I was excessively optimistic. Perhaps more optimistic in terms of the resilience of the Polish system, as it had developed by 1975, and more optimistic also in terms of the Soviet capacity to adjust to change. But obviously the pressures in Poland were enormous, or else we would not have seen this very fundamental eruption of popular dissatisfaction with the regime. I would not attribute what's happened in Poland so much to Polish 'romanticism' (although there are some people who *do* attribute it to that), or a lack of a sense of limits. I *do* attribute it to another part of my discussion, on the occasion you refer to, which is the unnatural character of the whole situation. Being unnatural it results, unfortunately, in the kind of situation we now have in Poland where the Polish government, and the Soviets, react to internal developments that have developed their own dynamic and which can no longer be contained by their methods of toleration. Then they resort to the methods of repression.

CHARLTON: But it was clearly your hope in the middle 1970s that such changes as were necessary and likely *could* take place within the Soviet sphere of influence, as it has come to be recognised. Isn't this a path which is now blocked by what's happened?

SONNENFELDT: Any change that takes place in Eastern Europe is *bound* to take place within a Soviet sphere of influence, because the Soviets are nearby and have an enormous power. And in the foreseeable future they are not going to move physically, nor are they going to lose their enormous power. So all change that takes place is going to take place in that setting. It looks as though it *is* blocked, in Poland. If that is so, I think it can lead only to an explosion. Something will erupt. Therefore I maintain the proposition that change *has* to take place and that Western policy should encourage the change that *comes out of the systems themselves,* and from the peoples themselves. At the same time, be conscious of the fact that the tragedy of this region is that change has to occur in the shadow of Soviet power. Therefore when one promotes and encourages change one has to be cautious and responsible.

CHARLTON: So you think that Soviet power is immutable and

unshakeable in the area and, in that sense, we are living in an Ice Age politically and diplomatically?

SONNENFELDT: Well, Soviet power is a fact, and it appears to be growing in the military sense, although declining in many other respects. My hope continues to be, even in this very grim time, that the Soviets themselves will adjust to change. That they will recognise that it is possible for them to have security needs met, even though there is quite substantial change among, and within, the countries of Eastern and South-Eastern Europe. Unless the Soviets come to recognise that security is *not* synonymous with having satellites, and with having replications of one's own political system, I'm afraid we're in for a constant repetition of these tragedies. Somehow one has to assume that, over time, somebody within the Soviet structure will come to this realisation. Without that, I'm afraid we have almost no scope for policy-making at all.

CHARLTON: Well, you've had an opportunity, given to very few, of actually sitting down and negotiating with the Soviet leadership, with Brezhnev. What's the lasting impression it made on you? Do these events contribute to any disposition to make shifts and accommodations in Eastern Europe – or do they see the whole thing as a purely tactical situation, in which they're going to force a return to the *status quo ante* at each and every available opportunity?

SONNENFELDT: In my day of active negotiations with the Soviets, Eastern Europe was never on the agenda as an explicit item. No doubt it was in the back of their minds, and in the back of our minds. However, we never talked about events in Eastern Europe as a predecessor generation of American diplomats did at the end of World War II. But the overriding impression I brought away from these negotiations with the top Soviet leaders is that they are extremely cautious, that they are extremely slow to move, and that they have a highly cultivated sense of their own needs and requirements and not much empathy for those of others. The progress one makes with them in negotiations is marginal, at best. 'Grand Deals', so often dreamed of by impatient people here in the United States (and in Europe too) in my experience were not 'do-able'.

Perhaps some other generation of Soviet leaders, and perhaps some Western negotiators with greater vision than I and the people I worked for were able to muster, can arrange 'Grand Deals' – but I'm very sceptical that this is feasible. As regards the division of Europe, as regards the Soviet Empire – with all its cracks and failings in Eastern Europe – I very much doubt that it is going to be a matter of negotiation along the lines of the great Congresses of the nineteenth century. My feeling is that evolutionary change, incremental change (and sometimes very painful in the internal circumstances of the East European countries) in the attitude of the Soviet élite is what we have to strive for.

CHARLTON: But do you think the situation in the satellite countries, particularly Poland, has or could become one which could destroy the stability of the bloc system – the post-World-War-II architecture?

SONNENFELDT: I believe that the pressures in Eastern Europe, produced essentially by what happened there at the end of the Second World War, *do* have a potential for explosion reaching beyond the border of any one individual country. Therefore I think it is inherent in the situation that it might, at some point, prove to be quite destabilising. I have always believed that.

CHARLTON: Well, if you agree that an explosion is possible in Eastern Europe, is it in the interests of a wider peace in this world that, for example, a direct Polish challenge to the hegemony of the Soviet Union should be repressed?

SONNENFELDT: I don't see the events in Poland objectively challenging the brutal, but unavoidable, fact that the Soviet Union is a superpower adjacent to Eastern Europe. I don't think that change, even of a very fundamental character, challenges the hegemony of the Soviet Union – in the sense that that hegemony is based upon an overwhelming Soviet military power. What it does challenge is the Soviet claim that by virtue of this power it can dominate the social, political, and cultural life of these countries. That is an unnatural pretension, which is bound to produce resistance.

CHARLTON: But may I press this? Do you think we are essentially saying to the Poles, or should give the Poles, or call upon *them* to give the same answer Churchill asked them to give at the time of Yalta, and the Curzon Line and the changes in their frontier, when he said: 'We have the right to ask you to make this sacrifice. . . .' He meant for the possibility of a new world order, and the continuation of the wartime alliance. Now all that did not come to pass. So when the chips are down, is it in our interests *still* that this Polish challenge – and such other challenges as may go with it – be repressed?

SONNENFELDT: I do not think it is in our interest that the challenge should be repressed, to the extent that this challenge deals with the internal order of things in Poland. If we made that our interest we would be a participant in an untenable and profoundly unnatural course of events; and I am against events in the affairs of men that run counter to historical experience. Historical experience is that alien repression is not going to succeed. On the other hand, Poland being where it is, geography being what it is, and history being what it is, I don't believe it would be realistic for a freer Poland to become a member of NATO! If that means a sacrifice on the part of the Poles, in this Churchillian sense, I suppose I would agree – that the Poles would have to sacrifice the option of joining a Western military association. But I do not believe that they should be expected to sacrifice the inherent right and necessity to have a more natural internal order of things, which provides for a greater individual freedom and the right of the Poles to express their national individuality.

CHARLTON: But that is contradictory, isn't it?

SONNENFELDT: It is a contradiction, and it is the tragedy and the dilemma that one faces when dealing with East European policy. It is the tragedy that makes it so easy for some people constantly to posture as though they were going to ride tanks into Warsaw to throw the Soviets and the Communists out. When the chips are down, the people who want to ride those tank columns into Budapest, or Prague, or Warsaw tend to be the first ones to duck out and say, 'Well, it is really better for the Soviets to do their worst – then Western public opinion can be roused from its illusions that the Soviets are, really, nice people.' That is always the other argument advanced by people who want to let the tanks roll into Eastern Europe. I have never denied that policy towards Eastern Europe in the present era of history – given who the Soviets are and what their power is – is riddled with terrible moral as well as policy dilemmas.

IN HIS MONUMENTAL HISTORY, *Decline and Fall of the Roman Empire*, Edward Gibbon nominated as one of the conditions for imperial success, 'a ready access to the subject peoples'. Geography, military strength and the political system imposed by Stalin at the end of the Second World War continue to assure that.

Even so, forty years after Stalin enforced the nature of the present state, Poland is a country where the Communist Party had to be rescued by the Polish armed forces in order to maintain Communist power. Polish workers in the Workers' State have burned Lenin in effigy and cast down his statues. They have chanted *en masse* 'Long live Reagan'.

Therefore the shortening cycle of discontents in Eastern Europe is becoming ever more difficult to dismiss, in the case of Poland, as the epiphany of its brilliant nationalism. Their real cause lies in the cultural amputation of Europe.

Norman Davies, the young British historian, has recently concluded a major historical study of the Polish state and nation.

DAVIES: I think the ties with the West are something which increase in proportion to the deprivation the Poles feel with regard to the world in which they live. It is not as though Western Europe has *imposed* its connections on Poland. Nobody in Western Europe insists that twice as many Poles go to church there as in any other Western European country. It is because of the shortcomings of life in the Communist world that the Poles exploit the ties which already exist and become more 'Western' than anybody in Western Europe – whether it's in their religious practices or in wanting the opportunity to see and know the richness and complexities of their heritage: far more so than we do.

CHARLTON: Is there a universal view among the Poles about Yalta – do they see it more or less as a permanent entrapment?

DAVIES: An entrapment, yes. Very few people would support Yalta.

Except of course those who argue from the pessimist standpoint. 'If we *have* to accommodate ourselves to the Soviet Union then this was inevitable.' But, when you say permanent entrapment, I think all Poles have the stubborn belief that they will outlast their oppressors. After all there is this great 'Messianic' tradition of Poland being fated to suffer for other people. It goes back at least 150 years, when it was formulated in the most ringing tones by the great Romantic poets in the early nineteenth century. Many Poles are saturated in this romantic nationalism – the feeling that suffering and agony is their lot but that, in the end, the skies will clear.

CHARLTON: But romantic nationalism is the very thing, surely, which the Western diplomats will say has cost the Poles so dearly: the air of romantic unreality they discern. Now would the Poles say that we're all being faint-hearted, or do they see positive opportunities, over which they have influence, for some change in the strategic position of the Soviet Union? Do they believe that they themselves are harbingers of it?

DAVIES: I do not think so. I think there is a great sense of fatalism in Poland. The idea that Poland today can somehow provoke the changes that are required is not held by very many people. After all, Solidarity, despite many months of activity, did not launch itself into the romantic uprising that some people might have expected. The threat of Soviet tanks, of Poland being flooded by two million men – an army of occupation to the next generation – is not a prospect which attracts. In spite of everything, Solidarity was extremely cautious on these issues. And, only at the very end, and in exasperation and desperation, did they begin to throw caution to the winds.

But, after forty years, the whole rationale of the Soviet Alliance is beginning to fall apart. The key event I think was in 1970, when Willy Brandt went to Warsaw. The sight of a German leader, kneeling in expiation for the crimes of the wartime period, is a sight which no Pole, I think, would ever forget. On top of that, of course, there is the younger generation. Stories of the Second World War are extremely remote for young people, and I think the time has come when you can no longer frighten young Poles with the Nazis and a resurgent Germany. Contemporary history is an issue of burning interest; and whereas a historian in England, you might say, would be fortunate to get an audience of fifty or one hundred people – in Poland in 1980–1 historians could fill a football stadium with fifty *thousand*, one hundred *thousand* people. There were lectures in factories, where the whole factory would halt in order to hear a lecture about contemporary history.

But the issues they were principally interested in were all the *taboo* subjects which nobody could mention before. In particular, Soviet–Polish relations. What was interesting for these audiences was not the battle against the Germans, about which, of course, every young Pole hears *ad*

nauseam at school, but: what was Rokossovsky* doing? What was the
Soviet side of that episode? What was the *Soviet* side of the 1939–41
period which included Katyn, and of the Battle of Warsaw in 1920, and
what was Pilsudski's policy against the Soviet Union? All these are issues
in history which are not answered for the young generation of Poles, and
which they are so fascinated by.

The Communist élite has a monumental inferiority complex about
itself – and it's very careful not to impinge on anything outside its own
little Polish parish. But the Polish intelligentsia, I think, has got quite the
opposite – almost megalomaniac – tendencies of seeing Poland as
carrying the torch for the oppressed peoples – certainly those of Eastern
Europe – as the saviour of the nation. There is this Messianic streak,
which is all mixed up with religious symbolism and, the more it is
repressed, the more powerful it becomes.

CHARLTON: To you, a historian, how significant is it that the Soviet
Union – claiming an ideology which is the ultimate revelation of politics
– has so signally failed in Poland when, plainly, it set out to do so much?
When it has moved frontiers, or caused them to be moved? When it has
taken away all the Polish minorities (the Jews had been removed already
by Hitler) and when the new frontiers include compensations for the
old, at Germany's expense, in the so-called 'recovered lands' in the West?
DAVIES: In my opinion you have to go back to the real nature of the
ideology which is, in many respects, far removed from what one would
think of as socialist, or as leftist, and which had so much in common in
fact with Nazi and Fascist ideology – especially on the national issue.
One thing Stalin was quite determined to do in Eastern Europe was to
segregate the various nationalities, each into their own exclusive reserves.
And in the period during and after the war something like twenty-five
million people were shipped around and sorted out. So much so that by
1948 you had a Czechoslovakia which was inhabited exclusively by
Czechs and Slovaks, a Poland which was exclusively Polish, East
Germany exclusively German, and so on. The result of this policy was of
course to remove many of the frictions between the national minorities
which had plagued Eastern Europe before the war. Equally, it has succeeded in cohering a mass of Poles together who have no diversions,
within Polish society, of the sort that existed previously, and who form a
much more resistant and politically and socially united mass than ever
was the case at any point in Polish history. After all, present-day Poland
is much more Catholic under Communist rule than it was at any previous
time in history *because* the religious, and national, minorities have been

---

* Konstantin Rokossovsky, Marshal of the Soviet Union, a Pole who spent his entire career
  in the Soviet service and was installed in Warsaw in 1949 as Vice-Premier, Minister of
  Defence, and a member of the Politburo.

removed. The new territory of Poland has been repopulated and resettled with Polish Catholics imported from the East. The consequence is a cohesive Polish, nationalist, anti-Russian population which in the long term will be much more difficult for the Russians to deal with than if they'd left things in place.

CHARLTON: So perhaps, as Frederick the Great said about the partition of Poland at an earlier period, 'This partition and this solution had its end in its very beginning'? That is, it has contrived the opposite of its intended outcome?

DAVIES: I think so. I think Stalin, in spite of everything, has sown the seed of an independent national Poland some time in the future.

THE BALEFUL SUPPRESSION of Solidarity has shown (if the demonstration were needed) that the possibility of change in Poland must still depend largely on the chances of change in the Soviet Union itself. As has also been suggested, such developments, in their turn, will depend to some, obviously unknowable, extent on Soviet perceptions of the West, and the positions it takes up.

The themes which have endured and persisted since Yalta present themselves in different guises everywhere. They do so before the audience of a new generation – in which the dominant age group now has no memory of the events which gave rise to them.

We come to the White House in the 1980s. Professor Richard Pipes, one of President Reagan's advisers on Soviet relations, has recently left the White House, after a two-year term with the National Security Council, to go back to Harvard and his old post as Professor of Russian History. Since Yalta, has the West ever done otherwise, in practice, than accept the immutability of the Soviet position in Eastern Europe?

PIPES: We accept the fact that these countries are, essentially, under Soviet occupation. But this country has never accepted this as a moral reality. There is a big difference between recognising a physical reality and accepting it as a *moral* reality. At Yalta we struck what we considered to be the best bargain possible for Eastern Europe. There were hopes that we could salvage the situation. These were very quickly disappointed, in the late forties. Then again, in the fifties – and, particularly in the sixties – there was a hope of 'building bridges' to Eastern Europe, partly through cultural contact but mainly through economic assistance. These definitely produced some results – in the sense that much of the ferment in Eastern Europe would not have been conceivable without this.

Ever since, we've conducted what we call a policy of differentiation vis-à-vis Eastern Europe – the official, if rather ugly, term. It means that we differentiate among the countries of Eastern Europe, and between the countries of Eastern Europe and the Soviet Union, in terms of our attitude. Those countries in Eastern Europe which either pursue a more independent foreign policy, or a more liberal policy domestically, receive certain tokens of appreciation from the United States – in the form of, for example, economic advantages.

Now, we cannot do very much about the fact that these areas are under Soviet occupation, but we do not acknowledge it *morally* and we hope that, some day, these areas will liberate themselves.

CHARLTON: All right, these are the arguments that we have lived with for getting on for forty years now. And in that time there has been the constant reiteration of the Soviet Union's feeling of 'insecurity', constantly put forward in their demands for the legitimisation of their position in Eastern Europe – as with the Helsinki Agreement. But taking stock now of the challenge to the Russians of economic and political crisis in Poland and elsewhere in Eastern Europe and at home, which arguments about how to 'coexist' with Soviet Russia do you find are being weakened and which are being strengthened by the present situation?

PIPES: I think you have to view the crisis of Soviet rule in Eastern Europe in a broader context. The Soviet Union is an empire. If you take all of the Soviet possessions – that is the Soviet Union and Eastern Europe together – you will find that the Great Russian population, the predominant population, is only approximately one-third of the total population. That *one*-third rules *two*-thirds. So what is happening in Poland, and what is happening elsewhere in Eastern Europe, also finds an expression in the Ukraine, in Central Asia and the Baltic states and so on.

Basically the Soviet Union is the last large empire – white man's empire – in the world. And it is now suffering the same problems that all other empires have suffered. Now Russian governments are always very slow in recognising realities; and they are being *buffeted* now by these problems. Essentially it is an *internal* problem. Our ability to affect the course of these developments is very limited. What the Soviet Union is experiencing is an internal challenge, which I think in the long run is going to lead to the break-up of that empire. We do not have to do very much about it. It will happen on its own.

CHARLTON: Isn't that tantamount to saying let the Soviet Union stew in its own juice?

PIPES: In a sense, yes. What we ought *not* to do is help them out of their dilemmas, by giving them economic aid, or by pronouncing 'doctrines' which seem to accept the Soviet domination of non-Russian areas. Yes, the Soviet Union's problems are self-generated. They are internal. I think the system ought to bear, and be forced to pay, its own consequences. We ought not to allow the Soviet Union to get off the hook of its decision not to decentralise the economy, not to provide adequate incentives, and to pour so much of its capital and resources into military hardware. We ought rather to say: 'Very well, if that is what you want, if that is what you have decided to do, then you must bear the consequences. We are not going to come and help you.'

THE CRISIS OVER POLAND and the general malaise and apathy reflected in the long death-watch of Mr Brezhnev's declining years have
served to reinforce the belief that the Soviet Union is finding it increasingly difficult successfully to order the economic life of its protectorate in
Eastern Europe without the help of the West. And therefore the impression that the Soviet Union faces harsher choices now than at any time
since Stalin died has gained ground.

Another who thinks that a previously favourable situation for the
Russians has begun to unravel is Seweryn Bialer.

BIALER: As in the history of every major empire we know of, the Soviet
Empire is also undergoing a change now that will lead to its decline and
end. From the economic point of view this decline of empire – which may
last a few decades – has already started. Eastern Europe is no longer an
economic asset to the Soviet Union. It is much more of a burden. They
hold on to it not for economic reasons but primarily for strategic and
political reasons. And there are signs that the *military* importance of
Eastern Europe for the Soviet Union is declining rapidly. We have a
situation where the key country in the Warsaw Pact was, for all practical
purposes, taken *out* of the Warsaw Pact. (The Soviets now have to think,
not about how to use Polish troops if there is a war with the West, but
how many of their *own* troops do they have to keep in Poland to prevent
Poles from rebelling!) There are signs in Soviet strategy and in their
strategic writings and deployments that they *know* it. They are trying to
create a southern corridor, for example, through Czechoslovakia, of supplies and logistics to their troops in East Germany facing NATO. And
there will come a time when they will have to commit more troops to the
defence and holding of Eastern Europe than they can take troops *from*
Eastern Europe to fight the West.

Now, thirdly, there is the political question. Eastern Europe is still an
asset *politically* to the Soviet Union – primarily with regard to the Soviet
population at home, which sees in Soviet domination of Eastern Europe
the symbol of just reward for what they did in the Second World War in
fighting the Nazis. Yet at the same time Eastern Europe is becoming a
major *embarrassment* for the Soviet Union politically, first of all because
of the Communist parties in the West. For example the Italian Communist Party broke with the Soviet Union completely – as China broke.
And then there are the West European countries with whom the Soviet
Union has *détente*, also deeply embarrassing them over Eastern Europe.
Frankly, I think the only thing that could change the minds of West European governments to move away from *détente* would be not Reagan's
pressure but Soviet misbehaviour and brutality in Eastern Europe. So,
from all these points of view, today we see the beginning of a major
decline.

THE MOUNTING EVIDENCE that the economy of the Soviet Union
will stagnate and even decay has to be weighed with the principal legacy
of Mr Brezhnev's time – his achievement and bequest of a preponderant
military might. In the past the Soviet Union has relied on force to solve,
or relieve what are euphemistically called 'contradictions' in its multi-
national empire. Hungary in 1956, Czechoslovakia in 1968, were both
invaded by the Red Army, and the present situation in Poland is fresh evidence that such difficulties for the Soviet hegemony are seen by them in
military terms in the last resort.

Those 'harsher choices' which, it is suggested, the Soviet Union is being
forced by circumstances to confront would seem to oscillate between two
extremes: a profound change in the nature of the Soviet economy, or the
possibility that the countries of Eastern and Central Europe might be
driven back to a new 'Dark Age'. Could another wave of darkness and
repression break over these resentful polities as it did in Stalin's day,
when he determined to communise them on the Soviet pattern? Mr
Gromyko's former personal political adviser, Arkady Shevchenko, chose
to answer this in terms of the likely consequences with which the Kremlin
would be faced.

SHEVCHENKO: I doubt that they could come back to Stalinist oppression, because it is not possible in the present situation. I dare to stress
that the East European countries have more independence – and then
there is the mood of the population: the Soviets know that if they *did* try
to return to the methods of the Stalin oppression they would face a
situation in *all* these countries like the one in Poland.

Even with all the military might of the Soviet Union, and that is its
nuclear might, I can tell you that really to control Eastern Europe,
seriously, by military force they need a huge army – a conventional army.
Why did they not intervene in Poland, directly, *themselves*? Because to
intervene in Poland directly, and by themselves, they needed an army of a
million men, at least. And if *all* the East European countries were in-
flamed, like Poland, they would need two or three millions. The Soviet
Union does not *have* such an army at all now. The *whole* Soviet army, the
Red Army, is now less than three million. And they have to keep at least a
million on the Chinese border, all the time. So, would they mobilise two
or three million men – all their reserves – and with all the difficulties and
the shortage of labour in the economy, with such difficulties as they are
going to face now? No, there are great difficulties here. I would dismiss the possibility that they could resort to Stalin's method. Don't forget
that in those days the Soviet Union was mobilised – the army and the
country had not yet demobilised after the Second World War. It was all
ready, it was a war machine at that time. The situation now is totally
different.

BOTH THEIR RELATIVE PROXIMITY to the Russians – and the resonance of history – have inclined the West Europeans in particular to be apprehensive of the possibility of unrest leading to fundamental change in the heart of Europe.

The Foreign Office, on the other side of Downing Street, is unlikely to be the only foreign service in Europe to remember a celebrated axiom of a French Ambassador to St Petersburg in the last century that 'Russia is never as strong – and never as weak – as she looks'. It is a judgement echoed, in part at least, by Walter Laqueur, the Director of the Contemporary History Institute in London.

LAQUEUR: We are certainly facing a new situation, but it is easy to exaggerate the acute dangers for the Soviet Union. In some respects, of course, the situation is even *more* acute and *more* dangerous than is generally appreciated in the West. It is not only a matter of Poland, it's a matter of most of these countries, including even Bulgaria, which was considered until recently a most faithful satellite.

On the other hand we should not forget that all the time the leadership of the Soviet Union is self-confident, and it disposes of such power that no movement of separatism has the slightest chance for success. We should not forget after all – let us look back for a moment in history – that but for the First World War, Poland would still belong to Russia. But for the First World War, Finland would still be a part of Russia. It took a total military disaster in the centre, meaning in Russia itself, for the success of secession, and I think we should not forget that. If there were to be a combined, united front of all East European countries against the Russians (which does not exist) then maybe. . . .

CHARLTON: In your view, then, was Solidarity doomed from the beginning?

LAQUEUR: Yes and no. Yes, because it was obvious that the Russians could not put up with a democratic movement of this kind. On the other hand, no, because unless in any given historical period there are people willing to risk their lives and their liberty there will never be progress. The possibilities are of continuing unrest; of the Soviet Union having to subsidise most of its allies – which is not very popular inside the Soviet Union. And, as far as the military aspects are concerned, I would not myself exaggerate the tendency to believe that the Russians cannot rely upon their East European allies. They probably will not use them as shock troops; but, the military in Eastern Europe is fairly tightly controlled, and I do not think this causes them many sleepless nights.

So in a way we should expect more of what we've had before – meaning that every five, ten or fifteen years a new generation comes up (these days a generation does not take as much as thirty years, things are much quicker), and there will be some form of resistance or rebellion – sometimes political, and sometimes, no doubt, more drastic. And the Russians will try to cope with this. The bottom line – to use an unlovely American expression – is that, unfortunately, there is not much for Eastern Europe to expect unless something changes *inside* the Soviet Union.

CHARLTON: But when you address that very question, what is the relevance of what *is* happening in Eastern Europe? Are the changes taking place on the periphery of the Soviet Empire of direct relevance to what is likely to happen inside the Soviet Union proper?

LAQUEUR: Well, there are two schools of thought. One is saying that the change may come from the periphery – as it came in the Roman Empire and as it came in other empires. But I'm afraid this one is probably different. I think that only if there should be a rift inside the Politburo, or some movement towards a greater – I would not say democracy, but less of a monolithic bloc – only in that case could there be more freedom for Eastern Europe.

CHARLTON: Why is this one different from the Roman Empire?

LAQUEUR: Modern technology. Because it took a long time for a courier from Rome to march to Asia Minor, whereas, these days, you have it in seconds. Within minutes you know what is happening in Poland, Czechoslovakia and Hungary, and the Russians can act. Now I may be a little pessimistic. Fortunately history, in contrast to popular belief, does not always repeat itself.

CHARLTON: But this is George Orwell's prescription for that apocalyptic era of his to be ushered in by 1984. So it's an invitation to speculate whether modern tyrannies – as he seemed to suggest in *Nineteen Eighty-Four* – are almost inevitably successful, given the support of modern technology in the manner you've suggested.

LAQUEUR: I'm afraid there is much in it. Perhaps not in the exaggerated form which Orwell, as a novelist, described. Many people thought, and certainly most of us would have welcomed it, that there was a chance of 'Finlandising', not Western Europe, but Eastern Europe. Unfortunately, you see, from the Soviet point of view this would be an intolerable retreat. If these countries had never *been* Communist, then they would probably accept it today. But, once they have been part of the Warsaw Pact, then it would be almost a declaration of bankruptcy – and that the Soviet Union simply cannot afford, or thinks it cannot afford. Perhaps it could, but they are head of a camp, and they cannot simply abdicate their leadership.

AFTER STALIN DIED, Khrushchev rid the Soviet Union of most of the institutionalised violence and terror of the old Dictator's time. But he also drew the limits of how far those changes could be allowed to go without weakening the hold of Lenin and Stalin's system of power. Under Brezhnev the all-pervading greyness of Stalin's bureaucracy was essentially consolidated. It is still Stalin's system, his apparatus of dictatorial administration which, by and large, is in place; and it remains a strong, secretive and jealous centralised power.

Viewed in this context Poland cannot be dismissed, in company with Hungary and Czechoslovakia in 1956 and 1968, as being of only circumscribed relevance to that power at the hub of the Soviet Union, in Moscow. According to Richard Pipes, it signals a further dismantling of Stalin's architecture.

PIPES: I believe, personally, that what we are witnessing is really the end of the Stalinist system. It is approximately fifty years old. Though some of the most horrible aspects of the Stalin years – its mindless terror – have been eliminated, the system which you have in the Soviet Union today is still, basically, the Stalin system. That system had its uses when Russia was making the transition from an agrarian to an industrial power, but no longer has any uses today. It has become a hindrance. It is intact but eroding, and it has eroded to the point where one wonders whether, in fact, it is intact. Let me remind you that approximately 40 per cent of all the construction work in the Soviet Union – and something like one-third of all the foodstuffs (except for grain) – are produced by private sectors.

CHARLTON: But in institutional terms the system Stalin created is still intact?

PIPES: It is in place, but there are so many cracks in it that the question is whether you can continue this system or whether you need very major reforms. I think things have reached the point where Brezhnev's successors now have a choice of doing one of two things – but they will *not* be able to continue along the present course. They will either have to go back to the old Stalin system which means, as you've pointed out, a crackdown (on corruption, laxity in work performance – with very heavy penalties) – and all combined with a retrenchment of imperial adventures as too costly. This would possibly solve Soviet problems for a short time but would be catastrophic in the long term. Or they must introduce cautious reform – both economic and political. This I think would be the more reasonable course.

CHARLTON: With the success of Solidarity there was a strong argument advanced that empires can be made to change by such changes at their outer limits. I suppose the British have a particular and recent experience. Kipling's poetry is full of premonitions about the overstretching of Britain's capacities in places like the North-West Frontier in India. Where do such arguments stand, in your view, after the unexpected success of the Soviet Union – at least, the unpredicted success – in producing General Jaruzelski as the solution, for the time being anyway, to Solidarity? Are such changes, or challenges, going to be reflected internally in the Soviet Union itself?

PIPES: Well, I would not call Jaruzelski a solution – it's a stopgap measure. The problem which has arisen in connection with Solidarity is enormously threatening to all the other countries of Eastern Europe, to the Communist parties of those countries, *and* to the Soviet Union. The reason they had to destroy Solidarity was because of the threat, not so much to Poland, but to the rest of Eastern Europe *and* to the Soviet Union. Now, there is evidence that the more intelligent people in the Soviet apparatus in Eastern Europe, outside of Poland, are aware of this.

But what is not likely to be transferred anywhere else is the replacement of Party rule by military rule. That is extremely unlikely in the Soviet Union, or anywhere else, and has to do rather with the peculiar traditions of Poland. But Solidarity – the rise of the working class against the Communist regime – makes a mockery, of course, of that regime's claim to represent the working class. And it poses a problem that the more intelligent Communist leaders must realise cannot be solved by repression.

CHARLTON: Sitting as you are here now – just down the corridor from the White House and the President's office – what are your perceptions, in this building, about the extent to which the Soviet Union's behaviour in Eastern Europe is influenced by your responses to what they do?

PIPES: I would not exaggerate the effect we have. It's true that, in the case of Poland, the Polish authorities and the Soviets blame everything that happens on Radio Free Europe, or the CIA, or President Reagan – but clearly this is not so. And, I say again, the problem is internally generated. I would not deny that the President's position and the sanctions which we've imposed boost the morale of Solidarity for example, and keep up the courage which might waver if they felt they were being abandoned. But the whole movement of Solidarity and the Church movement are internally generated, and only marginally influenced by what we do.

CHARLTON: Yet the Russians must know, when they consider the record, that the United States in historical terms – both after Versailles at the end of the First World War, and again with Roosevelt at the end of the Second World War – does not think that Eastern Europe is worth fighting for, worth going to war over?

PIPES: Well, I think this is probably true. But there is a great deal of difference between abandoning Eastern Europe to the Soviet Union and going to war over Eastern Europe. And as you watch developments in Eastern Europe they are fundamentally very encouraging in the long term. What we would like to do is to assist at least morally, and if possible economically through aid, those forces in Eastern Europe – be it in Poland, or Hungary, or Romania – that work towards diversity and towards more liberal forms of government.

CHARLTON: What is the capacity of these countries *themselves*, divorced from the will of the Soviet Union, to destroy the stability – the uneasy stability – which followed the Yalta compromise? Do they have such capacity themselves?

PIPES: Yes, I think they do. Since the end of the Second World War there have now been major uprisings in three countries of Eastern Europe, two of which had to be dealt with by Soviet troops. They know they are intensely disliked in all these countries by the vast majority of the population – the Soviet leadership must have very few illusions – and they must realise that the moment their coercive capacity in this area diminishes, then these countries will go their own way.

I was in Prague a month before the Soviet invasion in 1968 and I was astonished how all signs of both Communist government and Soviet hegemony had disappeared. I was in a country that seemed very shoddy, poor, but still Western. That shows how very little Communist rule, and Soviet domination, have really penetrated in these countries. And the same thing I think was true of Poland before December 1981 and the military takeover.

THE MASTERFUL, ORDERING TOUCH with which the Russians imposed Communism on Eastern Europe after the war was one end of that rainbow which, for the Communist parties installed in power there, has continued to recede. Then there was terror – but also idealism. Idealism was a galvanising ingredient which has gone now. It has left the grey residue of a political and economic system which the former Yugoslav leader, Milovan Djilas, has described to us as 'Industrial Feudalism'. The guns and butter policy of the Brezhnev years is in jeopardy. At the same time there is the awakening of a certain introspection inside the Soviet Union – down as far as the inchoate popular level – about the 'People's Democracies'. This evidence is supported by Arkady Shevchenko in so far as the leadership is concerned. As he has indicated, 'Pessimism may be too strong a word – but there is certainly concern.' Shevchenko thinks that the burden of growing liabilities in Eastern Europe has become such – or is certain to do so – that Moscow would countenance an experimental latitude.

SHEVCHENKO: As far as economic change goes – I mean, changes in the economies of Eastern Europe – they can swallow that. What they're afraid of is independence in the international arena. Romania comes immediately to my mind. They get mad when, let's say, the Romanians try and enter some kind of special relationship with the Western countries or with the United States. That is their preoccupation – that it could lead to more and more freedom and then it would be much more difficult to exercise strong control over them.

But I'll tell you another thing. They cannot *do* for these countries what they have promised to do in the economic field. They have been taking advantage of these countries of course, and taking a lot from them. They see their growing reluctance to have economic relations with the Soviet

Union which do not pay world market prices. If the Hungarians can sell to the West and get both hard currency and normal prices, what is the inducement to take roubles from the Soviet Union – which is paper, for which they can get nothing?

CHARLTON: But your personal experience of the leadership's attitudes: what, for example, can you remember people like Gromyko saying about these persistent challenges to Soviet domination?

SHEVCHENKO: If I read the mind of Gromyko, I tell you frankly that my impression is that Gromyko considered it would be better not to have them, and that these countries were a burden for us. He never said so, in so many words of course, but my feeling has always been that Gromyko would prefer not to have them at all, and not to have all the problems. And he does not like to deal with them. I know that it is always painful for him and that he was always angry, Gromyko, to meet with all these leaders or to go there. He did not show it openly, but that is the feeling I have.

But in the Soviet leadership Gromyko belongs to those people who consider that the most important thing for the Soviet Union, in foreign policy, is the relationship with the United States and the major European countries – the United Kingdom, France, Germany. His philosophy is a little bit different. He does not consider that these East European bloc countries give anything for the Soviet Union. And that was also my position, when *I* was Soviet, and before I changed my mind and broke with the Soviet government. I also considered – what the hell, let's leave these countries to be on their own. Why should the Soviet Union *need* to control them? There are so many *domestic* problems in the Soviet Union at the present time.

I would say that most of the Soviet population would share this opinion, because they want changes *in the Soviet Union*, improvement of the economic situation *in the Soviet Union* – which is absolutely terrible now. The scale of the economic disaster in the Soviet Union is tre-mendous. If you look now – even in the Soviet press – I never in my life saw so much open criticism, even on the pages of *Pravda* and *Izvestia*, saying how poorly managed industry is – not just agriculture, which was always recognised as a problem. So there is a feeling that the Soviet leadership should better look at their own affairs – and leave all these countries alone.

CHARLTON: And yet you say these are impressions. I find them fascinating coming, as they do, from the Soviet Foreign Minister about Eastern Europe, but they are only 'impressions'? It would seem, from what you say, that it is not within the permissible limits of discussion to air views like these openly in official circles, in the leadership.

SHEVCHENKO: Of course they will not ever discuss that in such a way. I had this kind of discussion only with some of my very close friends in the Foreign Ministry, because it is a heresy. Here we have the duplicity and the hypocritical approach. No one can openly say what I said to you, as a Soviet leader. There is the ideological thing. There is a conflict between the pragmatic approach to foreign policy and that of the theoretical, ideological people in the Central Committee, who will think in terms of the Marxist–Leninist approach to world development. There are still these people; and that is the opinion of quite a body of influential people in the Central Committee, or in the two departments of the Central Committee which are very influential – the International Department, which is headed by Ponamarev, and the Department for Relations with the Socialist Countries, which is headed by Russakov. They are strong powers.

As Shevchenko in the end makes clear, there is, therefore, a link between economic changes and political development which is indivisible, and which leaves the present generation of Soviet leaders trying to accommodate their square pegs of economic reform in the political round hole.

Seweryn Bialer is a frequent visitor to Moscow, with access to senior levels of Soviet Party power. Has he gained the impression – heresy or no – that there are the beginnings of a policy debate in the Soviet Union about Eastern Europe?

Bialer: I do think that there are some discussions in the Soviet Union about the East European situation – particularly Poland. Poland was an extraordinary shock to them. Martial law and its establishment was an act of desperation, not an act of planning for the future. Now they have so-called peace in Poland but, in reality, they do not know what to do; and they *are* terribly pessimistic about the future of Poland, and the future of Eastern Europe. For the first time one can see an article in *Pravda* which informed the Soviet public how difficult the situation is, and creating the impression that it will remain critical for many years ahead.

So obviously there are discussions. But this generation of leaders in the Soviet Union, political and military leaders, will *not* give up Eastern Europe. So there is a paradoxical situation. They're even pushing these countries to make economic reforms which may improve their economic situation – but those reforms may at the same time create political pressures also for change, and those political pressures for change could explode.

Charlton: Kissinger put this in the form of an equation I think. He thought that it boiled down to some sort of race between East and West – a race between that time when, he thought, the Soviet Union's empire in the East would inevitably break up, and the ability of the Russians to conduct the policies of *détente* in a manner calculated to weaken and divide the West – to get it to succumb as the result of prolonged relaxation.

BIALER: I do not think Kissinger was the first man who said it. There were many people before him who said it too. I think there is a basic truth in the saying about 'competitive decay'. It's a question who will decay first and faster – the United States or the Soviet Union? The Western Alliance, or the Soviet Empire?

I must say that there are some reasons for fearing that there will be this kind of decline, and that unfortunately the Soviet Union, because it has a repressive regime, and its policy does not depend on the opinion of a large professional class – or public opinion – may be able to hold out longer. But I think this is a very shallow view. Today there is a crisis in the Western Alliance, but still an alliance between free people has flexibility that permits it to have disagreements and nevertheless have a commitment to the common goal – at least to the military goal of keeping Russia at bay. On the other hand when you have repressive regimes – when you have an empire – every minor problem, when it is unsolved, grows and becomes more dangerous. That is what happened in Poland.

In Poland, in the last twenty years, they have had three uprisings of workers and finally, after the third uprising, a completely new situation was created. What will happen in the 1980s if, which is very possible, not one country but *many* countries in the Soviet bloc have bad economic times? What would happen if the Soviet Union has to deal, not with one, but with three or four countries at the same time?

This is a danger of war in the heart of Europe – created by the Soviets. So I think that their problems are greater than our problems.

THE POLITICAL FRAMEWORK within which change in the Soviet Union can even be considered, let alone take place, is remarkably constricted. The satellite countries are not thought of as matters of foreign policy, but are harnessed directly to the forum of power at the very top of the Soviet Union, the Central Committee. Just how confined the processes of argument and decision are, within that tightly-drawn arena, is conveyed in Shevchenko's revelation that Mr Gromyko, although Foreign Minister of the Soviet Union, can be unaware of how, and why, decisions are taken as between the Communist leaders in the capitals of Eastern Europe, and Boris Ponamarev in Moscow, the Politburo member who deals with them.

SHEVCHENKO: The Foreign Ministry role is so marginal – it just participates when the leaders of the East European countries are to be briefed on some aspect of Soviet foreign policy, or when that is being coordinated with them. That is the role of the foreign ministry and of Gromyko. But the *real* relationship with these countries lies not in any Foreign Minister – it is direct, and in the hands of the Central Committee and its two departments. Between the Central Committees of these countries and the Central Committee of the Soviet Union. In Hungary

and the other socialist countries, they have direct telephone communications with the Central Committee. I was in Budapest, and the
Secretary of the Party – in my presence – he just called Ponamarev up
and discussed problems with him, but not with Gromyko. The Foreign
Minister, the Foreign Ministry, perhaps never even knew what they're
talking about or what they're doing.

It is this self-enclosed, claustrophobic exercise of power –
Lenin's creation, largely unchanged since he brought it with him to the
Finland Station – which makes it more or less inevitable that the fore-
most responses of the Soviet leaders to the difficulties they face will be
authoritarian. But the era since the death of Stalin – which was one without the threat of terror in the mass – was also one in which the standard
of living rose steadily. This is the prospect which has now come to an
end – for an indefinite period. With the spectre raised by the events in
Poland, consequences are unpredictable. A special standing as an
authority on the economies of Eastern Europe is enjoyed by Michael
Kaser, of St Antony's College, Oxford.

Kaser: The economies have been decelerating markedly. Their own
periods of rapid growth coincided with those of a dynamic expansion by
us of East–West trade and were due partly to their sudden access to
Western technology (which transformed their outdated structures) and
because they had access to immense supplies of labour. I think, of course,
of the agrarian countries of the Balkans and the Soviet Union itself,
though less, obviously, of East Germany, Hungary and Czechoslovakia,
where there were far fewer reserves of that nature to draw upon.

But massive availability of manpower clearly allowed the East European countries to choose their priorities, and to choose rapid-expansion
sectors, even though they were labour intensive. These conditions, too,
have changed. The labour is no longer available. There may be a little
available in Bulgaria still, and it may be available in Central Asia (with
the problems of resettlement in Siberia for people who are certainly un-
used to Siberian winters and the rigours of remote regions). But, by and
large, the whole area has to be much more *capital*-intensive. Yet, at the
very time that the economies *have* to become capital-intensive, the availability of that capital, either by lending from the West, or from raising
the efficiency of their own capital by better technology, seems to have
been eliminated.

Then also, I suggest, there is a running out of *élan*. There was at least
a certain degree of enthusiasm for economic growth. These were
changing societies, they were displacing an old ruling group by a new
ruling group, and the new ruling groups were ambitious. They were
almost entrepreneurs in nationalised industry. However, now that
nationalised industry is bureaucratised, and there is no 'ideology' left, the

whole spirit of expansion has gone. Consequently, they're in a state of lethargy, seeking new ideas but simply not getting them.

CHARLTON: What are the disciplines, what are the austerities which you think it likely these governments are going to force the peoples of Eastern Europe to accept?

KASER: Well, the austerities are already at work. The burden for the Soviet Union is unlikely to be carried for too long. The Soviet Union's own problems are too large for that to be a permanent feature of Eastern Europe. The East European countries must bestir themselves for an export surplus, and try to find some way of promoting their exports on the Western markets.

The fall in East–West trade in 1981 was almost entirely due to the sharp cut-back on imports of all the East European countries, with heavy debt services to undertake and in some cases their inability to effect that service. East European countries have, as a whole, drawn in their horns where imports are concerned. That cannot go on for a long period. Much of their technological equipment needs spare parts and the gains from international trade are far too rosy, despite the depression in the West, to be entirely forgone. And the prospects of integrating their economy totally with the Soviet Union are none too enticing. Their problems would be helped by a resumption of lending; but much more it will be a siphoning-off of all the national income increments generated by past capital invest-ment, so leaving very little for any real consumer income increases.

It is a belt-tightening period for the consumer in Eastern Europe and, obviously, it is touch and go whether that might lead to further uprisings – as it did so patently in Poland in 1980.

CHARLTON: But it is not a unique experience to have shortages in Eastern Europe. They've been endemic. Are you saying this will now be a period of *greater* shortage than experienced in the past?

KASER: Shortage, like beauty, is in the eye of the beholder. If you have a higher income and the money you earn seems larger, in comparison with your past experience, and then you can't *spend* that because the goods are not in the shops – no matter what the aggregate of goods you may be getting compared to the past – you feel more deprived.

It is *repressed inflation* which is the worst symptom of the present tight economic situation in Eastern Europe. People feel more upset by having to queue – by being turned away by empty shelves – and having the money rattling in their pockets. In earlier periods of shortage, they did not *have* that money – indeed, there was much more specific rationing, as a carry-over from the wartime period. When, in the Stalin period, more cash was rattling around in people's money-boxes than could be matched by goods, there was a new monetary reform. In the period of the early 1950s a number of East European countries simply decimated their cur-rencies by saying, 'We are changing over to a new money – and all your old money is worthless.' That can't be done these days. Therefore East

European governments have got to live with a situation of shortages. The shortages *do* seem worse, of course, and that is largely because repressed inflation is worse.

CHARLTON: Would you expect social disturbance on a wider scale than we've seen it?

KASER: If the present economic structures remained intact and rigid, that surely would be the answer. Yet the political monopolies that are the Communist Parties of the area are not unaware of the dissatisfaction arising. So I feel sure that there will be changes, simply in order to nip in the bud the riots and unrest that could arise. I am sure that 'Poland 1980' is engraved on the minds of every Party leader elsewhere in Europe. I feel that the political authorities will do their best to alter the situation. If they do not do it in the present conditions of adversarial politics by borrowing or assistance from the West, then they will obviously have to turn to the Soviet Union. Then the Soviet Union must put its own house in order to continue to provide raw materials to keep industry going in Eastern Europe. It's certain that much will depend, as far as Eastern Europe goes, on *what* opportunities are provided by the Soviet Union towards its partners in Comecon.

CHARLTON: Is it not perhaps mistaken, in historical terms, to hold out such a prospect – of a hard and a soft line? After Stalin's death were not exactly the same arguments advanced as between Malenkov and Khrushchev, with Malenkov wanting to widen the opportunities for the consumer in the Soviet Union? Now, in historical terms, there is not much comfort offered to the people of Eastern Europe or to the Russians, because that argument was lost. The Party could *not* reform itself or chose not to.

KASER: Certainly the Party was extremely important – both at the time of the overthrow of the Molotov/Malenkov group in favour of Khrushchev, and then in subsequently dismissing Khrushchev in favour of Kosygin and Brezhnev. It is the leadership at the regional level (not so much the very central authorities, but the men who run the Oblast Committees) whose vote probably counts particularly. Although they would, by virtue of their ideology and their insistence on bureaucracy, prefer the continuance of a high degree of centralisation, there is much to be said in their interest for having a much more flexible *middle* level of Soviet administration.

One of the most interesting examples in the field of specifically economic reform, reflecting the interests of the regional authorities (a sort of pent-up interest that 'We must get in on the act', and 'We don't like the central ministries') came in a series of articles which were to be published between about October 1980 and March 1981 in the Soviet Central Press. Only one of that series was ever published – by a little-known economist called Laksis. He was advocating the union of de-centralised nationalised industries with the local authorities, and using as his peg the New Economic Policy – Lenin's NEP.

Now, the rumour goes that there was to have been an escalation of these articles, at various intervals, until they reached the anniversary of the 10th Party Congress (the one at which Lenin launched the NEP and the return to 'the Market' in 1921), in March 1981. Again, it is said the Central Committee, the Politburo, had cold feet and only the first of that series ever appeared. When, of course, the Party anniversary did come in March 1981 the whole of the market economy in Lenin's thought was given short shrift. But it does seem (in conversation with Soviet economists it *has* been suggested) that it is the view of the professionals that *some* form of regionalised system may well provide the flexibility required – and it would also respond to substantial strata in the middle Party administration.

CHARLTON: But would you agree that when that choice has been faced before it was made unequivocally in the *other* direction. So, unless you think the compulsions now are of a different order and more insistent and more urgent, what really are the chances that the decision will be any different next time, no matter who or what will stand in line of succession to Brezhnev and Andropov?

KASER: The compulsions are very much more urgent because the economy in the Soviet Union is so much more complex, and because the cost of the border lands is so much higher. Not only is there the five billion dollars the Soviet Union lent in 1981 to the East European countries – there is another 2½ billion that goes to the developing countries in Comecon; and with problems further afield in Ethiopia, Angola, Mozambique, costs will rise. Consequently the demand for more efficiency and more flexibility is very much greater than it was in 1957 when, for example, Khrushchev did in fact decentralise.

But what Khrushchev did then was merely to set up mini-Ministries in a hundred regional capitals. It was one of the 'hare-brained schemes' of almost impulsive decentralisation which did not respond to Soviet conditions. A much more measured reform is called for, which would allow such enterprises to compete among themselves on a regional basis and certainly not to concentrate everything in the hands of *one* authority for *all* of industry in each region.

Khrushchev's reform was no more than a devolution. The ideas which seem to be circulating among progressive Soviet economists today involve decentralising the big industrial corporations, but making them compete on the basis of market relations – a real sense of flexibility which might respond to Party requirements also.

CHARLTON: Nearly all you say seems to me to suggest ways of improving the bloc system, of suggesting ways in which a stability plainly lost in Eastern Europe might be consolidated or restored. Yet isn't it the lesson of these last forty-odd years, since the map of Europe was redrawn, that that is the very thing which is being challenged? Isn't it simply that the people of Eastern Europe are mounting at shortening intervals, and more

and more outspokenly, a challenge to the whole idea of Soviet Communism and hegemony in Eastern Europe?

KASER: That is certainly true. And, because the Soviet Union is interested
in having a stable area on its frontier (just as it was worried enough by
destabilisation in Afghanistan to invade on its Eastern frontier), so it is
very concerned to have a stable economy and policies on its Western
frontier. To that extent therefore rather more liberalised, somewhat
market-oriented, certainly privatised sectors in Eastern Europe could
bring more stability: a stability which would help the maintenance of
that political power without which the Soviet Union would no longer
have confidence in the governments of its client states and yet, at the
same time, would open up a true dialogue between those holders of
monopoly power in East European capitals and those in the Kremlin.

CHARLTON: Providing only that the leading role of the Party is maintained – the very instrument of Soviet power which is increasingly challenged or rejected by Poles, Hungarians, Romanians?

KASER: This of course is the permanent dilemma. The East European
countries, with fresher memories than the Soviet public of a non-
Sovietised period, are, of course, anxious for a change in the system. But
the options for change are very few. That is why I see much more
expectation of reorganisation *within* the Party monopolies of power than
of any fundamental variant in the exercise of that power.

A NEW SPECTACLE has taken shape over the last ten years. It is the
Western banks falling into the arms of the planned economies of Eastern
Europe and they, in their turn, accumulating massive indebtedness to the
West. It has been a mutually nigh-ruinous embrace.

Since the lightning flash in the East of the Hungarian Uprising in
1956, an unspoken compact has existed between the rulers and the ruled,
in Hungary and Poland particularly, but also more widely in the Soviet
protectorates. It is that *rule* by the Communist Party would be passively
accepted – only in return for *performance*, and the demonstrated benefits,
of the better life. By the 1970s in Poland it had become the political
priority for the Communist leadership to give the workers more in real
wages and more to buy. That meant turning to the West for huge credits
to modernise and develop new export industries to pay for the new consumerism.

During this period, Eastern Europe amassed an obligation which, even
by the statistically-bloated measurements of health and sickness of the
present day, sounds demoralising. It is in debt to the West to the tune of
£40,000 million. It is unlikely that debt can be repaid. There is now a
huge reverse flow of money – £5000 million a year, in the minimal
repayments of interest alone, leaving these Communist countries each
year. It leaves them also having to confront their populations with the
renunciation of the 'unspoken compact' – and the prospect of a former,

deadening austerity. Lawrence Brainard, of the Banker's Trust of America, is a member of the steering committee of twenty Western banks negotiating the attempted salvage of Eastern Europe's debts to the West, and those of Poland particularly.

BRAINARD: Most of these countries came into the 1970s acutely aware that they were lagging behind the West European countries in levels of consumption, and in levels of technology. They wanted to try and catch up, and most of them felt that what was lacking was really a will to invest. As the international banking system began growing in the early 1970s – and credit became more freely available – many of these countries availed themselves of bank credits in particular. They applied a strategy which meant that they took credits to invest in their domestic economies, and they hoped that there would be exports at the end of the line that would repay these debts they were incurring.

As we look back on the 1970s we can see now that, for the most part, these strategies have failed. They have failed, chiefly, for two reasons. One reason is that the West has had the major rises in the price of oil, and this has severely affected Eastern Europe's ability to sell in the Western markets: the recession in the West has particularly affected demand for their goods. The second reason is that the very nature of these economies – their dependence on 'planning' – makes them inefficient in investment. They have taken credits, but they've not used them wisely. They've not brought projects on stream in time, and so we have not seen the productivity. Their ability to compete, therefore, in an increasingly competitive world market, has not kept pace. Their exports grow very much more slowly than some of the other major exporting countries.

In Poland, initially, the banks got involved in providing these resources because it was a country which provided some very interesting possibilities for development of raw materials. Very early on the banks became disillusioned, because the country got into very severe balance of payments problems, and then Poland turned to Western *governments*. After 1975 Poland became very dependent on loans from our own governments – from the United States, from the United Kingdom, from Germany and from France. It was in fact our desire to promote this 'consumerism' – and with it a different face on the Communist regimes – that kept their head above water. By 1981 it was obvious that it simply could not continue and that the country could not depend on more and more government money to bail it out. Hence we see the crisis we have seen in Poland.

CHARLTON: Now both economic systems – East and West – had therefore to address the question of Poland afresh in the 1970s. Presumably the Soviet Union had to make up its mind whether to assist this 'development' strategy in Poland (which the Polish Communists believed necessary in order to placate the working population) – without which there would be trouble. Why was it left to the West to make it possible for the Polish Communist government to avoid the harsh choices?

BRAINARD: That is a very intriguing question. I'm not sure I have the answer, but I think the Soviet attitude at this time was not to incur longer-term liabilities. The Soviets didn't want to give any kind of guarantee on the Polish borrowings, and were very clear in telling the Poles: 'Don't come running to us if you strike problems.' They also told the *bankers* not to expect Moscow to bail *them* out. Many of the continental banks, whose own governments were heavily involved in *détente*, were committed to the notion of the 'Umbrella Theory' – that the Soviet Union *would* help any of its allies in Eastern Europe. In other words, that a default by an East European country would so affect the credit rating of the other East European countries that they just could not let it happen. That was the thinking.

As to why the West provided the financing, I think there were two reasons. One, there was the illusion on the part of the Western governments that these resources going into Poland would be productively used. The fact that it didn't turn out that way is prima facie evidence that we did not have adequate, and accurate, information on the state of the Polish economy. That is one inescapable conclusion. Secondly, I think we were misled by a country that had a lot of resources, and which seems to enjoy a certain popular political support in the West. Certainly President Giscard d'Estaing was one of the close supporters of the Polish government at this time, as was Helmut Schmidt and the West German government, and for that matter, so was our own government here in the United States during the Carter administration.

CHARLTON: What is the proven effect of Western bank lending on domestic policy in the Eastern bloc countries?

BRAINARD: If you think of a loan which has a repayment period, the monies that went in will have to start flowing back as the loan is repaid – and these are payments both for interest and principle. The biggest impact the banks have had on Eastern Europe is simply by demanding the repayment of the monies. The only way the East European countries can repay these monies is by squeezing their own domestic economies. That means to cut off imports, to cancel or postpone investment projects and to cut levels of consumption – to take very drastic austerity measures. The disciplines are very basic and unpleasant ones that are reducing real incomes, and are creating havoc in their own economic plans. These countries really have very few choices.

CHARLTON: So, how would you characterise the degree of *de facto* influence the West has now acquired inside these Communist governments? Can one go so far as to say that when their Politburos meet to review, say, the Five-Year Plan, that there is an extra chair around the tables – inside the highest reaches of these governments – which is a chair occupied, in fact, by the West?

BRAINARD: I would not go so far as to say the Western governments have any kind of direct and specific influence in the East European economies, in the sense that we can tell them which policies to follow. But what I would say is that there are some very clear disciplines that result from their involvement in Western banking markets. In terms of drawing up their economic plans they have to take into account the disciplines of the market-place as regards private credit and the private banks.

But, had we all seen the Polish problem with the kind of clarity which hindsight brings, we would have been infinitely more cautious when it was evident that their economic strategy was not working. Instead the Western governments really convinced themselves that we ought to keep the experiment going – an experiment which had no economic logic. It was a purely political logic we were supporting. In a sense we were buying a chance to reform the Soviet or Stalinist system. I believe that was certainly the kind of thinking that was predominant in the White House at the time. And what kind of a mess did we get ourselves into! We all got a bit carried away with the ephemeral benefits of *détente*.

My view is simply that if these countries are not able to show us the productivity – to show us the exports that are going to come out of the investments that keep our workers employed – be they British, German, French or US workers – then we ought not to get into this business of giving them credits.

I think Western governments have to consider, obviously, the longer term, and whether they can support this kind of effort to become more independent within a sphere of Soviet influence. I would not like to answer that question. I think there will be a lot of interest in reforms. But, as you may gather, I'm somewhat sceptical whether these reforms can really alter things in any fundamental way. Many of these countries have found themselves now in a vicious circle. The very means by which they save their necks is also putting at risk their longer-term growth. What we are seeing is a period of stagnation – worse than stagnation – a period of very severe recession in Eastern Europe. We are into a period of perhaps some years – out into the mid-decade at least – of decline, on a year-by-year basis, in their standard of living.

THE SOVIET UNION IS BEING forced to climb down from the pinnacles of that once 'complete explanation' furnished by Ideology, to confront more openly the confounding, persisting realities. While the crisis of the Communist parties is primarily that of the economies they manage, it is also political and moral.

A central stimulus of the embattled discontents in Eastern Europe has been the corruption in high places, which has spread out among the new class ironically called 'the priviligentsia'.

In Poland it was the evidence of pervasive corruption (which Solidarity succeeded in making public) that carried the sparks of the workers' revolt over the high gates of the place with the unassailable name – the Lenin Shipyard – in Gdansk and out to the nation, where they set alight feelings among the whole population. The Prime Minister, eighteen Ministers and fifty-six Deputy Ministers were arrested for bribery and theft in the State hierarchy alone. In the Soviet Union itself, the arrival of Mr Andropov at the top (and as happened when Khrushchev succeeded Stalin) coincided with the official acknowledgement that the cancer of corruption had spread.

The ubiquity of a word like 'crisis' devalues its meaning. But, after fifty years, the political and economic architecture erected upon Lenin's gospel is being subverted by forces it refuses to accommodate and yet cannot eliminate. Given its enormous resources, however, how should the ability of the Soviet Union to shore up its position at home and abroad be understood? Seweryn Bialer returned this answer.

BIALER: The Soviet capacity to restore Eastern Europe economically – to inject into the economic situation there an element of stability and growth – depends on the performance of the Soviet economy in the Soviet Union itself; and this performance is even worse than the per- formance of Eastern Europe. The situation still exists – and it is very rare in the history of empires – where every single country of Eastern Europe has a higher standard of living than the Soviet Union. Therefore you have an empire that from almost every point of view, except the military, is inferior to those countries, yet still rules over them. The chances that the Soviet Union, in the coming decade, will be able to improve, radically, its declining economic position are, in my opinion, close to zero. That is to say, such an improvement can occur only if the Soviet Union itself undergoes a radical reform.

But a radical reform will have such a high political price that it is much less dangerous to do little rather than undertake it. Those who think that they will institute a reform like the one in Hungary are wrong in my view. The Hungarian reform is not fit for the Soviet Union. It is an economy of a different size, with a different role for the military sector – different workers, and different managers. So I don't think they will move in that direction; rather, they will stop very far short of it. And it will once again be a situation where an 'experiment' is undertaken, just as has been the case in the last twenty-five or thirty years – 'experiment' after 'experi- ment', every few years something new, and all turning out to have no real effect.

I made an interesting study at Columbia when I had some students in an advanced seminar on the Soviet Union. I took some editorials printed in *Pravda*, of different periods from the death of Stalin to today – about ten editorials on the same subject – on agriculture. I erased every reference to any date and I asked them to select a chronology, to say in what sequence those editorials were written. It is impossible to do it. Not a single student was able to do it. I could not do it, and the Soviets themselves would be unable to do it. In other words we're speaking about a chronic disease, you know. And aspirins will not suffice to cure it.

CHARLTON: But that points only in the direction of crisis and perhaps, as you've suggested earlier, the danger of war in the centre of Europe. This lack of flexibility – did you have the feeling that the gap between what is necessary and what's possible is widening?

BIALER: I think it is widening in the Soviet Union itself, but I don't think that in the Soviet Union itself there is a high probability of an explosion. I do not share the views that many 'Sovietologists' in Europe, and some in the United States – let us say that the Reagan administration – share, that the Soviet Union, as a political system, is declining so fast that another push, and it will fall apart; that Soviet armaments are so expensive that we can spend them into bankruptcy; or that we can create a situation where the Soviet leaders, instead of being preoccupied with their position in the international arena will redirect their attention to internal matters. I think that those are all unrealistic goals of American policy.

CHARLTON: What is the central flaw in that view?

BIALER: Simply that the Soviet Union is a great state which has enormous reserves of stability. It is not built simply on repression – although repression very much exists. It is a police state, but it is based not only on fear. It is also based on social controls that are very important. For example, the whole question of the intelligentsia in the Soviet Union – the professional class. I would not call it the intelligentsia, I would call it the professional class.

CHARLTON: The 'priviligentsia'?

BIALER: It's not the intelligentsia; there are some elements of the professional class which I would call intelligentsia – in the nineteenth-century sense – but this I think is a misuse of the word intelligentsia, which was a state of mind, not simply the acquisition of education. The educated classes in the Soviet Union today are basically 'in-system' classes. That is to say, they do want to manipulate the system to their own advantage, and they want to improve it, but they do not want to abolish it. They want to repress some of the things, but they don't want to fight against it. In this sense this attitude is, in my opinion, an element of stability. The other element of stability is mobility within the stratification system of the USSR. It may surprise you. I think I have checked this sufficiently, and despite the fact that there are, of course, major differences between classes in the Soviet Union the differences between – let us call it the intellectual class – and between a skilled worker has narrowed in the last ten years. It was narrowed by Brezhnev. I remember some professors in the Soviet Union telling me that they had not had a rise in pay in the last nine years. So, you have a number of social controls.

Let me give you an example with the nationalities. The non-Slav nationalities are kept by a very clever policy of stick and carrot. The peasant in Georgia lives better than the peasant in Russia – he is bribed by the regime. At the same time he is dealing with the local élite who are native. The ordinary citizen in Uzbekistan seldom has dealings with *Russian* officials. Those officials are found at the higher and middle levels. On the lower levels, and at the lowest level he is dealing with his *own* officials – the Uzbeks. Many other such clever devices make the probability of a blow-up in the Soviet Union low in my opinion.

NONETHELESS, THERE IS a theme in nearly all these informed judgements of men whose opinions have had an influence on the conduct of American, and therefore Western, policy towards the Soviet Union. It is that the Russians are buying time. Seweryn Bialer for example is 'deeply convinced that they do not know what to do'. And he adds the instructive rider that 'It is the area between immediate knowledge and analysis, and the trend which will break through in the future, which is the most difficult to contemplate and consider.'

The question was earlier put to Arkady Shevchenko, the former high-ranking Soviet diplomat, whether the Soviet Union might not try to deal with its resentful clients in Eastern Europe by unleashing another wave of darkness. Shevchenko thought the deterrent effects of a predictable explosion makes this improbable.

Richard Pipes, back at Harvard now after his time as a Reagan White House Soviet adviser, thought the historical analogies suggestive. What are the chances that, instead of contemplating a leap into the unknown with 'reform' or 'experiment', which Marxism–Leninism forbids, the Soviet leadership might have recourse to a system of government whose central operating principle is the 'proletarian coercion' practised by Stalin? Less euphemistically – fear.

PIPES: They might well do that, and not only in Eastern Europe but in the Soviet Union also. But, as I have said, I think that would be a catastrophic course. Doing that would almost certainly guarantee that the country is going to face an extremely explosive situation.

As a historian I can draw on historical parallels. It is very similar to the situation which Russia faced in the 1880s following a period of reforms which also created certain security problems. The government, instead of continuing the reforms, decided to crack down and engaged for a quarter of a century in extremely repressive measures. One can very well say that what happened between 1881 and 1904 *guaranteed* a revolution in Russia.

IF THE NATURE AND DEGREE of the Soviet Union's difficulties in Eastern Europe are accepted, then it is surely right that more eyes, more attentively, should be turned towards the gestation, in the heart of the Continent, of a new situation.

In Poland, Communist power has been compelled to wage war against its own society. The Party has been both demoralised and rejected.

One of the most warmly debated factors in the whole equation of East–West relations continues to be the extent to which the policy of the Soviet Union is conditioned by the perception, in Moscow, of the likely Western responses. Arkady Shevchenko would have us in small doubt.

SHEVCHENKO: The Western countries could, of course, respond much more strongly and that could affect the Soviets. What did the Western countries do in all these situations? Nothing! I mean the United States started some kind of embargo, which is now eroding – the West Europeans did not want to do anything at all. There is criticism in some of the mass media, but in fact they continue to deal with the Soviet Union like nothing happened. And, of course, the Soviet leadership understand that. What – tell me – what any European country *did* in connection with Poland? What did they do? Who *did* something serious, which could affect Soviet behaviour, or influence it seriously? What did they do?

CHARLTON: But *how* influential is that? We know now for example that Stalin, when he was very much weaker than we thought he was – and as Khrushchev confirms over and over again in his memoirs – in the aftermath of Yalta, that had we gone all out for a settlement of the European question . . . .

SHEVCHENKO: I am absolutely sure, if the West had been more strong – if Winston Churchill's views had been considered more seriously by Roosevelt at that time – it could be another settlement. . . .

CHARLTON: But where does your argument stand now? If you agree that the Soviet Union is very much stronger today, and the situation almost totally different in that respect, how can what the West is likely to do *force* changes in Soviet policy?

SHEVCHENKO: You know, the Soviet Union is still very much interested in relations with the Western countries. And the interest of the Soviet Union in maintaining relations with the Western countries lies, first of all, in economic cooperation. They really need advanced technology from the West. They are still not able to do that themselves. More than that, I can tell you – how will they survive without the supply of grain from the Western countries? They are *dependent* on that. Of course they are stronger than in the period immediately after the Second World War. They are strong because they have built a nuclear capability which is equal to the United States. Some people say even superior. I do not believe that. But at least it is equal. And there lies their strength – and they use it as a political weapon in general.

CHARLTON: But what are the limits? If the West refused to trade in technology or food – grain for food, and grain to feed the cattle to feed the people – were there to be curtailment of that, what effect do you say it would have on Soviet policy?

SHEVCHENKO: It would have a strong effect if the West were united. I believe it *would* affect them, extremely seriously, if it really were a united policy of all the Western countries. But the division of the West allows the Soviets to play their games. If they can't get it from the United States, well, they get it from Germany. The whole crux of the matter, and the problem, is the lack of a unified, solid policy of the whole industrialised West. I don't know whether that is possible or not. And the Soviets – they act according to their old policy, following Lenin's advice to use the contradictions between the Imperialist countries. That is what they are doing – and they are doing it successfully I would say.

THIS IS A TIME of danger and uncertainty. The Polish events place the tranquillity of Europe on the agenda once more. Unbearable and seemingly hopeless situations are hardly new in historical terms, and they are typical of a balance of power – as with the division of Europe. What is new today is the element of nuclear bombs. Shevchenko alluded to their particular significance in the Soviet case. Stalin said of nuclear weapons, 'They frighten people with weak nerves.'

But, accompanying the challenge to the *Cordon Stalinaire*'s political and economic stability, is the fear, nourished in the West, that from such unbearable situations nuclear war might indeed be a consequence.

Seweryn Bialer reinforces the importance for the Soviet Union of the nuclear arm as the ultimate determinant of relations between States. Therefore, in the continuing trial of nerve and will between the Soviet bloc and the West how should we assess the likelihood of misperceiving vital interests?

BIALER: Let me answer your question in two parts. First, I question the assumption that the most important thing in Soviet–American, or Soviet–West European relations are misperceptions. The basic thing is that we have different interests. You know, it is like the case of the paranoiac who really *was* followed by somebody! We suspect it only, but we *do* have different interests. They are a different country from our own countries, they have a different ideology and different values. They see the future of the world in different terms. So, it is not enough to sit at the table with them, and talk with them, as human beings. Of *course* they are human beings. They are a warm and good people. I personally love Russians. It is simply a question of their having different interests; and as long as they have different interests there will be competition. To think anything else is Utopian, totally Utopian. The question is how to control this competiton. It is not a question of misperception. So now the second part of my answer to you – and it is the question of nuclear weapons. I would say that the greatest beneficiary of nuclear weapons in post-war history has been the Soviet Union – and for three reasons.

The first reason is that the industrial and military potential of the Western allies – of the United States, Western Europe and Japan is five to six times higher than the Soviet potential. The difference today is probably even bigger than it was before the Second World War. So, the nuclear weapons here act as an equaliser – they simply made it possible for Russia to become an expansionist and expanding power. Without nuclear weapons, in my opinion, there would have been a war already many times and Russia would not stand a chance in such wars – conventional wars.

CHARLTON: Often advanced as the reason why Stalin was so cautious in Europe after 1945 and before they had the bomb in 1949?

BIALER: Exactly. Yes. So this is the first reason why nuclear weapons favour Russia and this is why I do not believe that total disarmament, or the abolition, of nuclear weapons would be accepted by the Soviet Union. It would be very much in our interests, not in the Russians'.

Secondly, because the idea of the nuclear umbrella – of deterrence to Russia – which America holds over Western Europe, and which is supplemented by the British and the French nuclear deterrents – has meant that the nations of Western Europe did not develop their conventional forces. If you compare what is now being spent on conventional arms in Europe with what was spent even in the First World War, or before the Second World War in times of peace, you will find that the percentage is much lower. In this sense nuclear weapons created a feeling of complacency in Western democracies with regard to conventional methods of defence. That is to say, the Russians use their much lower economic potential for much greater effect in conventional armament than the Europeans or the Americans do. This, then, is the second way in which the possession of nuclear weapons favours the Russians. And the third way is, exactly now, probably the most important way. The Soviet Union is a closed society, and it can do most things with regard to foreign policy without having to ask its people what they think about it. Of course public opinion is important in the Soviet Union but in a completely different way from its importance in the Western democracies. It is simply that the Soviets are able to manipulate the issue of arms control. I am not saying that they invented the Peace Movement or that the people in the Peace Movement are Russian agents. The point is that it is exploited by the Russians, regardless of its own interests and its own intentions. In this sense there is no balance or symmetry. They can influence, or not influence, a Peace Movement – but they can *rely* on a Peace Movement that develops indigenously in the West. We do not have a parallel situation in the Soviet Union.

IT IS ALMOST FORTY YEARS since Yalta. In that time a basic fatalism has come to underlie Western attitudes towards the other half of Europe.

Something akin to what Bismarck said about the Balkan Christians then under Turkish rule: 'I shall remember them in my prayers, but I may not make them the object of policy.' But the unadorned significance of the recurring efforts, East of the Elbe, to be rid of Soviet domination is that the West might have to contemplate more actively what it has hardly wished to do since Yalta – make the other half of Europe, 'the object of policy'.

Today a new generation is in place and is now the dominant age group on the continent of Europe. Like the king, in Exodus, who arose in Egypt, it is a generation 'which knew not Joseph' – and to whom the enforcements, and the architecture of the Stalin years are neither in mind nor experience. It is a generation which, although 'Americanised', exhibits an anti-American animus. These things complement a growing disposition to reconsider the orthodoxy which has taken shape since Yalta. They point in the direction of the secular trend, initiated by General de Gaulle, of 'a European Europe'.

To the sustained, epidemic resentments which are held down by military power in Eastern Europe must now be added the latter-day discomforts and divisions within the Western alliance. This is giving a new dimension to the legacy of Yalta – a legacy which Zbigniew Brzezinski, who was President Carter's National Security Adviser, believes the West should take the initiative in, gradually, trying to unravel. He has put the proposition in the following terms.

> We will do better if we focus on a longer term objective – which is more likely to associate the Europeans in a common endeavour with us. I have particularly in mind the need to gradually undo the legacy of Yalta – which so much conditions the specificity of the European outlook on East–West relations. Few Americans appreciate the extent to which Yalta is viewed by Europeans as, largely, an American–Russian arrangement historically imposed upon a prostrate Europe. To be sure, in a formal sense, the Yalta Agreement had nothing to do with the division of Europe. In a broader historical sense however, the aftermath of Yalta, shaped by the dynamism of the Yalta arrangements, led to the division of Europe, and certainly the division of Germany. In a sense the division of Germany is the fundamental reason why the Yalta legacy, the Yalta 'system' cannot endure because it is evident that it is only by external factors that the division of Germany is perpetuated. That division continues to act as a catalyst for change.

The apparent collapse of the foreign policy consensus in West Germany (which has accompanied the debate over the deployment of Cruise and Pershing missiles) dramatises one aspect of Brzezinski's personal view. Helmut Kohl, who succeeded Helmut Schmidt as Chancellor of West Germany, has after all said of these nuclear weapons, 'Our country's orientation in external affairs is at stake.'

Is some fundamental reappraisal of the bloc system in effect what Zbigniew Brzezinski is now calling for?

BRZEZINSKI: I would put it differently. I would say that what is needed is not so much a fundamental reappraisal; what is needed is a broad comprehensive initiative by the West. Ultimately I think most of us – to different degrees – realise that the system in the East is sick; that it is illegitimate; that it is not performing and that it is unpopular. But what is missing is some sustained and comprehensive Western initiative to take advantage of that condition in a creative and feasible manner. And, I have argued, in the last year of my tenure in the White House, and more openly since leaving the White House, that the moment is extremely ripe for a broad Western initiative which would combine far-reaching accommodation in the area of arms control with a comprehensive economic offer – in order to give the rulers in the East (and particularly in Moscow) a broad choice. Accommodate, and create new conditions for stability in the context of historical change, or reject this offer and face probably growing, intensifying and eventually dangerous crisis from within.

CHARLTON: But how would that differ essentially from the offer of the Marshall Plan which the Russians rejected in 1947/48?

BRZEZINSKI: It would not be quite like the Marshall Plan – because the Marshall Plan aimed more generally at the integration of Europe and it would have had (under the then existing conditions) far more immediately felt political consequences. What I am talking about is a longer range, and more modest, initiative – but one which would have as its purpose the gradual transformation of the inefficient Eastern economies into economies more capable of satisfying the needs of their peoples, and the growing of more cooperative links between the East and the West. This would not have an immediately felt effect but over the long run it would indeed alter the nature of the East–West relationship, and the Eastern systems. The leaders in the East have to face the fact that they can either rule by accommodation with their peoples – and we can help that – or by suppression of their peoples. The choice between the two is becoming sharper.

THE POLITICAL SETTLEMENT which, *de facto*, followed in the wake of Yalta was meant to provide for the security of the Soviet Union and that of the West. Mainly because of the doubts that it would prove acceptable indefinitely to the peoples of Eastern Europe there was always – notably in the instance of Churchill himself at the time – scepticism that it could be a lasting arrangement.

Zbigniew Brzezinski speaks of a *requirement* today for Western diplomacy to 'gradually undo the legacy of Yalta'. But is emancipation from the decisions of Yalta consistent with the tranquillity of Europe?

Some important undercurrents seem to have been stirred up within the American foreign policy establishment that carry themes which have been submerged since the time of Yalta itself. They seek to re-examine critically the split in Europe. American perceptions of increasing Soviet difficulties in the heart of the continent – with their, perhaps, ultimately nuclear dangers – combine today with their own concern at contemporary attitudes to the dominant role of the United States. They see themselves coupled, by the new generation, with the Soviet Union as the Montagues and Capulets of the balance of power. Calls for 'a plague o' both your houses' are a strand in both the nationalist and neutralist arguments in Europe.

Meanwhile Europe itself is falling to a less resigned contemplation of the forty years of facts and force which saw finally raised up, on either side of the old Europe – the outcome of its fratricidal wars – the two superpowers.

What one might call a 'Copernican' view of diplomacy in Europe is slowly rising just above the horizon. It is a feeling that, large and small, the planet states of Europe, and their hopes and discontents, could be arranging themselves in a new – or rather former – conjunction. Here is one such voice. He was present 'in the beginning', as it were, and an American diplomat during the building of the Western alliance, at the end of the Second World War. Walt Rostow has been a Special Assistant to the White House for National Security Affairs in the administrations of both President Kennedy and President Lyndon Johnson.

WALT ROSTOW: It is time for the leaders in the Soviet Union and the West to begin to think about an alternative. Because one can envisage without great difficulty a situation generating itself in Eastern Europe which would be incapable of management by, let us say, the technique of martial law as in Poland. A situation in which the Soviet Union would be forced to intervene and in which the military would either go against the Soviet Union – or split – in which case there would be the danger of an Afghanistan type of development in the heart of Europe. The outcome of this could not be predicted. The use of Soviet military forces against a resisting force in Eastern Europe could set in motion all manner of the greatest dangers. They would include nuclear dangers. Therefore it is time to think again about how the abiding, and legitimate, security interests of the Soviet Union in Europe can be satisfied by a progressive movement towards what you might call an Austrian/Finnish type resolution.

What really needs to happen is that the two halves of Europe draw together more normally. That means there must be very serious, agreed measures of arms control which the United States and the Soviet Union – both of whom have a vital interest – would continue to monitor. Let Eastern Europe take a normal place in the world and develop the kind of politics they want. Eastern Europe, since the Second World War, has been transformed in terms of industrialisation and in the average levels of education, in terms of its patterns of trade and production. My simple point is that what may have looked like a realistic, tolerably stable, if

second-order solution to the problem of Soviet security interests in
Eastern Europe – the division of Europe – is with the passage of time becoming less and less viable. In my view, therefore, rather than wait until
we are caught up in a crisis almost certainly coming, wisdom would call
for the Soviets and for the West to think seriously about a different path;
one by which we gradually, or quickly, undo this system and substitute
for it one that provides security for all, and political and economic freedom for all. And I think that is really do-able.

Now, the path from here to there could be convulsive, or a gradual
historical process. It could be one in which the Warsaw Pact forces and
the NATO forces were gradually and mutually reduced. It could be one
in which higher degrees of economic relations grew up between
Comecon and OECD – between the Eastern and Western economic
organisations. Should a crisis arise the Soviets should have in their minds
that there *is* some alternative between two dreadful outcomes. The one, is
that Eastern Europe break free – and in effect be free to join the West –
and so threaten the security arrangements of the Soviet Union. The other
that the Red Army has to be sent in against resistance. They should have
in their minds that there, on the table, is another option.

CHARLTON: I have put this to Arkady Shevchenko and others, but may
I repeat it? It was the view of the British Foreign Office, quoted home to
President Truman by your Ambassador to Moscow, Averell Harriman,
in May 1946. It seems to me that this particular Foreign Office viewpoint
was accepted by the United States and serves as the definition of the
problem as both sides saw it then.

> We British are agreed that the satellite regimes are not likely to wither
> away. We do not minimize the powerful domestic resentment against
> them, particularly in Poland. We do however wish to emphasise that, in
> our opinion, the USSR is willing to go to almost any lengths and employ
> almost any measures to achieve this end. The composition of the satellite
> regimes may change but their essential subservience to the Soviet Union
> must, as far as Soviet intentions are concerned, continue. If the foregoing is
> true then we are compelled to view Europe – not as a whole – but as
> essentially divided into two zones.

That was written in 1946 – would you question any of that, essentially,
today?

ROSTOW: Yes. After all the Soviets did accept Finland and Austria. So,
the notion that we are really discussing – the separation of their vital
security interests from their degree of political control – is not a notion
foreign to them. Secondly, I would guess that the Soviet analysts are
vastly more sophisticated than I am, in being able to detect and describe
the dangerous trends towards nationalism, and the desire for political
independence in Eastern Europe. I know for certain that one of the
reasons they moved into Czechoslovakia in 1968 was the fear of some

Soviet leaders of the impact on the Ukraine if Czechoslovakia became part of a kind of new order. The degree of tension between what goes on in Eastern Europe and the Soviet Union itself is a very serious matter, quite aside from national security interests. But, the growing up of Eastern Europe, as the generations pass, is going to be a fact. To some degree, it is recognised – in one form in Romania, in another form in Hungary. It was obvious, wasn't it, that the Soviet Union had the greatest reluctance to send its own forces into Poland? They have found this interim device of martial law by the Polish army. When you think of it that is a kind of abdication of Communist Party control – and the end of it cannot be seen. What may have seemed obvious, and was possible, as a Soviet basis of action in the immediate post-war Eastern Europe becomes less so with the coming of the generations that did not know the Second World War. They listen to the West, and they wear blue jeans, and they are very sophisticated about what is going on in Western Europe, which is not what they are *told* is going on. And these people are asking, and are going to go on asking, why are *we* denied even the most primitive form of self-expression? And the answer is going to be harder and harder for the Soviet Union to give with the passage of time.

CHARLTON: But history is not reassuring is it? Have there not been many uprisings suppressed in Eastern Europe, particularly in Poland, against the hegemony of the Russians?

ROSTOW: All of us have to think about military history. But this is not really an *age* for empires. And if there is any kind of rationality in good sense, and not in anarchy, it *is* an age for regional organisations among dignified nations. But, the transition from empire to that is not easy.

Poland is the key to Eastern Europe. After the Potsdam Conference, which quickly followed Yalta, the United States, except for gestures, accepted the takeover of Poland and Eastern Europe. Not quite. There were protests. But what lay behind it I think is something fundamental and which Americans very rarely articulate – our national interest. Yet if you play over American performance rather than rhetoric – without a soundtrack – what you can see is that, systematically, we are extremely sensitive to the balance of power in Europe. But we only act, in Sam Johnson's phrase, when our minds are clarified by the sight of the gallows.

Eastern Europe is simply not an area – in itself – on which the balance of power in Europe depends. And therefore, after the First World War, when Woodrow Wilson played a central role in the break-up of the Austro-Hungarian Empire and the creation of these small states, we then did nothing to *sustain* the countries of Eastern Europe. In the end it is not an area of the world where the United States is willing to go to war. The United States goes to war if a single, potentially hostile, power appears as though it is going to win control of *Western* Europe and control the Atlantic. So there was no great weight behind the American protests in

1946 and 1947, and Stalin gradually perceived that he could get away with the installation of Communist government in Poland, for example.

Now behind all *that* there was a debate between those who – following the British and the French – felt that the best we could get out of the war was to split Europe. The British and the French were very deeply affected by the uncertainty surrounding the United States' intentions and performance, but also I believe – in the back of their minds – not discontented with a divided Germany. I do not know how deeply the British and French weighed the long-run implications of a split Europe, but it was easy to see (as some of us in the State Department saw at the time) that this was going to mean an indefinitely protracted military confrontation with all the uncertainties that would go with that. There were some of us who struggled against the inevitability of that outcome. The alternative was to assert – credibly – that the United States' role in Europe was a permanent role. That is to say, the Soviets would face a permanent United States presence in Western Europe (and a *military* presence) and we would bring to bear all the pressure that we could – short of going to war with Stalin – *while holding up a positive alternative way* of satisfying Soviet security interests. We felt that we had a duty, before accepting this second-order alternative of a split Europe, to mobilise all our potential influence in the matter. Much as Truman did on Northern Azerbaijan where the Soviets, seeing a determined United States, backed away.

The alternative was a Europe in which, first, there would be arms control in Germany – virtual disarmament of Germany – in which the Soviets would be full participants. In fact what we proposed was a kind of special Security Council for Europe that would oversee arms control and the Treaties. And secondly, that Europe would be organised economically – so that the normal reinforcing strands between Eastern and Western Europe could come into play and that the United States would be prepared to back economically that kind of a United Europe. Out of our ideas then has been created . . . in a way that is not unusual in history – rather accidentally – the Economic Commission for Europe, which is a living instrument.

Politically, what was in the back of our minds was the kind of settlement which ultimately did take place, as I have said, in Austria and Finland – namely, the separation of the Soviet security interests (which we regarded as wholly legitimate) from the detailed Soviet control over the politics of all these countries. They would be rendered 'undangerous' by security arrangements which the Soviets would oversee, as would the United States. We felt the danger of a United Germany was not great so long as you had a multilateral framework around it and it could not deal bilaterally with each of the countries.

CHARLTON: But are you saying that Soviet policy was dictated then largely by its perceptions of what the West would tolerate? That what Stalin did was largely the result of the opportunities presented to him?

ROSTOW: I have no doubt that is true to the present day concerning the Soviet Union. Perhaps our greatest differences with our foreign service colleagues – many of them were my lifelong friends – was that they talked in terms of Soviet intentions. Our view was that there was no such thing as Soviet intentions independent of what the United States was prepared to put forward and seriously prepared to *do*! That is the plan we put up in April 1946. What happened is quite extraordinary in the American scheme of things. It never got to Truman. I have checked now with the benefit of the files. Byrnes (who was the Secretary of State) never took it up and never put it to Truman. My guess is that had it gone to Truman he would have tried it. He had a Secretary of State in Byrnes with whom he hardly communicated. Byrnes felt he should have been President, that he was better equipped than Truman. There is something of a wild card here in the personal relations between Byrnes and Truman.

I do not assert that if our plan had gone forward all would have been well. I do not believe in rerunning history. But I regret to this day we did not do it.

CHARLTON: And the connection, as you see it, between 1946 (and what may or may not have been neglected chances) and the present time?

ROSTOW: It is my judgement, for what it is worth, that the trend in Eastern Europe is going only in one direction – towards a greater assertion of national independence as one generation succeeds another. A more insistent thrust for human dignity in which political freedoms will become more, not less, important and that in those circumstances Stalin's East European Empire had already become a source of insecurity for the Soviet Union – not safety.

THERE IS CONSIDERABLE EVIDENCE that the last time the Soviet Union may have contemplated a radical revision of divided Europe, and of the divided Germany which lies at the core of it, was in 1953. That was during the time of profound uncertainty within the Soviet leadership which followed the death of Stalin.

Then, a softer wind began to blow out of Moscow, against a background of popular unrest in Eastern Europe. But then the realities of nuclear might were only shifting towards the more or less equal balance which now exists – and which is fundamental. And then again, tactical smiles have all too often been mistaken in the West for inner warmth.

With the changing of the guard from Brezhnev to Andropov, and more latterly Chernenko, this is how Zbigniew Brzezinski contemplates the political 'orrery' which has been constructed after forty years of fixed relationships established by Yalta.

BRZEZINSKI: Even Moscow is not capable of resisting the winds of change. I suspect there must be younger leaders in the Soviet Union who, while not prepared to dismantle their empire, might be willing to see some positive advantage from a more constructive relationship with the West. Otherwise the prospects for the Soviet Union are not all that attractive – intensifying conflicts, tensions, isolation. Perhaps even encirclement, if ties with China develop further, and also growing national unrest within the Soviet Union itself.

CHARLTON: But does your 'broad comprehensive initiative', which you think is called for now from the West, envisage the momentous question of the possible reunification of Germany?

BRZEZINSKI: I think it is sometimes unwise to put too many things on the table at once – just as in the Middle East we cannot move towards a complete peace by spelling out in every detail, and in every respect, what will happen to the Palestinians once they are part of a confederation with Jordan. So, I think it is premature to speak about the reunification of Germany. But, surely, in a less antagonistic, more cooperative East–West relationship, the nature of the division of Germany would undergo some further change?

CHARLTON: Yet we have faced periods like this before, haven't we? After Stalin's death, can I suggest, there was one?

BRZEZINSKI: And we failed to act.

CHARLTON: Well, did the opportunity exist?

BRZEZINSKI: We will never know. But we do know that there were disagreements and dissension within the Soviet leadership, particularly in regard to Germany. We do not know if a more forthcoming initiative by the West, occurring precisely at that time, might not have had some impact.

CHARLTON: But the realities intruded didn't they? As they always seem to intrude? The complexities and the obstacles appeared overwhelming to anything so fundamental as undoing, as you put it, the split in Europe.

BRZEZINSKI: I do not think one can undo it through an act or through an initiative. What I am talking about is not so much the undoing of the East–West split in Europe, but the setting in motion of processes which, over time, would have that effect. They would be more compatible with the internal historical drives of the Europeans themselves. We did not do that in the early 1950s. I think it is a pity we did not do so. I think we should try in the early 1980s. But a policy has to be guided by some sense of historical vision. That is what distinguishes really significant leaders from people who are essentially guided by the forces of inertia. I do not think we have such leaders right now. This is one of the reasons why the West is so fundamentally passive.

The kind of isolationism that existed in the twenties and thirties does not exist today in America. But there is no doubt that there is a fatigue, in contemporary America, with America's engagement in the world. I think it is a different 'mood', and the two are not the same. Nonetheless, the result could be in some ways analogous to American behaviour in the thirties. This is precisely what must be avoided.

But I see no reason why our existing leaders – Mrs Thatcher, President Mitterand, President Reagan and the German Chancellor – could not undertake a serious dialogue on the subject. I participated in four summits for the Western democracies and I can tell you that, as time goes on, these summits have become more decorous and less substantive. At not one of them were the large East–West strategic issues ever seriously discussed. It is about time that they were. I believe that we do have an opportunity – given the internal crisis in the Soviet world – to steer change in the Soviet Union in positive directions.

THE INVOLVEMENTS OF THE LAST twenty years or so, during the period known as *détente*, have made the Western countries both witnesses and participants in perhaps momentous events concerning Stalin's cloister in Eastern Europe.

The old Bolshevik, Karl Radek (who died a victim of the purges in Stalin's Gulag) once said that, 'Communism is not like a bath; something you can make hot one minute, cold the next.' In other words, its essence cannot be changed. But a society in decay is one which is naturally presided over by the unconstructive.

It is a measure of the cynical malaise which gnaws at the Soviet domination of the other half of Europe that a Communist of the rank and importance of Milovan Djilas can choose now as his metaphor to describe the nature of that domination 'Industrial Feudalism'. Djilas sees in the essence of Soviet Communist power similarities with the vast Ottoman Empire – only officially inspired, unconvinced, by a militant ideology, conquering where it could, and sticking to its conquests until decay set in.

It is 130 years since Karl Marx wrote the following words, possessed today of no little irony, for an article in the *New York Daily News* published on 12 April 1853. He was writing about Imperial Russia.

> But having come this far on the way to universal empire, is it probable that this gigantic and swollen power will pause in its career? . . . The broken and undulating Western frontier of the Empire, ill-defined in respect of natural boundaries, would call for rectification; and it would appear that the natural frontier of Russia runs from Danzig, or perhaps Stettin to Trieste.

Not quite a century after this was written Churchill was saying in his great speech at Fulton, 'From Stettin in the Baltic to Trieste in the Adriatic an Iron Curtain has descended across the continent. . . .'

For Karl Marx historical inevitability pointed the way – relegating history's accidents and its unpredictable points of departure. In the month following Marx's enlightenment of the readers of the *New York Daily News*, Lord Palmerston, Queen Victoria's Prime Minister, whose own career dislodged the first stones from the house of the old

Europe built by the Congress of Vienna, was writing to the Foreign Secretary, Clarendon, on 22 May 1853, the year before Britain confronted Imperial Russia in the Crimea:

> The policy and practice of the Russian Government has always been to push forward its encroachments as fast and as far as apathy, or want of firmness of other governments would allow it to go – but always to stop and retire when it met with decided resistance. Then to wait for the next favourable opportunity to make another spring on its intended victim.

The landscape is familiar. These are the woods and trees of present-day argument. They bow beneath the force of Churchill's perception of the aspirations and grievances which would attend the unnatural division of Europe and his warning to Stalin of what he forecast would be 'the long reproaches of the aftertime'. These gather and they accumulate.

The Yalta compromise – for almost forty years the axiom underlying the conduct of relations between East and West – is proving too artificial to endure, too circumscribed for the realities of the 1980s. The Russians are fighting a losing battle to maintain the present nature of their hold.

The summer lightning in the East illuminates the peaks of forty years of challenge to Soviet encroachment: Poland and Hungary in the 1950s, Czechoslovakia a decade later, and, in sharper relief this time, Poland now once more. On the far horizon – Afghanistan. It illuminates the failure and the fading of the ideology which is 'dead but indispensable', and which leaves only the Red Army now as the guarantor of the irreversibility of history.

And it lights up Churchill's majestic swoop of intuition that very first night after dinner at Yalta, when he said to Stalin, 'The Eagle should permit the small birds to sing. . .'

The Contributors

Abbreviations used in the following notes include:
Amb – Ambassador; Asst – Assistant; Coll – College; Conf – Conference; CP – Communist Party; Cttee – Committee; Dep – Deputy; Dept – Department; Dir – Director; Econ – Economic; Exec – Executive; Gen – General; Govt – Government; Inst – Institute; Int – International; LSE – London School of Economics; Mil – Military; Min – Minister; Perm – Permanent; Pol – Politics; Pres – President; Prof – Professor; Pte – Private; Rep – Representative; Sec – Secretary

BIALER, Seweryn (b. Berlin 1926). American historian, Prof of Pol Science, Columbia University and Dir of its Research Inst of Int Change. Formerly Polish citizen and research associate Inst Social Sciences, Warsaw, 1953–6; and at Inst of Economics, Polish Academy of Sciences, lecturer School of Planning and Statistics, Warsaw, 1954–6.

BRAINARD, Lawrence J. (b. 1944). American economist. Snr Vice-Pres Econ Dept, Bankers Trust Co. New York, Head of the Bank's Int Econ and Pol Analysis Division and responsible for organising the Bank's country 'risk' assessment.

BRZEZINSKI, Zbigniew (b. Warsaw 1928). American academic and politician. Russian Research Centre Harvard, 1953–6; Prof of Govt, Harvard 1956–60; Prof Public Law and Govt, Columbia 1960–6; President Carter's Special White House Adviser for National Security 1977–80.

CONQUEST, Robert (b. 1917). British writer and historian. Foreign Service 1946–56; Fellow LSE 1956–8; Fellow Columbia University 1964–5; Woodrow Wilson Int Centre 1976–7; Hoover Inst 1977–. Author, *The Great Terror, Lenin*.

DAVIES, Norman (b. 1939). British historian. Lecturer in History, School of Slavonic and East European Studies, University of London. Author, *God's Playground – a history of Poland* (2 vols).

DJILAS, Milovan (b. Montenegro 1911). Yugoslav Communist, Partisan General, member of Politburo. Joined CP Yugoslavia in 1932, subsequently arrested and imprisoned by the royal govt. Recognised as a poet and achieved notoriety as a revolutionary. Headed a military mission to Moscow 1944–5 as Tito's second in command, to have talks with Stalin and Molotov. Ideological disagreements with Tito and others in the leadership arose in 1953 when he wrote articles critical of the bureaucracy, which he later called the New Class. Broke with CP in 1955, lengthy terms of imprisonment under Tito. Lives in Belgrade.

DUCHACEK, Ivo (b. 1913). Czech diplomat and politician. Spent wartime in London; Czech Govt liaison to General Patton's 5th Army 1945; People's Party (Christian Democrat) MP in Czechoslovakia 1945–8. Served as Chairman of Foreign Relations Committee of Czech Parliament in this period.

GATI, Charles (b. Budapest 1934). Historian. Prof of Pol Science, Union College, Schenectady, NY; Visiting Prof of Pol Science, Columbia University NY 1972–; Member Council of Foreign Relations. Author, *Blue Collared Workers in Eastern Europe, The International Politics of Eastern Europe, The Politics of Modernisation in Eastern Europe.*

GILBERT, Martin (b. 1936). British historian. Fellow Merton Coll Oxford 1962–; Research Asst to Randolph Churchill 1962–7. Author, *The European Powers 1900–45.* Official biographer, *Winston Churchill* (3 vols).

GLADWYN, Lord (Gladwyn Jebb), (b. 1900). British diplomat; entered diplomatic service 1924. Pte Sec to Perm Under Sec of State 1937–40; Head Reconstruction Dept Foreign Office 1942–5; Exec Sec Preparatory Commission of UN 1945; Acting Sec-Gen UN 1946. Foreign Office appointments 1946–50 incl Dep Under Sec of State, Perm Rep UN 1950–4, Amb to France 1954–60.

GOLDSTÜCKER, Eduard (b. 1913). One of the leading figures of the 'Prague Spring' in the 1960s. Joined the CP before 1939, and after the Communists took power in Czechoslovakia in 1948 served as Amb to Israel. Condemned to life imprisonment during the Slansky Trial. Rehabilitated 1956, became Rector of Charles University, Prague, and Chairman of the Writers' Union. Has since been officially denounced and attacked by the present govt led by Gustav Husak.

HISS, Alger (b. 1904). Former American diplomat. Sec and law clerk to Supreme Court Justice Holmes 1929–30; legal asst to Senate Cttee investigating munitions industry 1934–5; Asst to Asst Sec of State 1936; Asst to Adviser on Pol Relations 1939; Spec Asst to Dir Office, Far Eastern Affairs 1944; Director 1945; accompanied Pres Roosevelt and

Sec of State Stettinius to Malta and Yalta Confs Feb 1945; Exec Sec Dumbarton Oaks Conf August 1944, Sec-Gen UN Conf on Int Reorganisation 1945; Principal Adviser to US delegation to Gen Assembly of UN, London 1946. Accused by Whittaker Chambers of espionage for the Soviet Union, tried and convicted of perjury 1951.

JACOB, Lt Gen Sir Ian (b. 1899). Mil Asst Sec to the War Cabinet 1939–46. Chief Staff Officer to Min of Defence and Dep Sec of the Cabinet (Mil) 1952. Dir-Gen of the BBC 1952–60.

KASER, Michael (b. 1926). British economist. Diplomatic Service London and Moscow 1947–51; UN Secretariat 1951–63; Professorial Fellow of St Antony's Coll, Oxford, 1972–. Author, *The New Economic Systems of Eastern Europe, The Soviet Union since the Fall of Khrushchev, Health Care in the Soviet Union and East Europe, Planning in East Europe, Soviet Economics.*

KIRALY, Bela (b. Kaposvár, Hungary, 1912). Career military officer. Chief Division of Educational Training, Min of National Defence, Budapest 1947–8. Major General, Cdr Infantry Land Forces, Hungarian army 1948–50; Supt and Prof of Mil History, War Academy General Staff College, Budapest 1950–1. Arrested, sentenced to death (sentence commuted 1955) in Stalinist purges, paroled 1956. Major General Chairman Revolutionary Council National Defence, Commander in Chief Hungarian National Guard and subsequently of Freedom Fighters 1956. Currently Prof Emeritus Brooklyn Coll, City University NY.

KOLAKOWSKI, Leszek (b. Poland 1927). Polish philosopher. Prof of the History of Philosophy, Warsaw University 1959–68. Expelled for political reasons 1968. Now Fellow of All Souls Coll, Oxford, and Visiting Prof Yale, Chicago and Berkeley Universities. Author, *Main Currents of Marxism* (3 vols).

LABEDZ, Leopold (b. Simbirsk, USSR, 1920). Of Polish origin, now a British citizen, writer and academic. Snr Fellow Russian Inst, Columbia University 1962–3. Visiting Prof Stanford University, Centre for Advanced Int Studies, Miami, and Fellow of Centre of Int Studies LSE. Member advisory board Royal Inst Int Affairs, Chatham House, and also of *Encounter* magazine. Editor of *Survey*, a journal of East and West Studies.

LAQUEUR, Walter (b. 1921). British historian and academic. Dir, Inst of Contemporary History and Wiener Library, London 1964–. Editor of *Survey* 1955–65; Prof Brandeis University 1967–71; Visiting Prof Harvard, John Hopkins, Chicago Universities; Chairman Research

Council Centre for Strategic Studies, Georgetown University. Author, *Weimar, a Cultural History, Europe since Hitler, Communism and Nationalism.*

LOEBL, Eugen (b. Czechoslovakia 1907). Asst Min for Foreign Trade in the Czech Communist govt of 1948. Joined the CP in 1931 and became one of the leading Marxist economic theoreticians in Czechoslovakia. Came to England in 1939 as economic adviser to Jan Masaryk, then head of the Czech Ministry of Reconstruction. Member of the group that included Rudolf Slansky (Sec-Gen of the Czech CP) and Vladimir Clementis (Foreign Minister) who were chosen in Moscow for the Show Trials. Arrested in 1949 and sentenced to life imprisonment at the Slansky Trial. Released in 1960; later 'rehabilitated' by the Dubček regime in 1968. Now lives in New York.

NOWAK, Jan (b. Warsaw 1913). Snr Research Fellow Poznań University. Acted as courier between Polish Govt-in-Exile in London and the Polish Underground in Warsaw during Second World War, making many trips across Germany in disguise to do so. Throughout the Warsaw Uprising was in charge of the English language secret radio broadcasts; at the end of the fighting he brought out the microfilm archives of the Uprising, reaching London with this material in Jan 1945 – just before the Yalta Conference. Head of BBC Polish Section after the war; and of Polish Section Radio Free Europe 1951–76. Consultant to National Security Council White House under Pres Carter and Reagan.

PIPES, Richard (b. Poland 1923). American historian. Prof of History, Harvard 1963–75; Dir Russian Research Centre 1968–73; Snr Consultant Stanford University 1973–8; Dir East European and Soviet Affairs, National Security Council under Pres Reagan 1981–2. Baird Prof of History Harvard 1975–.

RACZYNSKI, Count Edward (b. 1891). Polish diplomat. Entered Polish Ministry of Foreign Affairs 1919. Polish Min accredited to League of Nations 1932–4: Polish Amb to London 1934–45. Acting Polish Min for Foreign Affairs 1941–2; Min of State in charge of Foreign Affairs, Cabinet of Gen Sikorski 1942–3; Chief Polish rep on interim Treasury cttee for Polish questions 1945–7.

ROBERTS, Sir Frank (b. 1907). British diplomat. HM Embassies Paris and Cairo 1932–7; Foreign Office 1937–45; Chargé d'Affaires to Czech Govt 1943; British Min in Moscow 1945–7; PPS to Ernest Bevin as Foreign Sec 1947–9; Dep Under Sec of State FO 1951–4; Amb Yugoslavia 1954–7; UK Perm Rep North Atlantic Council 1957–60; Amb USSR 1960–2; to Federal Republic of Germany 1963–8.

Rostow, Walt Whitman (b. 1916). American economist and diplomat. Economic Commission for Europe 1947–9; Chairman Policy Planning Council State Dept 1961–6; Special Asst to Pres Lyndon Johnson 1966–9. Now Prof Economics and History at University of Texas.

Rupnik, Jacques (b. Prague 1950). Czech historian. Sorbonne 1968–72; BBC Overseas Service 1976–82. At present lecturer and Research Fellow, Fondation Nationale des Sciences Politiques, Paris. Author, *History of the Czechoslovak Communist Party*.

Schapiro, Leonard (1908–84). British writer and historian. War Office 1942–5; practised at Bar 1946–55; Dept of Pol LSE 1955–84. Prof Pol Science with special reference to Russian Studies LSE 1963–75. Author, *The Origin of the Communist Autocracy, The Communist Party of the Soviet Union, The Government and Politics of Soviet Russia, Rationalism and Nationalism in Russian Nineteenth-Century Political Thought*.

Shevchenko, Arkady (b. Gorlovka, Ukraine, 1930). Soviet diplomat. Joined Soviet Ministry of Foreign Affairs 1956; adviser with rank of Amb and close personal ties to Min of Foreign Affairs, Andrei Gromyko 1970–3; UN Under Sec-Gen 1973–8. Sought and granted residence in USA 1978.

Sonnenfeldt, Helmut (b. Berlin 1926). American govt official. US State Dept 1952–69; Dir Office Research and Analysis of USSR and Eastern Europe 1966–9; Snr Staff member for Europe and East–West Relations, National Security Council 1969–74.

Swaniewicz, Stanislaw (b. Daugapils, Russia, 1899). Economist; survivor of the Katyn Massacre. Student Moscow University 1917–18; Polish Army 1919–21; University of Vilna 1921–39 as student and research fellow; Breslau University and Kiel Inst of Econ Research 1938; Extraordinary Prof Economics Vilna 1938; Polish army 1939. Captured by Russians 1939; released 1942. In Middle East with Polish army under Gen Anders following amnesty 1942–4; came to London 1944 as adviser Polish Govt-in-Exile; Prof and Head of Econ Dept Polish University College 1945; subsequently LSE and Notre Dame University, Halifax. Author, *Lenin as Economist, The German Economy under Hitler* (the book that saved his life).

Szasz, Bela (b. Hungary 1910). A central figure in the Rajk trial, Budapest, 1949. Studied Budapest University and the Sorbonne, Paris. Joined the Hungarian CP 1932. In 1939 went to Argentina where he edited an anti-Fascist weekly and was Gen Sec of the Free Hungarian

Movement in South America; returned Budapest 1946. Appointed to Press Depts of Ministry of Foreign Affairs and the Ministry of Agriculture. Arrested and tried during the purge of Laszlo Rajk; sentenced to 10 years' hard labour. Now lives in London.

TABORSKY, Edward (b. Prague 1910). Sec to Czech Min of Foreign Affairs (Jan Masaryk) 1937–9; personal aide to Pres Beneš 1939–45. Prof of Govt, University of Austin, Texas 1949–.

VAS, Zoltan (1903–83). Former Communist Mayor of Budapest. Longstanding member of Hungary CP and associate of Rakosi. Spent war in Soviet Union, worked for Comintern 1940–3, thereafter posted to Soviet army as colonel. On return to Hungary was involved in 'salami tactics' as member of State Planning Bureau 1946–53; 1st Sec to Council of Ministers 1954–5; Dep Min of Foreign Trade 1956. On downfall of Nagy's government was deported to Romania, but returned soon afterwards.

Index

(Italic figures denote illustrations)